Hedge

Nicolas Colin began his career in the French civil service and then brought his clear understanding of regulatory systems across Europe to his work as a tech entrepreneur. In 2013, he became Co-founder and Director of The Family, a pan-European investment firm supporting early-stage entrepreneurs, now with a portfolio of 150+ fast-growing startups.

He sits on the board of Radio France, the French national radio broadcasting corporation, and teaches university courses on corporate strategy and public policy at Sciences Po in Paris. He has previously served as a member of the board of the French personal data protection authority.

Nicolas is a thought-provoking voice in the conversation about new institutions in the digital world. He has co-authored several works on technology, including a 2013 Report on Taxation in the Digital Economy (for which he was voted one of that year's ten most influential people by the *International Tax Review*). His articles regularly appear in both English and French publications, including *Foreign Affairs*, *The Financial Times*, and *Le Monde*. *Hedge* is his third book, and the first published in English.

Nicolas was born in Normandy, France and raised by musician parents, becoming an accomplished bass guitar player. He lives in London with his wife Laetitia Vitaud and their two children.

Advance Praise

"Brilliant, timely and urgent! This digital native takes my theory of technological revolutions and runs with it, applying the lessons of history to the complexities of the present day. An eye-opening primer to the technological present, this book speaks to innovators and entrepreneurs, proposing bold and imaginative solutions towards the creation of a 'Safety Net 2.0' and a better future for all."

— Carlota Perez, author of *Technological Revolutions and Financial Capital: The Dynamics of Bubbles and Golden Ages*

"Nicolas Colin is a path-breaking French entrepreneur who emerged from the world's most elite civil service to become a direct participant in and compelling analyst of the Digital Revolution. In *Hedge*, he brings together a deep reading of the history of economic development through transformational technology with his own direct experience as co-founder of a unique Paris-, London- and Berlin-based firm, The Family, dedicated to galvanizing a start-up culture first in France and now more broadly across Europe. Colin's understanding that economic disruption, especially of the labor market, must be balanced and buffered by relevant innovations in social policy makes *Hedge* must reading for everyone – on both sides of the Atlantic and around the world – wakening to the impact of the Digital Revolution."

— William H. Janeway, Senior Advisor, Warburg Pincus, author of *Doing Capitalism in the Innovation Economy*

"Nicolas has written a sharp and historically grounded analysis of how technology and the political economy of the West have evolved in tandem, and how we might lay groundwork for a society that has both a strong social safety net and supports entrepreneurialism and innovation going forward."

— Kim-Mai Cutler, Partner, Initialized

"This is an important book which poses profound questions about the social and political effects of technological change. Rather than adding to the growing backlash against tech, Colin puts forward specific and forward looking ideas about how we can strike a new balance between technological change and wider social stability and solidarity. In essence, Colin envisages nothing less than a reinvention of the welfare state to suit the modern entrepreneurial age."

— Sir Nick Clegg, former UK Deputy Prime Minister

"I have known Nicolas since the inception of his firm The Family, back in 2013. I've seen their capacity to transform the European startup ecosystem from the inside. As a former civil servant in the upper levels of the French government, Nicolas knows very well that politicians aren't willing or able to take the lead when it comes to technology. To save the tech industry from itself, he urges entrepreneurs of the world to build a "Greater Safety Net 2.0" that can provide economic security and prosperity for all. I've always praised Silicon Valley's unique ability to encourage contrarian thinking. *Hedge* should become part of its playbook, because we urgently need to come together and find ways to uplift humanity in these times of radical change."

— Vivek Wadhwa, Distinguished Fellow at Harvard Law School and Carnegie Mellon University

"Nicolas Colin has brilliantly interpreted a fundamental shift in the nature of the worker and the political economy, a shift to the Entrepreneurial Age. This must be met, he argues, by delivering a new Great Safety Net. Carefully documented yet contemporary, *Hedge* makes for compulsive and thought-provoking reading, which will hopefully stir you into action."

— Azeem Azhar, Founder, *Exponential View*

Nicolas Colin

Hedge
A Greater Safety Net
for the Entrepreneurial Age

The Family, 9ᵗʰ Floor, 107 Cheapside, London, United Kingdom, EC2V 6DN
www.thefamily.co
Information on this title: hedgethebook.com

First edition published 2018

ISBN-13: 978-1718917088

ISBN-10: 1718917082

*To Eckhard Strohschänk, who was my uncle,
and my political awakening.*

To Laetitia, Béatrice, and Ferdinand.

Table of Contents

Introduction: From Europe With Love   **13**

The Ticking Clock   **21**

1. The Tech Backlash   23

Do middle class workers dream of tech companies? – Big chances missed in the tech world – The shifting balance of international power

2. Technology and Institutional Change   43

Modern history is a succession of paradigm shifts – Different days, similar problems – How we once built the Great Safety Net

3. Stuck in the Dark Ages   61

The Western middle class's never-ending crisis – How the Dark Ages shifted risks onto individuals – Making the West great again

The Entrepreneurial Age   **81**

4. Entrepreneurs and the New Corporate World   83

A brief history of science and entrepreneurship – From personal computing to continuous innovation – Entrepreneurs are here to stay

5. Behind Entrepreneurs: The Multitude   99

How customers rose as the main force in the corporate contract – Production and consumption are increasingly blurred – What's a tech company, anyway?

6. Consumer Power: The Modern-Day Janus   117

We're all undergoing the 'Wal-Mart Effect' – Instability is the new normal – Getting from Great to Greater

The Collapse of the Cathedrals 137

7. The Safety Net in an Open World 139

Software is opening the world – The thalassocracies – A more open world calls for greater economic security

8. From the Old to the New Working Class 157

The old working class has been left behind – The new factory floor – The problem with proximity services

9. The Lost Art of State Intervention 175

The state as the solution to many problems – How bureaucracy reached the point of irrelevance – Reviving the state

A Greater Safety Net 193

10. Always Be Rebounding 195

Education is no longer the magic bullet – Occupational licensing for amateurs – Affordable housing for hunters and settlers

11. Institutions for Hunters 216

A new breed of consumer finance – Dealing a new hand in insurance – We should all be taxed like Donald Trump

12. A Hedge for the Networked Individual 233

The retreat of the corporate world – The new frontier in collective bargaining – The equation for creating good jobs

Conclusion: Basic Income Isn't Enough 251

Acknowledgments 263

Notes 269

Index 319

Introduction

From Europe With Love

"The new line is drawn between those who look back with nostalgia, trying to hold on to past practices, and those who embrace the new paradigm and propose new institutions to fit the new conditions. This blurs the previous connection between certain values and goals and the specific means of attaining them. Though the goals may remain unchanged, the adequate and viable means to pursue them change with each paradigm shift."
— Carlota Perez[1]

On February 7, 2014, my firm, The Family, received a letter at our office in Paris. The sender was an investigating police officer, inviting me to present myself before an examining magistrate. I was about to be indicted for defamation against Nicolas Rousselet, the CEO of Groupe Rousselet (then known as Groupe G7), a family-owned conglomerate that dominates the taxi industry in the Paris area.

The plaintiff had lodged a civil claim against me as part of a criminal case. Because French law lacks the broad principles of free speech that grew out of the First Amendment in the US, this is enough to trigger an indictment. With no room for prosecutorial discretion, the meeting with the examining magistrate was the first step toward a criminal trial that would take place a few months later.

Now why would the de facto chief of the mighty Parisian taxi industry file such a suit against me, a former civil servant who had just co-founded a small firm assisting startup founders?

It was quite simple, in fact. A few weeks earlier I had published a blog post, later republished by the newspaper *La Tribune*, that openly questioned the soundness of Rousselet's understanding of innovation. Initially, the article attracted a few thousand readers, which was somehow enough for me to appear on the man's radar.

Back then, the war between transportation startups and the local taxi industry was warming up. The French government had decided to enact a new rule: every car without a taxi medallion had to wait 15 minutes after the driver had received a booking before picking up the passenger. Obviously it was targeted at Uber and other ride-hailing startups, and it was a major blow for them. I wasn't particularly interested in the sector at that time. But the new rule was so stupid, and the discussion around it so heated, that I decided I had to learn more about the topic and form my own opinion.

Among all the available information, one document stood out: a filmed interview of Nicolas Rousselet, a proponent of the 15-minute rule, touting his vision of innovation. It was appalling. There was the bias for the higher end of the market, as Parisian taxis mostly transport business people and rich foreign tourists. There was the idea that innovation was all about improving existing products, not solving bigger problems and redrawing the contours of the market. And there was the arrogance of a man painting himself as a champion of innovation while actively lobbying for that ridiculous rule. What I wrote after watching that video was quite straightforward: *"Innovation as seen by Nicolas Rousselet deserves our attention because it is so derisory and so erroneous, virtually from beginning to end"*[2].

All in all, Rousselet's was an outdated vision of mobility in today's urban world. And it was coming from one of the most powerful persons in the Parisian transport sphere! If this man had such a backward-looking, narrow-minded understanding of innovation, it was no wonder why the local taxi industry was having a hard time competing against Uber and other tech startups.

Now, lawsuits are nothing new in the tech world. Among the many entrepreneurs I know, more than one has had to deal with the police or the magistrates—typically because their innovative value proposition didn't fit in the old boxes created by existing rules.

What's more, being sued by the leading figure of a disliked industry known for rent-seeking led to a warm wave of support. Many more people read my article and thanked me for opening a much-needed conversation on innovation and regulation. Pillars of the local tech community offered to serve as witnesses at the trial. Entrepreneurs trying to enter regulated industries approached us to join my firm's portfolio. In the end, I was eventually cleared by the court and left with just some fees for my (excellent) lawyer—and quite a few new Twitter followers. As for the 15-minute rule, it was never enforced and was later struck down.

Taxis are admittedly an extreme case. They're quite rough in their approach to business and very close to the government due to the high level of legacy regulations. But the legal dimension of what I call 'startup busting' exists in most industries. It is quite representative of what happens in Europe when fast-growing startups shake up the status quo. Politicians and corporate executives love tech entrepreneurs only so long as they look like harmless children frolicking on the playground. But as their businesses grow, entrepreneurs come to be seen as threats and are scolded accordingly, just as when children bring their roughhousing home and annoy the adults at the dinner table.

If you're in the US, this only reinforces what you think of Europe: just another example of why no dominant tech company has ever grown out of there! Yes, we in Europe can be forced to defend ourselves in a criminal defamation case for publicly discussing questions like *"What is innovation?"* and *"Couldn't we do better than the existing taxi industry?"*.

This is why many of us are tackling the problem of making entrepreneurship easier in Europe. Luckily, a good set of lessons is available to learn from thanks to our fellow entrepreneurs and venture capitalists in the US. And today, the overall European context looks rosier than it did when I went on trial four years ago: a healthier startup ecosystem; promising tech companies growing swiftly; the election of pro-entrepreneurship president Emmanuel Macron in France.

Yet as Europe makes progress, the US tech industry is encountering new problems of its own. Airbnb has been restricted in more than one US city. Uber is now an embattled company with many regulatory and cultural challenges to tackle. The election of Donald Trump has destroyed the support that Silicon Valley could count on in Washington under Barack Obama. Many decisions by the Trump administration, from suppressing net neutrality to booting out skilled immigrants, are direct blows to the US tech industry. Even the mighty Facebook appears to be stumbling badly. What is now known as the *"tech backlash"* seems to be underpinned by a generalized and widespread fear for economic security and prosperity in the face of technological change.

Again, for Americans, Europe may seem far away—different, and lagging behind. And yet, in the context of this worrying *"backlash"* I think that Europe provides valuable insight. One example is our attachment to economic security for the many. In the US, the workers' safety net has been methodically dismantled over the last decades. As for China, its singular political system provides little room to implement the kind of social compromise that once reconciled classical liberals and social democrats in the West. By contrast, most European countries still have best-in-class public services and a broad and strong safety net. These can even serve as platforms for entrepreneurs and give rise to European tech champions in sectors such as healthcare, insurance, housing, elder care, child care, education, and others.

Above all, Europe provides a distinctive institutional context in which caring for the greater goals of economic security and prosperity is critical for entrepreneurs to succeed. That's because European citizens, most of them still living the good life, have a lot to lose in the current paradigm shift. And dealing with such a widespread mistrust of change is precisely where European entrepreneurs can supply the US tech industry with a few useful lessons.

The truth is that technology will progress against all odds. But not every country will welcome it as an opportunity for further economic development. For a long time, we've had good reasons to be worried about Europe. But there are now reasons to question whether the US, too, will make the most of the current transition. Now it's the entire Western world that seems about to miss the opportunities brought about by the current great surge of development.

Many people in the tech industry think that they can fight back through the polarizing playbook of entrepreneurship. But in doing so, they neglect the institutional needs that underlie our economies and indeed our societies as a whole. Tech companies are only a part of something bigger: a paradigm shift, the kind that once happened with the deployment of railways or the rise of the automobile. And many obstacles are still barring their growth, among which is that nagging feeling that today's economy brings about neither prosperity nor economic security for the many.

Such concerns about technological change lead to startup-busting politicians, lobbied by all the Rousselets of the world, erecting barriers in the name of nostalgia. Elected officials, corporate executives, scholars, and journalists prefer to see entrepreneurs as the new *"Barbarians at the Gate"*[3] and slow them down rather than supporting them. They simply don't see (or refuse to see) the better world that the paradigm shift could bring about. And so the tech industry will prosper only if it helps reveal that perspective and participate in imagining new institutions for the new age.

Ultimately, imagining what I call a *Greater Safety Net for the Entrepreneurial Age* will prove beneficial for all tech entrepreneurs in the West. It will offer a more inclusive and reassuring perspective on what they are trying to achieve. It will also contribute to setting up the institutions these entrepreneurs need to maximize their venture's success. After all, most social and economic institutions built in the age of the automobile and mass production ultimately became pillars that enabled the Fordist corporate world to thrive—a sort of providential gift from union leaders, consumer advocates, and liberal and socialist politicians to the embattled corporate executives of the day.

That gift, which mostly dates back to the 1930s, has now been exhausted. And so we must imagine a new safety net that is more in line with today's economy. It's a long road ahead, and there's no reason to delay the departure any longer. Those who are willing to take the ride face an uphill battle. This book, *Hedge*, has been written for them.

Part 1
The Ticking Clock

Chapter 1
The Tech Backlash

*"Mr. Obama's campaign, conceived outside the party establishment
and built on a platform of online membership, felt like a high-tech
reimagining of politics. It seemed to presage an age of government that
could champion both individuality and community, a government that
made programs more responsive and flexible without eroding our sense
of shared responsibility."*
—Matt Bai[1]

Do middle class workers dream of tech companies?

Technology is not popular nowadays. As I write these words
in early 2018, it even appears to be an enemy of our entire way
of life: it disrupts whole industries; it displaces jobs; it widens the
inequality gap; it endangers our privacy; it undermines the economic
security that was at the heart of the post-war social compact; it even
threatens democracy as we know it.

In a way, it all started with the 2008 financial crisis. We all
remember that year as the bursting of the housing bubble, followed
by the cracking of the global banking system. Less remembered is the
fact that the iPhone had launched the previous year, with the App
Store following on July 10, 2008. These two unrelated events, the
crisis and the iPhone, ended up reinforcing each other. The potential of using the Internet through smartphones instead of desktop
computers was realized thanks to the post-crisis context. Businesses
started to consider technology as a lever to become more competitive.
And households needed to find new ways to make ends meet.

As a consequence, the crisis contributed to boosting a new breed
of technology company. Airbnb was first launched in 2008; its early

success was due to people having difficulties paying the rent. Uber started operating the following year; it relied on the smartphone as the most convenient device to order a ride, but also on the reserve army of would-be drivers—all those who, for lack of a better job, were ready to go work on the new platforms of the *"gig economy"*. 2008 was also the year when Facebook passed the threshold of 100 million users and Barack Obama was elected president.

With its growth fueled by the crisis, technology was now understood through a different narrative. Gone were the days when we thought, as once did the US Bureau of Labor Statistics[2], that technology would create more jobs than it would destroy. Now it came to be seen as a driver of the crisis: a new paradigm that made us suffer, worsening the hardships of the day rather than solving them. Once a motive for hope, technology came to inspire fear. The ebullient optimism all but disappeared. It left room for a new set of feelings that ranged from indifference to suspicion to outright hostility.

One front in the war around technology was fought over corporate taxation—a topic I know well, having co-authored a 2013 report for the French government on taxing the digital economy[3]. Starting in 2010, economic hardships created difficulties for governments trying to balance their budgets. It prompted a new line of questioning: were multinational corporations paying their fair share? A thundering article by journalist Jesse Drucker triggered a global conversation on corporate tax planning and the particularly low rate of taxation of large tech companies[4]. The G20 and the OECD started working on countering aggressive corporate tax planning. American states sought ways to force online merchants to collect sales tax, fueling a controversy over the so-called *"Amazon Tax"*[5].

Then came the war around privacy, which was started by Edward Snowden. When he fled to Hong Kong on July 20, 2013 and then revealed hints of a massive surveillance system powered by technology, it was a sudden blow for the entire tech industry. From then on, it was not about making the world a better place, but rather about invading people's privacy. I can testify that the Snowden revelations changed the tone of the conversation around technology. Those of us working in the tech industry in Europe had to make our apologies before we could continue promoting technology as a positive agent of change.

Then starting sometime in 2015 came the fear for jobs. It's unclear why automation suddenly became such a hot topic in the global media. But authors such as Erik Brynjolfsson and Andrew McAfee were writing about the progress of robotics[6]. There was a general weariness from years of unsuccessfully fighting unemployment. The rising spectre of the gig economy suggested that technology would put an end to the Fordist experiment of the steady job. Above all, progress in artificial intelligence led many people to realize that white-collar jobs in fields such as law and medicine were technology's for the taking, too. And if educated workers aren't safe, then nobody is.

2016 was a turning point. Until then, a generation of powerful and well-respected policymakers such as Barack Obama and David Cameron had sided with the tech industry, realizing its transformative power and burnishing its image for the general public. But then those politicians left the stage, being replaced by much less tech-friendly successors.

This was when everybody realized the impact technology was having on our democracy. Donald Trump unexpectedly won the US presidential election due to his masterful ability to manipulate attention, the support of online communities fueled by a populist sentiment, and an intrusion of foreign agents in the democratic process—all facilitated by social media. A few months earlier, in rather similar conditions, the British people had voted to leave the European Union out of fear that the new world was making their lives so much worse.

The question that led to writing this book was, *"How did we end up here?"*. Things were so different when I first became interested in technology back in 1992! True, I was a teenager then, and I firmly believed that the US was that terrible country presided over by the arch-conservatives Ronald Reagan and George H.W. Bush. Viewed from Europe, this was a country where sick people died in the streets because no one would lift a finger to help them.

But then Bill Clinton, *"The Man from Hope"*, rose from Arkansas with an agenda that included making the tax system more progressive, setting up universal healthcare coverage, and supporting new solutions to make the government more efficient and effective. I was intrigued by that more liberal version of the US and the forward-looking vision personified by its new leader.

HOW TECHNOLOGY IS VIEWED
(1961 TO TODAY)

1961 IT WILL HELP US GO TO THE MOON.

1969 "IT WILL MAKE THE WORLD A BETTER PLACE"

 1984 "IT'S ABOUT FREEING INDIVIDUALS"

"IT'S ABOUT CONNECTING **1992** **HOPE & CHANGE**
THE WORLD"

 1994 "IT WILL CREATE MILLIONS OF JOBS"

2000 "IT WAS A BUBBLE AFTER ALL"

2004

"IT WILL IMPACT CONTENT
INDUSTRIES ONLY"

 2008

"IT HELPED OBAMA WIN
THE PRESIDENCY."

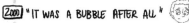

"WE'VE HAD ENOUGH OF TECH COMPANIES." [2018]

"TECH COMPANIES MISTREAT WOMEN." [2017]

"TECH COMPANIES HELPED ELECT TRUMP." [2016]

FEAR & WORRY [2015] "TECH COMPANIES DESTROY ALL THE JOBS."

"TECH COMPANIES INFLICT UNFAIR COMPETITION." [2014]

"TECH COMPANIES INVADE OUR PRIVACY!" [2013]

[2012]

[2010]

"TECH COMPANIES OWN WASHINGTON, DC."

"TECH COMPANIES DON'T PAY THEIR TAXES"

In particular, following his running mate Al Gore's inspiration[7], Clinton was pursuing the deployment of what was then called the *"information superhighway"*. At the time I mostly got news from *Le Monde diplomatique*, a radical, left-wing French magazine. This crowd was very suspicious of Clinton, a pro-business moderate. But they were also sensitive to the extraordinary promise of the Internet, a new infrastructure whose architecture and philosophy were rooted in the counterculture of the 1960s. It looked as if the Internet inspired optimism across all sides of the political spectrum.

My interest in that *"information superhighway"* eventually led me to specialize in technology. From 1996 onwards I studied telecommunications, electronics, and computer science. I was fortunate enough to access the Internet with a broadband connection when most of the world was still stuck with 56k modems. Computer science students like me would code their personal web page in HTML, send emails, chat on IRC, read newsgroups. We were thrilled to be taking part in that *"new economy"* that was bound to change the world. It only helped that in my home country of France mathematics and technology attract many of the best students. There, becoming a technologist is rewarded with a promising career, handsome salary, and privileged social status.

However the ebullient optimism of the mid- to late-90s didn't last. The Internet fueled a speculative bubble that eventually burst in 2000. A few months later, Al Gore himself lost that year's bitterly fought US presidential election, leaving the stage to a Republican administration that cared more about oil and steel than technology. Then 9/11 happened, which led most officials around the world to focus on the more pressing topics of fighting terrorism and ensuring national security.

In retrospect, the period from 2001 to 2008 was about more of the same rather than the radical change envisioned during the previous decade. The view was that technology would not disrupt everything after all. Increasing global trade made it possible to maintain a productive apparatus that served the same old mass consumption. The final dismantling of the Glass-Steagall Act in the late 1990s led to widespread access to credit, keeping consumers happy while fueling the emergence of a housing bubble[8].

For a time, the impact of technology was contained within a

narrow segment of the economy. The only ones to be unnerved were executives in the advertising and media industries. The Napster trial was the first showdown between a fast-growing startup and incumbents dominating an old industry. Then Google began its rise from being a better search engine to becoming a tech powerhouse. That was hardly a surprise. Music, advertising, and media were all about intangible assets. Technology was bound to eat those industries someday—as it was expected to leave the rest intact.

But now ten years have passed since the financial crisis, and the tech industry has eaten much more than that. As a result, it now has a big problem: the *"tech backlash"*. As tech companies are perceived as destroying good jobs and weakening liberal democratic values, they've ended up encountering a powerful adversary: not only the backward-looking elite, but the entire Western middle class. Many people now wonder if technology brings about progress, or if it's here to prolong the stagnation that has long reigned in Western societies, actively destroying their way of life in the process.

For me, this is all a huge disappointment. I was brought to technology by the extraordinary optimism that buoyed the Western world back in the 1990s. And I think it's become urgent to reconnect with this optimism as threats to our way of life are looming from so many directions. This is as much a challenge for Western governments as it is for the tech industry itself.

Big chances missed in the tech world

The problem with the *"tech backlash"* is that it provides those who've always hated technology with a fair amount of ammunition. Many in power circles are turning fiercely against tech companies. And this is a problem when you feel optimistic as to what technology can bring about. It's hard enough to convince non-tech people that technology is about making the world better. In the current context, it has become near impossible. The attitude of kind indifference or curiosity that entrepreneurs could count on in the past has now been replaced by mistrust and, in many cases, active resistance. In the US as in Europe, the idea of *"regulating"* tech companies has become a code word to suggest that we've had enough of technology. And as techno-skeptics of all kinds now have the upper hand, complacent incumbents and well-connected rent-seekers can finally seek their revenge against tech entrepreneurs.

To reverse the trend, my belief is that large Western tech companies—that is, US companies—should commit to building new institutions designed for economic security and prosperity. These companies are the ones that reveal the new techno-economic paradigm as they grow. And among their executives are leaders who best understand what is required to make it all work better. Thus they have a role to play as catalysts and enablers of a much-needed effort at radical imagination.

This is not to say that tech executives should replace governments when it comes to public policy. After all, it wasn't Henry Ford or Alfred P. Sloan who designed and implemented the New Deal. But nor was the New Deal the novel brainchild of Franklin D. Roosevelt—who in 1932 ran with essentially no program except for repealing Prohibition, balancing the budget, and an attitude of *"bold, persistent experimentation"*.

Roosevelt's eventual legacy was the result of a complex multi-player game running throughout an unexpected sequence of events. The first version of the New Deal revolved around founding the ill-fated National Recovery Administration (NRA). Inspired by Owen Young, then CEO of General Electric, it essentially consisted of a corporatist program to end deflation and raise prices by restricting supply. However it was soon declared unconstitutional by the Supreme Court for exceeding congressional power under the Commerce Clause of the US Constitution.

Following this major setback, the Roosevelt administration sought to regroup and started looking for new allies. Recovery and growth were eventually made possible, leading to Roosevelt's reelection in 1936, because capital-intensive industries and financiers made an alliance with labor to provide support for an upgraded New Deal. What they gained in exchange was the commitment of the US government and trade unions to support free trade. The lowering or disappearance of tariffs was critical for those industries as access to larger markets was needed to make the most of their massive investments[9].

And so trade unions, capital-intensive industries and finance (and a few other parties, such as segregationist Democrats in Southern states[10]) reached a compromise. This diverse, opportunistic coalition managed to circumvent the resistance of business executives opposed to worker-friendly policies and getting rid of trade barriers.

During the war, big corporations even became involved in covering social risks. The combination of a reduced workforce and wage controls forced them to compete for workers using healthcare and pensions, whose costs were tax deductible, rather than higher wages. Most US business executives ultimately turned against the Second New Deal's most liberal components. But this unique sequence of events reveals the corporate world's transient role in imagining and building the institutions that made the post-war boom possible.

As of today, what strikes me is that the same kind of alliance between capital-intensive, global-reaching corporations and liberal politicians almost succeeded with the Obama administration. Just as tech companies were becoming the largest in the world (in terms of market capitalization), they started throwing their full support behind Obama's agenda.

Until then, the Democratic Party had long relied on alliances that were less about building the future than preserving the past. Democrats forged an enduring bond with labor to perpetuate the New Deal, lasting approximately until Lyndon B. Johnson left the White House in 1968. Then, after two decades of uncertainty, they allied with Hollywood and Wall Street simply because they needed the money. Obama, despite the innovation brought about in his 2008 campaign, was no exception in that regard.

The shift between 2008 and 2012 can be explained by the financial crisis. Wall Street became discredited by its excesses, the fall of big investment banks (Bear Stearns and Lehman Brothers), and the widely unpopular bailout of the banking sector by the Bush administration in 2008. Then the Obama administration toughened banking regulations with the Dodd-Frank Act, upsetting its supporters on Wall Street. Vexed by their newly infamous image and angry at fresh regulations that they said made their business more difficult to operate, Wall Street power brokers abandoned the Democrats[11]. Now financiers were firm supporters of the Republican Party[12].

WHERE DEMOCRATIC PARTY SUPPORT LIES
(1932 to TODAY)

1932-1948 : FREE TRADE AND SOCIAL SECURITY
(AND SEGREGATION IN THE SOUTH)

1948-1968 : LABOR AND CIVIL RIGHTS

1968-1992 : ACTIVISM & MINORITIES

1992-2008 : BUSINESS & FAME

2008-2016 : TECHNOLOGY & CITIES

Fortunately for Obama's Democrats, Silicon Valley took over. It already had a bond with Obama himself following the 2008 election, in which the campaigning had become more technology-driven and startup-like[13]. But with Obama's campaign for a second term in 2012, Democratic fundraising from Silicon Valley exceeded that from Wall Street and Hollywood for the first time[14]. Tech companies—CEOs as well as employees—went on to become the party's strongest and most decisive supporters. And they brought a lot to the table: skills to win electoral campaigns[15]; the brand power of widely used consumer products; talent to reinvent the government and try to turn it into a platform[16]; the idea of building a better future; and a tremendous amount of money.

In exchange, Obama's second term was a boon for Silicon Valley. Large tech companies stood to gain from free trade, which Obama consistently pushed for during his presidency. They lobbied effectively to preserve net neutrality and prevent backward-looking copyright laws. There was widespread government support to financially hedge entrepreneurs and investors against failure while they wandered in relatively unknown technological territories such as solar power and electric cars.

Even the Affordable Care Act, the signature legislation of the Obama era, had a positive impact on Silicon Valley. Separating access to healthcare from stable employment effectively benefited entrepreneurs and self-employed workers finding gigs on technology-driven platforms[17]. And this is without mentioning the opportunity that the major overhaul of the US healthcare system represented for aspiring entrepreneurs in that particular industry[18].

Following Obama's reelection, many (myself included) thought that Democrats were about to tighten their grip on US politics for several more decades. They had found reliable allies in the increasingly dominant industry of the day. Their electoral base was now firmly located in urban areas, which bring together those more prone to tackle the challenges of the new paradigm. They appeared ready to make inroads in the difficult field of radical institutional innovation. And Hillary Clinton was setting out to cement Obama's legacy—just as Harry Truman had done for Franklin D. Roosevelt from 1945 onward[19]. Allied with entrepreneurs and prepared to imagine a better future, a new lineage of liberal, forward-looking US presidents was about to move decidedly towards the advent of the new age. US Democrats were about to lead the world out of the darkness and back into the light.

Obviously something went terribly wrong along the way. One worrying signal had been there since at least 2010: Democrats controlled the White House, but they were at their weakest in every other part of the complex US political system. And while tech executives overwhelmingly endorsed Hillary Clinton for the presidency, Obama's successor as Democratic nominee was from a different era. She may have been successful in a pre-digital political world, where her qualities might have been better rewarded. But she found insurmountable difficulties in a world where technology makes it possible for candidates to connect directly with the voters. The era when it was enough to compromise on a centrist agenda and court big corporate donors was gone. You could say that American voters supported Donald Trump for the same reason that they had elected Obama before him: now technology made it possible for them to make their voice heard and go against big donors and the establishment[20].

It appears Silicon Valley has lost a lot during this process. The Democratic Party has failed to stick to power and the piling up of revelations about technology contributing to the outcome of the 2016 presidential election is creating major problems for the largest tech companies. Tech's role in Trump's election has created suspicion in Democrats and greatly degraded Silicon Valley's image in the rest of the Western world. Meanwhile, its coastal progressivism makes it equally suspicious for Republicans.

And so the *"tech backlash"* is not about to subside, especially now that the US tech industry also has to deal with an enemy from within: its own government. The Trump administration is renouncing free trade. Legacy industries are winning battles against tech companies, as seen in the energy industry or with the fight against net neutrality. And the US government is cracking down on immigration, which is one key to prospering in the current paradigm shift.

All in all, technology almost became mainstream with Obama and the Democrats. But now that Trump and the Republicans have the upper hand, it's in danger of being labelled the enemy and sidelined in the political system. The US tech industry has squandered the opportunity to remain the center of the new age of ubiquitous computing and networks.

And so the clock is ticking. Silicon Valley is not alone in the world. China is gearing up to match American power and push its own model forward. What we're currently going through is a very complicated game being played out on the global stage. And it will decide the prosperity and stability of the Western world in the coming years and decades.

The shifting balance of international power

Alice Zagury, Oussama Ammar and I founded our firm The Family to pursue a simple mission: provide entrepreneurs with all they need to overcome the many obstacles encountered while trying to build great tech companies. Advancing the cause of tech startups requires building a healthy ecosystem. A key part of that is garnering support (or at least not too much hostility) within government, academia, the press, and the traditional business world. Lacking the sheer size and power of the US venture capital industry, European entrepreneurs cannot afford to make too many enemies.

In that regard, the interests of European startups and the US tech industry are aligned. The fear and anger of the European elite is primarily targeted at US tech giants and their supposed over-reaching. But the ones who pay the highest price are local entrepreneurs. They find it harder to grow their businesses because what they do is deemed a threat for incumbents, jobs, and existing institutions.

The Family was initially designed as an entity dedicated to nurturing ambitious entrepreneurs based in France. But when it was only two years old, my partners and I became convinced that we needed to expand internationally. The reason was that early stage investing had already become a global market, with an ever-increasing level of competition. It was impossible for us to compete at that level if our portfolio was confined to only one country. If we wanted to keep working with the best and most ambitious entrepreneurs, Europe had to become our playing field.

Unfortunately, Europe is not on the map yet. It's true that some entrepreneurs have had some success in certain European countries. But none of their companies has reached the level of a continental player. In theory, Europe is a single market. In practice, though, it appears that linguistic, regulatory, and, above all, cultural barriers make it extremely difficult for European entrepreneurs to rely on the continent as the domestic market that will jumpstart their global ambitions.

Meanwhile, there's a lot of talk about China rising as a developed economy and matching the US as the other world power of our time. Prominent authors such as Henry Kissinger[21] and the British scholar Martin Jacques[22] have published landmark books to tout the idea that China is about to reconnect with its glorious, imperial past. Journalists observe that the Trump presidency, with its avowed goal of pulling America back from world affairs, is effectively a boon for China. As written by Evan Osnos in an in-depth piece for *The New Yorker*, "*China has never seen such a moment, when its pursuit of a larger role in the world coincides with America's pursuit of a smaller one*"[23].

Technology is one of the battlefields on which China and the US are effectively pitted against one another. Like in the US, the Chinese digital economy is now dominated by continental giants, among them Tencent, Alibaba, Baidu, and Didi Chuxing. And as with their US counterparts, it's difficult to tell exactly what industry these Chinese tech giants belong to. Most of them diversified into various sectors —both to generate revenue margins when they couldn't do it on their original market and to compete with each other and secure a stronger alliance with the vast multitude of Chinese internet users. Their appetite for growth is unlimited, and they appear to be formidable competitors.

The reason why Chinese entrepreneurs are so good at this game was once explained by Henry Kissinger:

"*Americans think a stable world is normal. And so, when the world isn't stable, then it's a problem. And if there's a problem, you solve it, and then you go on to something else. Chinese leaders think that resolution of a problem is an admission ticket to another problem. So almost every Chinese leader that I've ever met has wanted to think in a conceptual way of policy as a process rather than as a program.*"[24]

Replace *"policy"* with *"business"* and you get the point. Chinese entrepreneurs were trained by their unique history and culture to evolve in the permanent instability that characterizes the current age. And so as part of the *process* of doing business in today's highly competitive economy, the Chinese giants diversify; they buy out other tech companies; they innovate constantly; and at a certain point, they seek to expand to other countries. That is when they might challenge US tech companies.

Expanding Chinese companies can count on their government. As laid out by Chinese leader Xi Jinping, the famous Belt and Road Initiative is about reviving the old trade routes that once linked China to Europe and Africa. And as once explained to me by a Chinese economist advising the government in Beijing, it's also about turning places such as Djibouti and Vladivostok (and maybe Tehran) into entrepreneurial ecosystems comparable to Shenzhen—all financed by Chinese capital and relying on Chinese infrastructure. As China records a perennial surplus in capital and financial accounts, it has all the resources needed to push forward such an ambitious plan.

With this initiative, backed by the newly formed Asian Infrastructure Investment Bank, China is becoming more of *"a shaper and maker of globalisation"*, as stated by Martin Jacques[25]. It's not that the Chinese want to colonize other countries. Like the Portuguese in the sixteenth century[26], China isn't interested in conquering land and submitting entire peoples to its power. Rather their goal is to pursue a trade-, investment- and connectivity-driven exploration strategy designed to confirm China's superior approach to innovation, expand their economic reach, and support the growth of their businesses in the process. If this all seems to resemble the US strategy following World War II, well, that's because it does.

Indeed the Belt and Road Initiative is not only a brand encompassing various investments in tangible infrastructures. I believe it's also a *process* by which Chinese tech giants such as Tencent and Alibaba will be able to expand their operations throughout Asia, Africa, and Europe. There are already ways through which popular Chinese applications such as WeChat and Alipay are adopted beyond the Chinese domestic market, mainly the Chinese diaspora and the growing number of Chinese tourists travelling abroad. But once the same applications are adopted in Central Asia, Africa and Eastern Europe, with the experience curve that comes from expanding to new countries and adapting to their particular customs, how long will it take for Western Europeans to get interested in WeChat and Alipay, too? Belt and Road could be to China what the Empire was for Britain in the Victorian era: an instrument to secure long-term global leadership—only this time it'll be in technology instead of finance.

Because they think in Western-centric terms, many people in the West thought that the first step for the expanding Chinese giants would be to try and enter Europe. Few realized that before considering the European market, the Chinese would warm up in Asia and Africa. Lifted by the Belt and Road Initiative, the underlying network infrastructure, and innovative trade and consumption practices, Chinese tech giants will eventually be able to spread their wings everywhere else. The technological and economic power accumulated in the process will then be harnessed to break onto the pan-European market, which will ultimately lead to a showdown between US and Chinese tech companies in Europe.

This is a challenge for us Europeans. The European continent becoming a battlefield for US and Chinese tech giants, all driven by superior technology, abundant capital, and powerful network effects, will make it harder for European startups to impose products on their own market. What's more, if China comes to dominate the economy both in Asia and Africa, Europe will be one of the last foreign markets left for the faltering American Digital Empire. Desperate US tech companies will tighten their grip, making it more difficult for European tech champions to emerge.

But beyond Europe, the rise of networked China is an even bigger challenge for the US tech industry itself—and for the US as a whole. So far America has had an extraordinary journey through economic history since the Industrial Revolution. While it was still a young, developing republic in the nineteenth century, it emerged as the core of two consecutive surges of development: that which led to the age of steel and heavy engineering (at the end of the nineteenth century), and that which led to the age of the automobile and mass production (during most of the twentieth century)[27].

This extraordinary outcome was made possible by a mix of trends and events. One was the wealth of the US as a seemingly infinite pool

The Belt and Road Initiative:
How China Will Conquer the Digital World

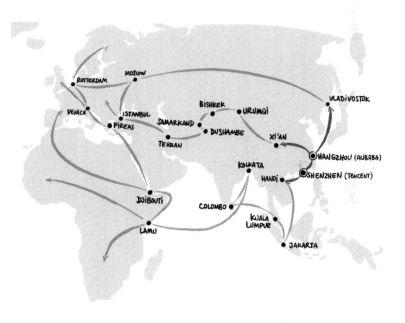

of land and other resources. Another factor was the disintegration of Europe, with Germany focusing more on its military than its industrial capacities from the end of the nineteenth century onward, and then the entire continent being wiped out by two consecutive world wars. A third factor was immigration. While Europe was losing itself to war and fascism, a massive influx of immigrants provided the US with an unrivaled entrepreneurial drive and an abundant workforce willing to fill the positions offered by the new industries of the day.

Until the 2008 financial crisis, it sure looked as if the US was going to strike for the third time in a row. It had once grown a world-class steel industry and then the mightiest car manufacturers in the world. Now America seemed poised to dominate the new age of ubiquitous computing and networks as well. It had invented the microprocessor, deployed the Internet, and given birth to what appeared to be the dominant corporate players of the age—the likes of Apple, Amazon, Google, and Facebook.

But the financial crisis turned the tables. For the Chinese, it first came as an unpleasant surprise. They, too, thought that we Westerners were firmly in control. Yet the events of 2008 proved we didn't have a clue how to manage the global economy in a sustainable way. In comparison, the Chinese financial system proved much more resistant than did that of the West, precipitating the dramatic power shift we've been witnessing ever since[28]. And so the 2008 crisis looks very much like a recurrence of the Great Depression, with China replacing the US as the emerging power. They have the stability that has deserted both the US and Europe. They're also racing ahead when it comes to growing the new businesses of the day and imagining the institutions that the new age calls for.

And that's really what is at stake here. Being the dominant power in a given techno-economic age is not only about nurturing the dominant corporations of the day. It's also about building the institutions needed to bring about economic security and prosperity. America has been the hotbed of three consecutive technological revolutions. But now that we're deep into the current age of ubiquitous computing and networks, it's entirely possible that the US will know the same fate as Germany at the dawn of the age of steel and heavy engineering. Despite having a headstart and everything needed to succeed, it could come up short and, taken aback by its own demise, experience the worst decades in its history. And if the US is the new Germany, then China is obviously the new US—and in that case we're not even sure what will become of Europe and the Western world as a whole.

Key takeaways

* *Technological progress was long seen as a boon for the Western economy. But since the 2008 crisis, it's been perceived more negatively, leading to the current "tech backlash".*

* *Now that tech companies are in a bind, it appears they've missed a once-in-a-lifetime opportunity: allying with the Democratic Party and building a better future together.*

* *While Donald Trump seemingly leads the US into the ground, China is rising as an economic and technological powerhouse. Now the dominant position of the Western world is at stake.*

Chapter 2
Technology and
Institutional Change

"The corporation managed the risk so well... that it created an innovation known as the steady job. For the first time in history, the risks of innovation were not borne by the poorest. This resulted in what economists call the Great Compression, when the gap between the income of the rich and poor rapidly fell to its lowest margin."
—Adam Davidson[1]

Modern history is a succession of paradigm shifts

I'm an engineer by training. So when I look at things I tend to see them in terms of a system. I divide what I see into elementary components. Then I hunt for the forces that explain the relationships between those components. This provides me with a model that I can reuse in many other situations.

Systems come with rigidity and they can thus become a mental trap that narrows your view of the world. But when you combine them with frequent reality checks, systems are a most powerful tool to interpret the world and share your interpretation with others. When you've crafted your own system to comprehend things such as politics, history, technology, the economy, or business, you can harness it to push in favor of radical, positive change and get things in motion.

Another systems lover that I've discovered in recent years is Carlota Perez. I first encountered Carlota's work by reading William H. Janeway's landmark work, *Doing Capitalism in the Innovation Economy*[2]. I then had the opportunity to meet her thanks to an introduction by Yann Ranchère of the investment firm Anthemis, which supports Carlota's work through the Anthemis Institute.

Carlota was born in Venezuela in 1939. Her first career there was as a civil servant specialized in energy and innovation policy[3]. Later in life, she switched to academia, settling in the UK where she started to focus on the relationship between technological change and financial markets. Almost by coincidence, her only book to date, *Technological Revolutions and Financial Capital*[4], was first published in 2002, right after the bursting of the technology bubble of the 1990s. In the post-bubble context, the book caught the attention of influential venture capitalists such as Fred Wilson[5], Marc Andreessen[6], and Chris Dixon[7], who then used it to nurture their understanding of the market.

It has since triggered a positive feedback loop. A significant part of the venture capital community has adopted Carlota's system as the bedrock of their investment theses. In turn, investors echoing Carlota's ideas in their day-to-day practices have had the effect of getting her even more interested in technology. As of now, Carlota has become one of the most important living authors of the new age as she contributes to revealing and even directing the current paradigm shift.

In Carlota's system, a *"great surge of development"* is a phenomenon that only happens once or twice in a century. The sequence always goes through two different phases. The *"installation phase"* is dominated by financial speculation and revolutionary entrepreneurial drive. In the *"deployment phase"* that follows, governments take the lead and set up the institutions that are needed for the new economy to enter a *"Golden Age"*. A *"major technology bubble"*[8] always marks the turning point of the surge. The exuberance of a bubble is necessary to attract capital, explore the many applications of the new technology of the day, and finance the infrastructures necessary to sustain the transition from one great surge to the other over the long term.

To devise her model, Carlota identified several consecutive great surges of development in modern economic history, from the spread of mechanization at the end of the eighteenth century to the rise of the automobile industry at the beginning of the twentieth century. In between those two periods, the world economy also went through the age of steam and iron railways and the subsequent age of steel and heavy engineering (civil, naval, electrical, chemical).

Carlota describes each of these revolutions as *"a powerful and highly visible cluster of new and dynamic technologies, products and industries... a strongly interrelated constellation of technical innovations, generally including an important all-pervasive low-cost input, often a source of energy, sometimes a crucial material, plus significant new products and processes and a new infrastructure."*[9] Each has spawned its own *"techno-economic paradigm"*, which is a set of best practice principles for innovation—the new common sense that organizations need to embrace if they want to remain competitive in the economy of the day.

The first great surge of development began in 1771, when English merchant Richard Arkwright built his legendary Cromford mill. By combining labor, capital in the form of machines, and energy generated by a paddle wheel (later a steam engine), Arkwright's mill inspired a widespread effort to mechanize the production of textiles. This period marked the beginning of unprecedented productivity gains and a radical transformation of the Western economy. Cotton-spinning mills were built everywhere. Canals were dug to transport goods and commodities in large quantities[10]. Productivity gained steam at the macroeconomic level and propelled economic growth to unprecedented heights[11]. The period of dramatic prosperity that followed the rise of the textile industry proved a radical break in economic history. This is why we remember it as the Industrial Revolution.

The next great surge began in 1829 with the triumph of Robert Stephenson's Rocket steam locomotive in the competition to propel the newly formed Liverpool-Manchester Railway. Thanks to the speculative Railway Mania that ensued in the UK, the development of railways brought about radical changes in the economy, with the shortening of distances and the possibility of transporting goods, people, and information in a much shorter time frame. Sources of energy started to diversify, with steam coming after coal. Increasing mastery of iron metallurgy allowed progress in industrial production and opened up yet another period of Britain-centered prosperity, the Victorian era. This was a time when UK was at the height of its industrial and military power. In turn, the US, Germany and France deployed their own rail infrastructures and gradually caught up in terms of economic development[12].

The third great surge was born with the development of a new, pervasive, low-cost input: steel. From the middle of the 1870s onward, technical progress in the manufacturing of alloys made it possible to mass produce steel at ever-lower prices. The abundance of cheap steel allowed the development of heavy engineering: the construction of the first large factories, the deployment of the transcontinental railway lines, the construction of steamboats, and the installation of submarine cables that enabled instantaneous telegraphic communication from one continent to another. Thanks to cheap steel and a whole set of new institutions, the economy entered a phase of globalization. Capital was also deployed to produce, transport and distribute electricity, a new form of energy that would later lift production and consumption up to an even larger scale.

The fourth great surge of development was marked by the eruption of cheap oil into the economy. First used for lighting, oil would gradually reveal its ability to propel engines[13]. Meanwhile, the *American system of manufacturing*, which promoted interchangeable parts, had led to the development of the typewriter, sewing machine, and bicycle. As they began generating demand for precision machine tools, the industries that grew up around these products became forerunners of a new approach to industrial production, paving the way for the emerging automobile industry. Henry Ford launched production of the Model T in 1908 and applied the principles of both the *American system* and scientific management to assembly lines producing cars for mass consumption. One after another, all industries embraced the new techno-economic paradigm discovered by the pioneering car industry. The mass production of goods and services began to serve ever larger consumer markets. After World War II, the deployment phase of the age of the automobile and mass production gave rise to one of the longest periods of prosperity in economic history—an episode known as the post-war boom[14].

The origins of the current great surge, the fifth since the end of the eighteenth century, dates back to 1971 when the first microprocessor was developed by Intel, a company founded three years earlier by Robert Noyce and Gordon Moore[15]. Thanks to the integration of all the key components of a computer on a single chip, the microprocessor would give birth to the microcomputer. Driven by this breakthrough technology, computing would find its way out of the world of large corporations, universities and government agencies to finally reach the general public—notably with the burst of personal computing in the 1980s orchestrated by companies such as Apple and Microsoft.

The microprocessor is the breakthrough innovation that, 25 years later when the US government opened the Internet to the private sector[16], brought the frenzy of a major technology bubble. In turn, the bubble would lead to the triumph of ubiquitous computing and its revolutionary impact. The spread and exploitation of new technologies depends on the construction of relevant networked infrastructure. And bubbles are often the only way to weave the network together before the investments pay off. It's in the nature of infrastructures to be all or nothing, and bubbles allow capital gains to replace potential dividends as the bits are being joined, with profits destined to form only much later in the future.

With this fifth great surge now nearing its deployment phase, we are definitely leaving the age of the automobile and mass production. Much like in the last century, we are witnessing a new techno-economic paradigm expanding into more and more industries, with new entrants harnessing the power of computing and networks to impose a new mode of production and consumption. Today is not about big, pyramidal organizations seeking supply-side economies of scale to mass-produce standardized goods and services for mass consumption. It is about agile, innovative firms obsessed with using technology-driven network effects to produce an exceptional experience at a large scale.

Transitions from one age to another are never easy. Even once the age of the automobile and mass production had entered its long period of senile decay, we had to wait quite some time before a new techno-paradigm emerged—and we were only prompted to better understand it by prescient authors such as Carlota Perez. The hesitations in our vocabulary bear witness to this as we alternatively use the vague terms of a *"post-industrial economy"*, a *"post-Fordist economy"*[17], a *"knowledge economy"*[18], the *"immaterial economy"*[19], *"network economy"*[20], *"digital economy"*[21], or simply the *"next economy"*[22].

The 2008 crisis accelerated the decomposition process of the old age and pushed forward the new techno-economic paradigm, helping us to see it more clearly. We needed new infrastructures to emerge and multiply the performance of transportation and commu-

THE FIVE GREAT SURGES OF DEVELOPMENT

1771 THE INDUSTRIAL REVOLUTION (UK)

1829 THE AGE OF STEAM & RAILWAYS (UK)

1875 THE AGE OF STEEL & HEAVY ENGINEERING (GERMANY, US)

1908 THE AGE OF THE AUTOMOBILE & MASS PRODUCTION (US)

1971 THE AGE OF UBIQUITOS COMPUTING & NETWORKS (US, CHINA)

(INSPIRED BY CARLOTA PEREZ)

nication systems while reducing their costs to unprecedented lows. The change imposed on the economy as a whole has given birth to new companies. But that change has also exposed individuals to a new form of economic insecurity, which largely explains the ongoing crisis of the Western middle class.

Different days, similar problems

One symptom of the crisis is the difficulty most of us have in understanding blue-collar jobs and their place in our collective psyche. On the one hand, our social contract has seemingly been designed around the core message that social climbing was about escaping those blue-collar jobs and sparing your children from even considering them. The main reason for doing well in school is that it enables you to head to university and obtain a degree that shields you from manual labor.

On the other hand, there's a sense of nostalgia for the lost manufacturing jobs that have been wiped out by the winds of globalization, financialization, and automation. Donald Trump's *"Making America Great Again"* are mostly code words to signal that the US will be bringing manufacturing jobs back. It's appealing to large swaths of (white) American voters because of the pride and security that once used to be attached to manufacturing jobs, regardless of their position on the income ladder[23]. It's all the more appealing because what most people see in the rising age of ubiquitous computing and networks is fewer jobs, diminishing wages, a wider inequality gap, and rising economic insecurity.

We can hardly prove those people wrong. The *"Great Decoupling"* is how Erik Brynjolfsson and Andrew McAfee describe the widening gap between productivity gains and real household income[24]. Fast-paced technological progress makes it possible for businesses to maximize output per worker. Yet unlike what happened during the post-war boom, higher labor productivity isn't translating into greater purchasing power for workers. On the contrary, the impression is that the more technology we deploy, the further workers fall down the social ladder. And so while technology could be seen as the solution to our current economic and social problems, in the actual state of things it's seen as only making the situation worse.

Too many people accept the pessimism inspired by an imagined past and a difficult present. For them, inequalities are bound to rise and jobs are bound to disappear. The only way to preserve balance in society would be to slow down technological progress (the solution of the neo-Luddite[25]) or to implement universal basic income (the solution of the politically inexperienced Silicon Valley engineer, which I'll discuss later in this book).

Another group of people, however, correctly observe that the same decoupling happened one century ago, just when we entered the age of the automobile and mass production. As the labor historian Nelson Lichtenstein has noted[26], in the 1920s *"output per worker in [US] manufacturing leaped upward by a remarkable 43 percent, while wages barely held their own."* In other words, what we're currently going through is not unprecedented. Rather it is to a great extent a recurrence of what happened in the 1920s and '30s when the Western world transitioned from the nineteenth century age of steel and heavy engineering to the twentieth century age of the automobile and mass production.

With *The Great Transformation*, published in 1944, the Hungarian-born historian and economist Karl Polanyi offers one of the best accounts of that techno-economic transition[27]. Although it's not autobiographical, the book is deeply rooted in Polanyi's life. Like many who grew up in Budapest and Vienna before the Great War, he witnessed first-hand the downfall of a civilization. As a soldier in the Austro-Hungarian army on the Eastern front, he experienced the violence and absurdity of World War I. As a socialist Jew, he fled the persecutions that later contributed to bringing down Europe. And as an intellectual, he felt the urge to write about it. This gave us *The Great Transformation*, one of the greatest political and economic tales of the troubled twentieth century.

Polanyi's work is often described as a harsh critique of *laissez-faire* in the tradition of classical liberalism[28]. But in my eyes it's also helpful to think about the institutions that are needed to support the market system and make it more sustainable and inclusive. The overarching concept brought forward by Polanyi is that of the *"double movement"*[29]: driven by technology, the market starts imposing its dynamics onto society; then, reacting to the harshness of the unrestrained market and the suffering it brings about, society reacts and ultimately reshapes the corporate world to channel its power and serve the many instead of the few. The *"Great Transformation"* is the painful process a society must go through to imagine and set up these indispensable institutions—a process that includes softer methods, like elections and collective bargaining, but also more destructive paths, like revolutions, fascism, and war.

Indeed what Polanyi describes in his book is the long techno-economic transition between two very different worlds. One is the nineteenth century economy, which mostly relied on the gold standard. Its prosperity during the age of steel and heavy engineering remained characterized by extreme economic inequality and limited access to the political process. The other is the twentieth century Fordist economy that gave birth to the age of the automobile and mass production, accompanied by the widespread expansion of voting rights.

Toward the end of the nineteenth century the old economic order began to unravel. At work was the rise of various forms of protectionism, from tariff barriers to colonial empires. When several pillars of that system began to falter, the resulting tensions mounted up toward World War I, which completed the destruction of the nineteenth century world order and proved to be the final crisis of the gold standard. As written by Polanyi, *"the breakdown of the international gold standard was the invisible link between the disintegration of the world economy which started at the turn of the century and the transformation of a whole civilization in the thirties"*[30].

Another world began to emerge, in which production and consumption proved radically different from what they used to be. Many works of art, among them Upton Sinclair's *The Jungle* (1906)[31] and Charlie Chaplin's *Modern Times* (1936), dealt with the fear that the new system of production inspired in astounded intellectuals and artists of the time. Today, the Fordist system — mass production of standardized products along giant assembly lines ruled by scientific management—may inspire nostalgia for those lost, secure jobs in manufacturing and giant bureaucracies. But at the time, it was a frightening world of insecurity and alienation. Absent were the institutions that would finally put the Fordist economy on the path to economic security and prosperity. As Joseph Stiglitz wrote in the introduction to a recent edition of Polanyi's book, *"rapid transformation destroys old coping mechanisms, old safety nets, while it creates a new set of demands, before new coping mechanisms are developed"*[32].

The fact is that the first half of last century was marked by the long and violent crisis that confronted two powerful movements. On one side were the established tenants of *laissez-faire*: backward-looking business leaders and elected officials who favored restoring market mechanisms as they had known them. On the other side was the emerging labor movement. Immediately following World War I, which had marked the failure of the ruling elite, empowered union leaders and socialist politicians tried to make the most of the extension of voting rights to advocate for their cause. Harnessing the democratic process, they demanded that the business community and the government finally put in place a safety net that would provide economic security to the rising industrial working class. The thriving big Fordist factories brought about new risks for which new coping mechanisms needed to be deployed.

The impossibility of settling that dispute amicably led to the unraveling of Europe. Again according to Stiglitz, *"when neither movement was able to impose its solution to the crisis, tensions increased until fascism gained the strength to seize power and break with both laissez-faire and democracy"*[33]. Even though Europe paid the highest price, fascism appeared in different places around the world. This suggests that fascism was not linked to a particular cultural or political context as much as it resulted from the tensions brought about by the transition itself.

Indeed the path from cheap oil and assembly lines to the prosperity of the post-war boom wasn't easily traveled. The Great Depression signaled the exhaustion of the age of steel and heavy engineering. The growth of the Fordist mode of production imposed suffering on workers and instability on markets driven by the booms and busts of mass consumption. In the aftermath of the trauma that was World War I, the incapacity of legacy institutions to hedge individuals against the critical risks of the day led to unrest in the workplace, political turmoil, the rise of fascism, and the race to yet another world war. It was only after World War II that Western governments were finally able to install a whole set of new institutions for the techno-economic paradigm of the new age.

How we once built the Great Safety Net 1.0

The central question of this book is this: *Where do prosperity and economic security come from?* I believe they don't come from a single magic-bullet mechanism like wage subsidies, a robot tax, tougher antitrust measures, a higher minimum wage, or universal basic income. Rather they can only emerge from a complex macro mechanism that goes way beyond the narrow definition of the safety net (e.g. the welfare state). In the age of the automobile and mass production, what I call the 'Great Safety Net' used to rely on three major institutional pillars: social insurance, the financial system, and collective bargaining.

The first pillar was *social insurance*: programs designed to cover certain critical risks to which individuals are exposed, such as old age, illness, and unemployment. One of the first such programs to have been deployed by government authorities was Germany's occupational accident insurance in 1884. The goal of then-Reich Chancellor Otto von Bismarck was not to cater to the demands of the labor movement, which he hated. Rather, it was to undercut the nascent trade unions of the time as they were gaining strength in propagating dangerous socialist ideas.

Occupational accident insurance was a breakthrough in that for the first time employers had been given a legal responsibility for the well-being of their employees. After Bismarck's inroads in the field of social insurance (an achievement later known as *"state socialism"*), the UK followed suit with the Old-Age Pensions Act of 1908 and the National Insurance Act of 1911. Then in 1935 Franklin D. Roosevelt and Frances Perkins, his Secretary of Labor, oversaw the creation of Social Security in the US. A consensus started to emerge around this unprecedented approach: covering households against critical risks was best implemented at the level of entire industries or nations; as such, it required state intervention.

Social insurance had an impact in many dimensions. It hedged individuals against critical risks, thus ensuring economic security for households. It also contributed to steadier consumer demand at the macroeconomic level because in the presence of such programs, households consume no matter what—even when people are injured, sick, unemployed, or simply too old to work.

At the dawn of the Fordist economy, widespread instability on large consumer markets had led firms to renounce investment, which in turn had fueled unemployment, which in turn had depressed consumer demand, and so on and so forth down to the Great Depression. Social insurance proved the most adequate remedy to such instability, a non-distortive way to provide economic security to individuals. Unlike mechanisms such as price controls or prohibiting layoffs, social insurance was a market-friendly solution that protected households and lifted up businesses at the same time— thus supporting what Will Wilkinson, of the libertarian Niskanen Center, calls *"the freedom lover's case for the welfare state"*[34].

But social insurance, however wide, was not enough to deliver economic security in a customized and sustainable way over the long term. The Great Safety Net wouldn't have been as effective without a second pillar, the *financial system*.

The idea that finance complemented social insurance may sound odd in today's context. But you shouldn't underestimate the power of finance when it comes to mitigating the risks to which households and businesses are exposed in their respective spheres.

For instance, with a little help from the US government (through organizations such as Fannie Mae and Freddie Mac, which provided government backing for mortgages), financial markets made it possible for American households to buy houses, which under certain conditions contributes to strengthening economic security. The financial system also played a role in making pension plans more sustainable over the long term (though poor stewardship could obviously produce the opposite result). Additionally, it provided individuals with the cash they needed to consume durable and expensive goods such as cars and appliances, and it occasionally covered daily consumption thanks to consumer credit.

Mobilizing the financial system to serve the masses was good for corporations in many ways. It wasn't only that consumer finance consistently fueled demand at the macroeconomic level. Inviting households into the financial system also made it possible to harness their savings to finance the mounting capital needs of ever-larger companies tackling ever-more capital-intensive industrial challenges. To finance the heavier industries that arose from the age of steel and heavy engineering onward, financial capital had to be organized beyond the small-scale merchant banking deals of the past. And households joining as capital providers in the corporate game was yet more proof that hedging individuals against critical risks was ultimately a good thing for the corporations themselves.

Far from being exclusive or independent of one another, social insurance and the new financial system ultimately came to be seen as two sides of the same coin. Because social insurance contributed to stabilizing household income even in the presence of critical risks, it became a key argument to prove solvency and reassure lenders. Thanks to social insurance, households borrowing money to buy a house or a car would always be able to pay off their debts whatever the ups and downs of the income derived from their labor. Conversely, the constant growth of consumer credit made it possible to sustain mass consumption at an ever larger scale, contributing to higher tax revenues and an improved capacity to bankroll broader social insurance systems.

Yet the two pillars of social insurance and the financial system, although complementary, were still not enough to ensure economic security and prosperity in the fast-growing Fordist economy of the time. The Great Safety Net also needed a dynamic force to grow from being simple to being comprehensive and adaptative. This force—the third pillar—was found in the *trade unions*. With collective bargaining, unions established a balance of power with employers. And with assistance from the government, they were able to gain the advantage and eventually obtain a larger part of the added value for workers.

It's true that union leaders, especially in Europe, used Marxism to bring industrial workers together. As a result, most people, including terrified politicians and business owners, saw unions as active agents of the destruction of capitalism. But in the nascent age of the automobile and mass production, there were two pressing problems with capitalism that only trade unions could address.

First, unions contributed to solving the problem of underconsumption by imposing higher wages in exchange for productivity gains. Complementing new legislation enacted by the governments around the world, they helped put a floor on wages and prices as well as a ceiling on hours and efforts, industry by industry. For that, collective bargaining at the company and industry levels was critical. As explained by Nelson Lichtenstein, *"labor's voice was essential to... industry self-regulation, because only the trade unions possessed an intimate, internal knowledge of business conditions. Only they could 'enforce' government-mandated minimum-wage standards and maximum-hour regulation"*[35].

Second, unions contributed to promoting the idea of *"industrial democracy"*[36]. Empowering workers meant promoting a higher standard of living, which included both economic security for the workers, and social security for the others (the old, the sick, the families). Thanks to industrial democracy, workers had their say in company matters, which led to a less rebellious workforce.

All in all, much like social insurance, collective bargaining benefited both households (under the form of higher wages and industrial democracy) and businesses (under the form of increased consumer demand and a more diligent workforce). Henry Ford dreaded unions, but he also famously understood the virtuous circle that linked consumption and production in the age of the automobile and mass production: *"One's own employees ought to be one's own best customers"*[37]. (Still, above all he wanted to reduce the huge employee turnover in his factories.[38])

Germany, France and the UK were among the first to enact new rules designed to protect and empower industrial workers. The US resisted assisting unions longer, probably because universal (white male) suffrage preceded industrialization, thus alleviating the pressure from the working masses. But from 1935 onward, it caught up with what has been called the Second New Deal, which included the National Labor Relations Act of 1935 (also known as the Wagner Act). Widespread assistance of unions by the US government lasted for over a decade, until Congress enacted the Taft-Hartley Act in 1948.

With the US catching up (even for a mere 12-year period), the principle of empowering workers came to be widely accepted in Western countries as necessary for providing economic security and prosperity. It prevented unrest in the workplace, sustained higher productivity gains, and contributed to redistributing wealth. Thanks to state-assisted unions, increasing wages finally caught up to productivity. The Great Safety Net was finally bringing the *"Great Decoupling"* to an end.

State assistance for unions proved to be the ideal complement to deploying social insurance and upgrading the financial system for the new age. With stronger unions, workers were now able to *voice* their demands for better working conditions. Meanwhile, thanks to the social insurance regimes and a more effective financial system which combined to make them less dependent on their employers, they could also *exit* when their unions couldn't reach an agreement with management. If the company went bankrupt because of the resulting strike, unemployment insurance was there as the safety net that workers needed to rebound. Likewise, if what they earned in exchange for their labor was not enough to purchase expensive goods, they could rely on the banking system to access additional capital.

This grip of voice and exit, explained in Albert O. Hirschman's famous framework[39], proved particularly powerful. Workers' bargaining power led to higher wages which, in turn, led to more tax revenue to bankroll social insurance regimes and a more widespread access to capital on financial markets—all of which improved the workers' bargaining power even more. These three pillars were stitching together the Great Safety Net that delivered economic security and prosperity in the age of the automobile and mass production.

Building the Great Safety Net differed a great deal from one country to another, even though national systems performed largely the same functions. In the US, it was a long process from the end of the nineteenth century to cementing Roosevelt's legacy during the post-war boom. There were many setbacks and shortcomings, and attacks against the Great Safety Net were never far away. One with the most long-term impact was the Taft-Hartley Act of 1948 that dramatically weakened state assistance to trade unions. And of course the US never achieved the goal of providing universal healthcare insurance, coming closest with the fragile (and incomplete) achievement that was Obamacare[40].

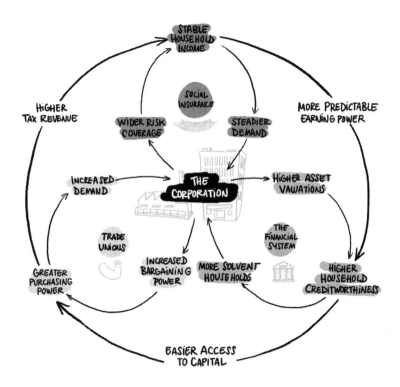

THE GREAT SAFETY NET 1.0
(AGE OF THE AUTOMOBILE & MASS PRODUCTION)

STABLE HOUSEHOLD INCOME

SOCIAL INSURANCE

HIGHER TAX REVENUE

MORE PREDICTABLE EARNING POWER

WIDER RISK COVERAGE

STEADIER DEMAND

INCREASED DEMAND

THE CORPORATION

HIGHER ASSET VALUATIONS

TRADE UNIONS

THE FINANCIAL SYSTEM

GREATER PURCHASING POWER

INCREASED BARGAINING POWER

MORE SOLVENT HOUSEHOLDS

HIGHER HOUSEHOLD CREDITWORTHINESS

EASIER ACCESS TO CAPITAL

Our European versions of the Great Safety Net were more ambitious and eventually more comprehensive. Indeed the trauma of World War II was significantly greater in Europe than it was in the US. But the war also provided a blank slate on which to build new institutions, and we knew that we had quite a lot to catch up on in terms of economic development and security at a large scale.

The German Great Safety Net was designed in line with the legacy of Bismarck's *"state socialism"*. Despite what the term *"state"* suggests, the German macro mechanism is organized industry by industry, mostly operated by employers and trade unions. Its explicit goal from 1945 onward was to hedge German households and businesses against the widespread instability and economic insecurity that had once paved the way for the rise of the NSDAP.

The UK took a different path. Following the conclusions of the landmark *Beveridge Report* of 1942, it opted for a more universal approach than the German corporatist system. The deeper involvement of the state culminated with the establishment of the National Health Service immediately after the war.

And as for my home country of France, we picked a little bit from both worlds, as is our way. Our national Great Safety Net was initially organized at the industry level, like in Germany; but over time the state became more and more involved, like in the UK, so as to take a more universal approach to economic security and prosperity.

All in all, the West's economic history since the 1908 Model T can be read as the long struggle to shape and improve this 'Great Safety Net 1.0'. At first, it had to be imagined. It took the sheer will of the labor movement and a great deal of help from governments (as well as the Great Depression and two world wars) to succeed. Then it bore fruits with the post-war boom.

As explained by Carlota Perez, each techno-economic paradigm involves a new understanding of the current means of production and consumption. In turn, it imposes a new way of life and thus calls for new institutions. Only with a new *"socio-institutional framework"*[41] in line with the new age can society enter a period marked by the redistribution of wealth to the many, the massive creation of jobs, and widespread prosperity. No technological revolution can deliver both economic security and prosperity if it doesn't trigger Karl Polanyi's concept of a *"double movement"*[42].

This is exactly what happened after World War II. In a society traumatized by global conflict, Western governments had to counter market instability by providing businesses as well as households with increased economic security. For a few decades in the twentieth century, a new set institutions was effectively shaped in the interest of both households and businesses. Thanks to the Great Safety Net 1.0, individuals were empowered and protected against critical risks. Meanwhile, corporations could count on sustained and growing consumer demand that made it possible for them to serenely invest in their businesses and make more profits. Indeed, what was there not to like? And, above all, can we once again rise to such a challenge?

Key takeaways

• *We're currently going through the fifth great surge of development since the Industrial Revolution, one that is leading us into the age of ubiquitous computing and networks.*

• *During the previous great surge, that of the automobile and mass production, the installation period culminated in problems similar to those we're experiencing today.*

• *Those problems were solved by deploying the 'Great Safety Net 1.0', a macro mechanism designed to deliver economic security and prosperity to both households and businesses.*

Chapter 3
Stuck in the Dark Ages

*"A country approaching the fascist phase showed [common] symptoms,
among [them] the spread of irrationalistic philosophies, racialist
aesthetics, anticapitalistic demagogy, heterodox currency views,
criticism of the party system, widespread disparagement of the "regime,"
or whatever was the name given to the existing democratic setup...
Fascism was an ever-given political possibility, an almost instantaneous
emotional reaction in every industrial community since the 1930s."*
—Karl Polany[ii]

The Western middle class's never-ending crisis

I've always felt part of the middle class. My parents had good,
stable jobs. My siblings and I had the opportunity to go to good
schools and attend events such as art exhibitions and jazz concerts.
I learned musical instruments (clarinet, saxophone, piano, and then
bass guitar) and played a few sports, including fencing and tennis. At
the same time, we didn't often go to restaurants and we never traveled much. But life felt relatively rewarding and we were imbued
with a solid sense of economic security.

Today the vast majority of people in the West still identify as
middle class. But the very concept of the middle class has evolved
through time. When I grew up in the 1970s and '80s, the cardinal
value of the middle class was stability. Most people had a fixed place
in the world and defined themselves through what they were doing
in life. As for today, being part of the middle class looks more like
the main character in Steven Soderbergh's *Magic Mike*: laboring
during the day as a construction worker, making money as a stripper
in night-clubs and private parties, and steadily describing himself as
an *"entrepreneur"*.

As in the case of Magic Mike, gone is the sense of economic security that provided middle class workers with a clear identity. Now we live in a world where job situations are unclear. People are no longer certain about what the future holds or even what their occupation is. Is Magic Mike a construction worker, a stripper, or an entrepreneur? Nobody knows, and so he is forced to decide for himself—in what the *Financial Times* columnist Simon Kuper calls the *"great middle class identity crisis"*[2].

What defines the middle class today is less stability than the dream of climbing up the economic ladder and, simultaneously, the nightmare of potentially falling down it. Values such as risk-taking and self-reliance rather than stability and solidarity become more central in the day-to-day experience of most households. Instability is creeping in to nourish the feeling of a looming and perpetual crisis. The middle class is now less about status and more about aspirations and fears.

And yet middle class workers didn't wait for computers and the Internet to identify threats to their status. In reality, their identity and economic problems have been in the making since at least the 1970s. Before that time, the middle class, buoyed by economic security, was enjoying the fruits of post-war peace and prosperity. Then everything changed.

The macroeconomic context of the time was transformed by many factors. Less developed countries started to catch up on the US, imposing an unprecedented level of competition on Western businesses. The Nixon administration abandoned the Bretton Woods system and let the dollar float, which led to more volatile exchange rates. The oil shocks of the '70s and the sharp increase in the price of oil resulted in a widespread energy crisis.

These changes took place atop a cultural and political crisis, revealed in many countries by the turmoil of 1968-69 and made even worse by degrading economic conditions. Every Western country went through the same feeling of decline, with the youth voicing demands for emancipation, workers fomenting unrest at the workplace, unemployment rising again after three decades of prosperity, and the simultaneous rise of inflation (an unprecedented phenomenon known as 'stagflation'). There were also occasional conflicts in every region of the globe, the intensification of violence in the

Middle East, and even frequent terrorist attacks in Western countries such as Germany and Italy. Viewed from the Western middle class, the 1970s were the beginning of a long, grim period of crisis. Again, all this was long before the Internet was a thing.

That decade of crisis triggered an institutional response in the form of neoliberalism. This new set of ideas, inspired by the likes of Friedrich Hayek and Milton Friedman[3], sought to draw lessons from the failures of state intervention in the 1970s. The stagflation of the time motivated an outright rejection of Keynesianism[4] and established the triumph of the rational expectations hypothesis[5]—an attempt at rejuvenating the concept of nineteenth-century *laissez-faire* at the macroeconomic level. In the US, it culminated with Fed chairman Paul Volcker battling inflation with higher interest rates from 1979 onwards. A series of tax and fiscal reforms was also designed to boost investment while trying to contain rising deficits[6]. In Europe, Germany led the way in promoting stable currencies and low deficits, using the (long) path to forming the Eurozone to impose its macroeconomic discipline across the continent[7].

In the end, the world economy decidedly pulled out of stagflation and entered a new phase of both stability at the macroeconomic levels (a phenomenon known as the *"Great Moderation"*[8]) and accelerated institutional change[9]. Neoliberalism, the ideology encompassing the new economic thinking of the day, was championed by prominent conservatives such as Margaret Thatcher and Ronald Reagan. It also changed center-left politics, with the French Socialist Party taking charge of deregulating the domestic financial system in 1985 and Chancellor Gerhard Schröder orchestrating the famous *"Hartz reforms"* to render the German labor market more flexible from 2003 onward.

International institutions played their role, too. The European Union promoted the principles of neoliberalism as it began building the European single market in 1986. The so-called *"Washington Consensus"* provided many countries with the standard package of reforms to convert to a neoliberal approach. After the fall of the Berlin Wall, a vast ideological offensive was launched to convert the rising elite in Eastern European countries. At stake was their support for democracy but also the assurance that pro-market leaders would have the upper hand.

Over time, the neoliberal offensive bore fruits as it contributed to accelerating the development of less developed regions and lifting many people out of poverty, actually narrowing the global inequality gap[10]. But for the Western middle class, there was a price to pay. Increased global competition forced flexibility onto the labor market. Jobs in manufacturing and then in services were destroyed and replaced by cheaper jobs in other regions of the world. Stagnating wages and rising unemployment made it difficult to finance the most advanced welfare states. Taxes were raised and benefits were decreased.

The shift accelerated with a radical transformation of the corporate world. From the 1970s onward, most businesses born in the prosperous age of the automobile and mass production experienced a sudden and unprecedented pressure that forced them to redesign their entire system of operations to make them more efficient. Trade barriers and tariffs came down, facilitating the integration of corporate operations on a global scale. Corporations grew even larger, industries became more concentrated[11], and global value chains were consolidated by geographical arbitrage and changes in the tools and methods of business[12]. These all played a key and positive role in increasing the competitiveness of firms. But they also contributed to weakening the Western workers' bargaining power. What David Weil calls the *"fissured workplace"*, which relies more on outsourcing and contracting[13], now leaves fewer steady jobs to be had by Western workers.

Similarly, finance's going global meant that corporate shareholders grew more powerful at the expense of workers. At one point in the 1930s, General Motors had more individual shareholders (half a million) than it had employees (a quarter of a million)[14]. That division of shareholders' forces helped CEO Alfred P. Sloan dictate his terms and do as he pleased, without paying too much attention to what individual shareholders had to say.

But from the 1970s onward, power shifted. Households now invested their savings through large and powerful intermediaries such as pension funds and mutual funds. The rules that had been set up to protect individual savers against the greed or incompetence of corporate executives were now leveraged by professional agents with billions of dollars of assets under management[15]. What's more, the financial services industry came to rely more on information and communication technologies, concentrating itself in a very few select cities rather than being spread all over the world. With this unprecedented concentration and the related emergence of global financial powerhouses, increasingly short-term constraints began to be exerted on public corporations[16].

At some point in the 1990s, the overall pressure on employment and wages became a macroeconomic threat to mass consumption, even in the presence of cheaper products. To maintain the middle class standard of living, the financial system was summoned to support mass consumption through the rise of private debt. Western households were eventually showered with cheap and abundant banking credit so that they could keep on consuming and buying houses. But the end result was the 2008 financial crisis and its destruction of any remaining delusions as to the state of the Western middle class.

All in all, the long period from 1968 to 2008 was tough on the middle class from many points of view. Innovation slowed down[17], the inequality gap widened[18], economic insecurity reached heights unknown since World War II[19], and populism rose again[20]. The rise of technology has hardly eased the pain. Over time it has even made some things worse.

This is why I call this period the *Dark Ages*: a long and ambivalent period between the fall of the Empire (the fading age of the automobile and mass production) and the Renaissance (the flowering age of ubiquitous computing and networks). We could make the most of this Renaissance and harness technology to increase economic security and prosperity for all. But first we need to understand how much the Great Safety Net of the past has been dismantled in recent decades.

How the Dark Ages shifted risks onto individuals

2008 revealed the advanced decay of the age of the automobile and mass production. In the previous decades, we had managed to

WHY THE US MIDDLE CLASS
FEELS IN CRISIS

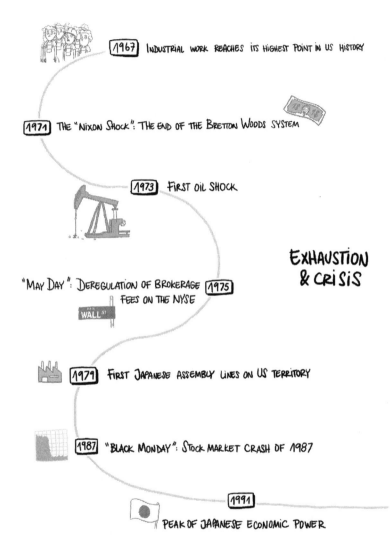

1967 INDUSTRIAL WORK REACHES ITS HIGHEST POINT IN US HISTORY

1971 THE "NIXON SHOCK": THE END OF THE BRETTON WOODS SYSTEM

1973 FIRST OIL SHOCK

EXHAUSTION & CRISIS

"MAY DAY": DEREGULATION OF BROKERAGE **1975**
FEES ON THE NYSE

1979 FIRST JAPANESE ASSEMBLY LINES ON US TERRITORY

1987 "BLACK MONDAY": STOCK MARKET CRASH OF 1987

1991

PEAK OF JAPANESE ECONOMIC POWER

CHINA IS THE WORLD'S LARGEST
ECONOMY IN PURCHASING POWER PARITY **2018**

US LIFE EXPECTANCY FALLS FOR THE SECOND YEAR IN A ROW **2016**

2011 SOFTWARE IS EATING THE WORLD

REBOOT
& PARADIGM SHIFT

2008 FINANCIAL CRISIS & THE FALL
OF DETROIT

 MARK ZUCKERBERG LAUNCHES FACEBOOK **2004**

 CHINA BECOMES A MEMBER OF
THE WORLD TRADE ORGANIZATION **2001**

1994
 JEFF BEZOS LAUNCHES AMAZON.COM
amazon

prolong the life of an exhausted techno-economic paradigm by using levers such as the rise of mass consumption in China, Brazil, Russia, and the Middle East, the possibility of making products cheaper by producing them offshore, the expansionary monetary policy that followed the terrorist attacks of 9/11 in the US, and the development of fracking to prolong the era of cheap fossil fuels. Governments used these to keep buying a few more tenths of a point in annual economic growth to counter unemployment and appease their voters. But the crisis brought all that to an end.

The problem is that the conversation on what should be done has been focused on the wrong issues. Because the agony of the previous techno-economic paradigm was revealed in a financial crisis, most discussions have been focused on finance itself. In her global best-seller *Makers and Takers*, Rana Foroohar has called for tackling the issue of financialization *"to ensure not only more sustainable growth, but more stable politics"*[21]. Harvard University's Clayton Christensen has dedicated a great deal of thought to how financial ratios have trumped corporate strategy and led the economy into the ground[22]. And in the US, the Dodd-Frank Act, the main regulatory response to the financial crisis, is still touted as a major part of Barack Obama's legacy[23].

Yet the extent of the crisis goes well beyond finance. The fact that the financial system is oversized and prone to systemic crisis doesn't call for regulating it more while leaving other policies untouched. Rather we must realize that the financial system has gone awry because we've left it as the only remaining pillar of the Great Safety Net 1.0, without the other pillars of social insurance and collective bargaining to complement it. This can be seen in how conservatives keep on stressing the importance of *"ownership"* as the best safety net for households[24], the inflating bubble of student loans, or the excessive reliance on consumption driven by credit card debt. With the financial system as the only mechanism for sustaining production and consumption, today's problem is less with the excesses of that particular system than with the failures of the Great Safety Net as a whole. And so tackling finance as the cause of our current problems is like prescribing cough drops to someone who's suffering from lung cancer.

One key feature of the Great Safety Net was the pooling of risks through social insurance. This was a major advance when compared with the past, when risks would only be covered by the family or small-scale pooling mechanisms such as mutual aid societies. The pooling of risks at a much larger scale boosted consumption because people were not required to save based on an excessive fear of what potential disaster tomorrow could bring. It also unleashed geographic mobility because workers were not required to stay close to their families and could pursue job opportunities elsewhere.

Alas in the past decades the old social insurance mechanisms have been dismantled or rendered less effective. Many risks are being gradually shifted back onto individuals again. The cost of healthcare has risen, and so households bear a larger part of the financial burden that comes with leaving work when they're sick and receiving treatment. The redistributive power of the pension system has been weakened as well, with the gradual replacement of traditional 'defined-benefits' pensions that provided a fixed benefit for life with 'defined-contributions' plans like the 401(k) which, as Jacob Hacker reminds us, *"offer neither predictable nor assured benefits"*[25]. It's now expected that more and more senior citizens will spend the last years of their lives without sufficient income[26].

There's also the misalignment between legacy mechanisms and the risks that dominate today. A key component of social insurance in the age of the automobile and mass production is that it was focused on salaried workers with steady jobs. Yet today steady jobs are increasingly the exception rather than the norm, at least for those who are newly hired. In the new age, individuals go through more diverse professional situations marked by occasionally violent ups and downs—a far cry from the linearity of yesterday's careers.

There are many reasons for the end of the steady job. One is simply the growing aspirations of people who like to change jobs from time to time. A more individualistic culture that promotes emancipation and innovation rather than community and continuity necessarily leads to more uneven career paths. Another reason is that technology, notably the abundance of information, makes the job market more efficient. If it's easier to learn about other jobs and to be trained to occupy them, then people will find it easier to think about switching jobs, and will act on it more often than not.

A third reason is that firms are simply more prone to failure. Today's economy is one in which more people embrace entrepreneurship. But their ventures also have a higher probability of disappearing in the near future. In the previous age, individuals could work for a long time in the same company no matter its size. But the new age will see an increased number of workers joining startups, which by definition are in search of their business model[27] and likely to disappear in a matter of years or even months. Others will have seemingly secure jobs at 'giants with clay feet'—large companies which, like Kodak or Toys "R" Us, will abruptly fall as they are unable to adapt and survive.

The intermittent nature of today's careers creates an unprecedented set of problems for social insurance. Such mechanisms that were designed for linear career paths are ill-fitted to respond to the needs of individuals whose working lives have become increasingly diverse, discontinuous and multiform. Because traditional social insurance is often linked to a stable job, it becomes discontinuous, inadequate or non-existent when individuals begin to change employers and employment status at a higher frequency.

With the unprecedented income discontinuity, intermittency itself becomes a risk that affects an increasing proportion of the population. No social insurance currently covers such a risk. Unemployment insurance, in particular, provides benefits only to employees who have contributed through their payroll taxes over a relatively long period. And by the way, a non-linear working life also means non-linear tax revenues because individuals don't contribute during the intermittent periods when they aren't earning a regular income.

Another adverse shift is that various social insurance mechanisms have failed to account for changes in the composition of households. Working families are evolving, with declining demographics, more blended families, older relatives that must be cared for much longer, and more single young parents—mostly women[28]. This new kind of 'atypical' working family has not made its way into our representation of the world. The institutions that were once designed to hedge families against critical risks still have the traditional 'working father / stay-at-home mother' family as the model.

Yet another risk shift is found in what economist Enrico Moretti calls the *"new geography of jobs"*[29]. Today, activities and jobs increasingly concentrate in the densest urban areas. Skilled workers gather in these areas in order to join the most dynamic and innovative companies whose growth and innovation efforts are fueled by the fact that they're close to each other. For less skilled workers, these areas of increased economic activity become magnets, too, as they need to be closer to where their job opportunities are. The problem is that these powerful clustering effects cause a steady increase in the price of real estate assets. And so a growing number of individuals are exposed to an unprecedented critical risk: not being able to afford to move into the cities where most of the jobs, social interactions and networking opportunities are located[30].

There is a close relationship between the rise of intermittency and evermore unaffordable housing. Intermittency makes housing more difficult, as it complicates the proof of solvency vis-à-vis landlords or lenders. Conversely, the difficulty of housing aggravates the intermittence of career paths. Many jobs in areas with high housing prices cannot be occupied in a stable way if people can't afford to live nearby. If the new economy creates relatively few jobs, it is not because it eliminates the needs that could be met by these jobs. It is rather because it makes it difficult to create those jobs due to the ever-increasing tension on the housing market. In other words, many jobs are not created because the majority of those who could occupy them are unable to find proper family housing in the areas where they are needed.

Collective bargaining, another pillar of the Great Safety Net, has also been weakened—even more than social insurance. In the past, state-assisted unions contributed to integrating a growing number of individuals in the workforce—including immigrants and minorities who formed a large portion of the unskilled workers toiling away in industrial facilities. For many decades, unions effectively wielded their newfound power to advance their members' interests, forcing employers to back down and share the wealth with workers. Thus state-assisted unions were instrumental in turning the working class into the middle class and inspiring the modern standard of living[31].

One reason why collective bargaining worked so well is that workers' unions bargain for the longer term. Unlike taxation or social insurance, the terms they negotiate are not in danger of being reversed at every electoral turn. Another distinctive feature is that unions, to quote Nelson Lichtenstein[32], are the only ones possessing an *"intimate, internal knowledge of business conditions"*. Finally, thanks to the power of polarization, bargaining in and of itself is a powerful means to achieve change and promote the workers' interest.

Alas today's unions are a mere shadow of their former selves[33]. Their demise was initiated in the 1970s. There was a growing indifference on the left as well as counter-measures such as 'right-to-work' laws and other union-busting mechanisms on the right. As a result, the working class has gradually turned away from legacy organizations that now fail to bargain on their behalf. Today's unions hardly serve as a proxy to advance workers' interests. And with their diminished influence on the political process comes rising economic insecurity for middle class workers[34] and a growing inequality gap.

This demise of most of the Great Safety Net 1.0 is mirrored by the transformation of the corporate world. During the post-war boom, the Great Safety Net was tied together by what Adam Davidson calls *"the single greatest risk-mitigating institution ever: the corporation"*[35]. As the entire economy consolidated around large, integrated firms[36], the government learned that it could rely on them as a proxy to implement policy in fields as diverse as collective bargaining, social insurance, and taxation. Big corporations, instead of being a foe, became a critical ally to help the state secure individuals.

Yet today big corporations are much less present. The more globalized ones are mostly beyond the state's reach: their restructuring into global value chains[37] has emptied their substance in many countries and made them reluctant to have too many dealings with governments. And big corporations employ fewer and fewer individuals as they've embraced contracting and outsourcing as their preferred way to access and exploit the workforce—again David Weil's *"fissured workplace"*[38]. As a result, policy primarily targeted at big Fordist corporations and using them as a proxy for risk-mitigation is bound to leave the vast majority of individuals off to the side. Employees of small and medium businesses, self-employed workers[39], students, job seekers, and startup founders are all out of reach for most institutions that used to be part of the Great Safety Net 1.0. The vast majority of workers are outsiders in a world where risks are covered only for those employed by large domestic corporations.

Even worse, the corporate world has mostly turned against the very principle of a Great Safety Net. As firms have to become more competitive, they've come to see the Great Safety Net as a burden to be sloughed off. The rise of imported products means that the Fordist positive feedback loop of mass production and mass consumption is becoming less obvious[40]. And the financial difficulties affecting the welfare state provide conservatives with anti-welfare state arguments and lead to regressive policies.

As a result, the macro mechanism that was the Great Safety Net 1.0 was slowly unraveled from 1968 onward, with social insurance programs becoming less sustainable and less effective while unions got weaker and lost their political clout. With the rise of neoliberalism, the remedy to this disturbance was the gradual removal of those two pillars. It left us with a radical bet on the financial system as the sole means to provide economic security and prosperity to both households and businesses.

That attempt at what Colin Crouch names *"Privatized Keynesianism"*[41] didn't work well and eventually went over the cliff with the 2008 financial crisis—a direct result of the economy's excessive reliance on household debt. When one's home became not only a shelter but also an investment for old age as well as collateral on which to borrow and consume, it exposed households to a potentially catastrophic failure of the financial system. Without the complementary balances provided by other pillars of the Great Safety Net, the goal of providing economic security and prosperity was submitted to the financial system's own key performance indicators. Hence the rightful impression that the Dark Ages have been a time of vertiginously rising financialization.

Making the West Great Again

The United States is a country that's always been dear to my heart. Just like Bill Clinton and Al Gore's *"information superhighway"* led me to study computer science, my curiosity for the US as a whole was also inspired by the 1992 presidential election. Following that year's campaign, I read extensively about American politics and history. Then I chose American studies as a major when I pursued my education at Sciences Po (a leading Paris-based university specialized in political science and public administration). When I later started working in the tech industry, my knowledge of the US helped me decipher the history of Silicon Valley, the spirit of the frontier, the strengths of the US political and legal systems regarding innovation, and the unique and inspiring American entrepreneurial culture.

And yet today there are worrying signs that suggest America could lose it all in the coming decades. I obviously don't wish that fate for a country I admire so much. But every day that passes since Donald Trump's election inspires in me this uneasy feeling: *we're witnessing the fall of the American Empire*. Many see this unexpected turn of events as an opportunity for Europe. Myself, I mostly feel sad that I have to witness a great nation go down the terrible path of debasement and destruction. And I dread the damage for the entire Western world and the values we all cherish.

According to the great political scientist Louis Hartz[42], one key to understanding the US is that it was originally founded as a democracy. Unlike Europe, which was burdened by its aristocratic heritage, that democratic legacy enabled the uniquely American set of values that for two centuries was the hotbed of such vibrancy and prosperity. Alas today there are signs of a shift leading to an unprecedented aristocratic ethos in the US: suppression of the estate tax; disinterest in busting monopolies; subsidies for dying, unproductive industries[43]; circumventing democracy in the interest of the rich and powerful; creating tariffs. What we're witnessing today very much looks like the end of what Louis Hartz calls the *"liberal tradition in America"*[44].

There are also signs of the US now lagging behind in terms of development. The inequality gap is widening[45]. Infrastructures are crumbling. Life expectancy is decreasing[46] for the first time in decades. In certain parts of the country, the population is afflicted by the extremely worrying opioid crisis[47]. The government looks like it has been circumvented by a clique of plutocrats that are as obsessed with exploiting the state for their own interests as they are indifferent to the economic insecurity experienced by their fellow citizens[48].

When Barack Obama was president we could expect the US to lead the Western world into imagining an upgraded version of the Great Safety Net—precisely what happened during the New Deal. But with Donald Trump in the White House, such a scenario has become highly improbable. So I now see three scenarios when it comes to the future of the Western world.

In the first, it would be China, rather than the US, which imagines and builds a 'Great Safety Net 2.0' for the new age and offers it as an example to follow—first in Southeast Asia, Central Asia and Africa, then maybe in Europe. China has many assets that indicate it could succeed on that front. It is unified and stabilized by an old civilizational heritage and a strong regime, enjoying unparalleled (if authoritarian) stability in a world otherwise dominated by chaos.

As it has emerged from the depths of under-development and the shock of Mao's Cultural Revolution, China is also unencumbered by the legacy institutions that still dominate Western societies. And so it's better positioned to imagine a new set of institutions that make the most of the current techno-economic paradigm. We can already see the outlines of a Chinese version of a modern-day Great Safety Net with the deployment of a national pension system[49], the widespread role of trade unions affiliated with the Communist Party[50], the fast-paced innovation in consumer finance[51], the diversification of the housing market[52], the first hints of interest in upgrading the healthcare system[53], and the ambiguous experiment that is China's now-notorious social credit system[54].

Additionally, China is not inward-looking anymore. Some have doubted that, unlike the US at the time of the Marshall Plan, China would have the slightest interest in trying to expand its social and economic institutions elsewhere in the world. What they don't realize is that with its vast economic footprint, the Belt and Road Initiative, and a deeper engagement with global institutions, China is not simply in a position to imagine a new Great Safety Net for the new age for itself. It also has the means and drive to implement and promote it on the world stage.

The problem, obviously, is that a Great Safety Net 2.0 imagined in China will probably not comply with Western liberal democratic values. With China as the core of the age of ubiquitous computing and networks, Western nations would be confronted for the first time with a dominant economic and strategic power that doesn't share their history and political heritage.

Furthermore, if the Great Safety Net 2.0, that of the twenty-first century, is imagined in China rather than in the Western world, Western nations might be the last to embrace it. More likely it will be deployed in other countries, those best capable of leapfrogging, before it's replicated in Europe and the US (if at all). And as a Great Safety Net is key to economic security and prosperity, China taking the lead will eventually lead to a sharp reversal in development trends, with the West falling behind while the Chinese world leaps forward.

In a second scenario, it is Europe that would forge ahead and tackle the new institutional challenges without relying on the US anymore. But this scenario is uncertain at best. As world leaders and experts look at Europe, what they see is a continent in disarray—one that is *"disappearing into itself"*, as it was once put by Kevin Rudd, the former Prime Minister of Australia (and an expert in many things related to China)[55]. There is the economic and financial imbalance following the budgetary crisis in Greece. There is the decision by British voters that the UK would leave the European Union. And now there are the tensions due to the rise of populism in many countries across the continent, including the authoritarian turn by some governments in Eastern Europe.

Because it hasn't grown large tech companies, Europe also lacks the intimate understanding of the new techno-economic paradigm as well as the economic power that it takes to effectively exert strategic power at a global level. As Kevin Rudd noted, *"once you have economic power, it in turn engenders political power; it in turn makes possible to have security power through the acquisition of military capabilities, which in turn generates foreign policy power, which in turn generates strategic power"*[56]. Europe still has power due to its economy and its legacy position within the global institutions founded in the aftermath of World War II. But it's drifting backward in comparison to both the US and China, whose strategic positioning at the global level is immensely strengthened by their harboring today's largest and most potent tech companies.

The third scenario is that the Western tech industry itself realizes that its interests lie in imagining a new Great Safety Net for the new age of ubiquitous computing and networks—and that it shouldn't wait for feeble Western governments to take the lead. The critical (if transient) role the corporate world played in securing the legacy of the Second New Deal is one precedent. An even more relevant one is that of utopian British industrialists such as Robert Owen (1771-1858), a leader in the development of cooperatives and the trade union movement, and William Morris (1834-1896), who promoted craftsmanship as a way to restore the workers' dignity and wholeness in a more industrial world[57]. Yet something was lacking in both cases. The grand vision of the New Deal was never completed in the US due to a backlash against trade unions and fierce resistance against deploying universal healthcare insurance. As for the British initiatives in the Victorian era, they never scaled to nationwide social significance.

This is where ubiquitous computing and networks can make a difference. Now non-governmental institutional change seems possible at a large scale because tech people congregate in their own kind of nation—what my friend and partner Oussama Ammar calls the *"Internet nation"*[58], echoing Balaji S. Srinivasan's idea that *"software is reorganizing the world"*[59]. After all, the rise of the printing press and the mass distribution of the written word once lead to the emergence of nationalism and the formation of nation states[60]. Now the power of networks (and related increasing returns to scale) makes it possible for tech people to build their own institutions without relying as much on governments.

In my view, the US tech industry doesn't really have a choice. Not only is it being cornered by the current political situation, but with pro-technology leaders such as Obama and Britain's David Cameron gone from the stage, there's really no Teddy Roosevelt or FDR in sight, is there?

These three scenarios—new institutions being imagined by China, Europe, or the tech industry itself—should be borne in mind as we go further. But for now we need to revisit the recent history of technology to have a shared understanding of what the new age is all about.

Key takeaways

• *The crisis of the Western middle class has been long in the making. It took the form of globalization and financialization before it was accelerated by technology.*

• *The Dark Ages of financialization led to shifting more risks onto individuals, effectively dismantling the Great Safety Net 1.0 and imposing an excessive burden on the financial system.*

• *Now that we're shifting to a new techno-economic paradigm, it's time to imagine new institutions for prosperity and economic security. The question is: Who will tackle that challenge?*

WHO WILL UPGRADE THE GREAT SAFETY NET?

PROBABLY CHINA
IN THE END
(BUT THE WEST MIGHT
NOT LIKE IT)

NOT THE US
(BECAUSE OF TRUMP
& THE GOP)

HOPEFULLY THE TECH INDUSTRY
& INTERNET USERS
(BUT THEY'D BETTER HURRY)

NOT EUROPE EITHER
(BECAUSE IT LACKS
ECONOMIC POWER)

THE CLOCK'S TICKING!

Part 2
The Entrepreneurial Age

Chapter 4
Entrepreneurs and
the New Corporate World

*"For entrepreneurs, there is no tradeoff between quality and scale.
The job is to do both—not one or the other. If it can't be done, you
innovate. Quality without scale is not entrepreneurship—it is a
tree falling in the forest with no one around. Scale without quality
is also not entrepreneurship—it is business as usual. And it leaves
businesses exposed to competitors who steal its customers (and, worse,
employees). Anyone who attempts to serve a customer at a new level of
quality and scale is an entrepreneur. Anyone who does not, is not."*
—Babak Nivi[1]

A brief history of science and entrepreneurship

My firm The Family has had the good fortune to be seen as a
place where people have a real viewpoint on entrepreneurship, technology, and innovation. As a result, we're often visited by various
people who on occasion ask us to provide expertise. Approximately
four years ago, a particular category of visitors emerged: local officials
and business owners who wanted to build their own Silicon Valley.
All were counting on the related entrepreneurial drive to trigger
local development, create jobs, and attract outside resources.

The question recurred so often, in fact, that we decided to act upon
it. Instead of providing the same answers over and over again (*"It's
difficult"*, *"It took decades"*, *"There was a particular context"*, *"There's
only one Silicon Valley"*), we decided to write it down once and for all
to have a document ready for anyone with questions related to creating
the next Silicon Valley[2]. In the process, we learned a lot about the

history of entrepreneurship and discovered many facts and ideas that most people ignore[3]. Above all, we unearthed many misunderstandings and clichés that too often pollute discussions on entrepreneurship.

One of the most potent clichés is that innovative entrepreneurship is about science. Many people confuse entrepreneurs with lonely, misunderstood scientists who hunt for breakthroughs in their basement. The vision is entertaining, but it is also misleading. Very few entrepreneurs (if any) are actually like Doc Brown in *Back to the Future*.

In fact, for much of the nineteenth century, science and business grew worlds apart. On one side, scientists were producing knowledge and conducting experiments in university laboratories or their homes. On the other, as stated by Olivier Zunz, mechanical tinkerers invested *"in labor-saving machinery and interchangeable parts to produce large quantities of technologically complex products"*[4] (otherwise known as the *"American system of manufacturing"*). Countries such as France and Germany, which had already created formal engineering schools, were pioneering new forms of cooperation between academia and business. But in general scientists weren't interested in entrepreneurship and there was not much use for science in the entrepreneurial world.

From 1875 onward, the transition to the age of steel and heavy engineering changed those conditions. Learned societies, notably of engineering, began to position themselves at the crossroads of science and business[5]. Local ecosystems of technology-savvy investors had to exploit available science to form opinions on new technological ventures[6]. Scientists began to express an interest in their work's applications in the business world, and entrepreneurs were now paying more attention to science.

Because entrepreneurs and scientists remained in two different categories, however, the rise of a more entrepreneurial approach to inventions needed a functioning market for technology where technological assets, both tangible and intangible, could be bought and sold at arm's length[7]. Key institutions such as patent law and licensing contributed to making that market efficient. Andrew Carnegie's Edgar Thomson Steel Works—the steel mill whose construction Carlota Perez marks as the Big Bang of the new technological age[8]—was built in 1875 in Pittsburgh, using the process for manufacturing cheap steel patented by Englishman Henry Bessemer twenty years earlier. Like Alexander Graham Bell (whose invention, the telephone, was turned into a corporate empire by the likes of Theodore Vail[9]), Bessemer ultimately had to rely on others for his invention to become the cornerstone of a new industry. The market for technology made it possible for scientists to work with entrepreneurs.

Yet at some point, the bigger corporations brought about by consecutive techno-economic transitions decided that they wanted to employ their own researchers rather than buying from lone inventors on the market. During the twentieth century, the rise of big, integrated corporations was facilitated by key trends: the structuration of modern industries and the emergence of the Great Safety Net that made steady mass consumption possible. Those trends contributed to concentrating the necessary resources—financial, human, technological—in unprecedentedly large corporate firms. In time, those firms developed an approach for managing research and development within their organizations.

It was not an easy task. Scientists were obviously eager to access the capital-intensive research facilities that only big corporations could pay for. But most of them were reluctant to relinquish ownership of their work. Similarly, individual autonomy was a key condition for success in the world of science, which contradicted the core principles of Frederick Taylor's scientific management.

To make up for the contradiction, scientific research had to be undertaken within specific departments. Strict separation was a way to provide autonomy to the researchers rather than locking them into the main organization. It was also a way to isolate the main organization from the apparent chaos that reigned in the realm of scientific research.

In 1925, Western Electric Research Laboratories and part of the engineering department at AT&T were consolidated to form Bell Telephone Laboratories, Inc., later known as Bell Labs. Corporate labs such as this, Lockheed's Skunk Works, and Xerox PARC all ultimately fit the same model: a separate entity in a corporate organization within which talented researchers were given a measure of freedom in the hope that their findings would help consolidate the parent company's long-term competitive advantage. Science was

seen as a privileged way to improve existing products, achieve efficiency gains, launch new products, and conquer new markets.

The history of corporate inventions reveals the importance of
in-house R&D in the progress made by technology all along the
twentieth century, from the weapons systems that helped the US
win World War II[10] to technological breakthroughs in synthetic
fibers, avionics and energy and on to the transistor that was invented
by John Bardeen, Walter Brattain, and William Shockley at Bell
Labs. With those successes, research and development gradually
became an issue of organizations rather than the market.

World War II also brought about a massive upheaval of public
spending in science. After the war, following the advice of science
policy overlords such as Vannevar Bush[11], governments started to
design new programs to support science's industrial applications.
The result was an obvious bias for large organizations rather than
small businesses or new entrepreneurial ventures. Like the widespread (and controversial[12]) R&D tax credit, most programs targeted
big corporations rather than the lone inventors and tinkerers who
had made possible the techno-economic transitions of the nineteenth
century. And when the government did try to support technological
research in the more entrepreneurial parts of the economy, it often
failed due to an excess of paperwork and risk-averse decision-making
processes[13].

As a result, during most of the twentieth century, those with a
scientific background didn't really consider entrepreneurship as an
option. If they were attracted to innovation, they had to be ranked
at the top of their class, join a big corporation, and innovate within
it and on its behalf. Entrepreneurial innovations, those undertaken
by lone individuals, looked like they would be permanently margin-
alized. If you were smart enough and wanted to make a difference
through technology, the corporate labs were where you had to be.
The nineteenth century was the century of entrepreneurial tinkerers and lone scientists; the twentieth was the century of corporate
researchers.

William Shockley, the same who co-invented the transistor at
Bell Labs, played a fleeting yet key role in the shift from corporate
research to the next era of innovation. After the transistor, Shockley
decided that his future was not at Bell Labs. He wanted to found his

own shop, explore applications for his invention, and contribute to creating a new industry. He located his new venture, Shockley Semiconductor Laboratory, in the small California town of his teenage years, where his elderly mother still lived: Palo Alto. This was also where Shockley's wartime colleague Frederick Terman was turning Stanford University into a scientific and entrepreneurial powerhouse[14].

The rest is history. Shockley recruited eight brilliant young men, all recently graduated from the best universities in the country. Then in 1956 he won the Nobel Prize in physics. Then he became insufferable. Led by 30-year-old Robert Noyce, the eight young men defected the following year to found a new company, Fairchild Semiconductor (a subsidiary of Fairchild Camera & Instrument, a family-owned industrial business located on the East Coast). This marked the beginning of a new era in innovation: the age of the young, radical entrepreneurs[15].

That's because there was a key difference between Shockley and Robert Noyce. The former was famous and respected, notably by potential investors. The latter was unknown and had everything to prove. He did it, impressively, and overcame the considerable risks he had taken with his seven co-founders.

These were risks that not many young people were willing to confront at the time. Founding a startup seems like a rational choice nowadays because steady jobs are scarce and corporate organizations look like they're going through unbearable agony. But in the 1950s, leaving your employer to found your own company was rare. For young, promising talents, corporate jobs came with high wages, social status, management responsibilities, job security, and ever-ascending career paths. For that alone, the role of the *"Traitorous Eight"* in the advent of a more entrepreneurial age cannot be stressed enough.

Robert Noyce's character gave a particular twist to the history of what was to become Silicon Valley. Noyce was neither an opportunistic businessman, nor a corporate manager obsessed with control, nor a misunderstood inventor willing to prove everyone wrong, nor the son of a poor family determined to have his revenge. He was, in a way, far more ordinary: born in the Midwest, raised in a happy middle-class family, an astute researcher with a genuine passion for transistors, a dedicated salesman, a leader who inspired all those who had the chance to work with him. With his partners, Robert Noyce created a new, lasting entrepreneurial culture that mixed enthusiasm, ingenuity, and ambition.

All in all, since the second half of the nineteenth century, entrepreneurship went through very different eras: that of scientists and entrepreneurs ignoring each other; that of the market for technology; then that of the corporate research lab. Entrepreneurship as we know it today only emerged with the rise of a new general purpose technology: the transistor.

From personal computing to continuous innovation

The link between Robert Noyce and today's entrepreneurs such as Mark Zuckerberg, Brian Chesky, and Travis Kalanick seems far-fetched. In the 1960s, after all, Frederick Terman's Stanford University was a place dedicated to conducting research for the military. Fairchild Semiconductor was no exception to its era: it was mostly a contractor for the US government, especially NASA. But sometime in the 1960s Noyce grew tired of Fairchild Semiconductor's parent company and the constraints it imposed on his day-to-day business. He wanted to explore consumer applications and soon left with his partner Gordon Moore to found a new venture, which they named Intel. There he helped invent the microprocessor, which became the cornerstone of the personal computing industry.

From the 1970s onwards, a new generation of entrepreneurs decided to focus their attention on this nascent industry. Under Andy Grove's leadership[16], Intel ultimately specialized in designing and producing microprocessors, those *"computers on chips"* that are at the heart of personal computers. Thanks to the microprocessor, personal computing went beyond a narrow circle of hobbyists to finally hit mass markets. In 1976, Steve Jobs partnered with Steve Wozniak to build and sell the first personal computers successfully designed for non-experts. With the Macintosh in 1984, Jobs commercialized the graphic interface and the mouse, revolutionizing what it meant to use a computer. In 1991, the demilitarization of the Internet made it possible to connect all computing devices on the planet, giving birth to powerful networked applications...and the technology bubble of the 1990s.

With the rise of personal computing and networks from the 1970s onwards, entrepreneurship took a new direction. The goal was not to best the Soviet Union at any cost, but to serve the general public, to improve people's daily lives, to change the consumer's world for the better. Entrepreneurs have always been key figures in the history of the industrial economy. But it was personal computing that really gave birth to tech entrepreneurs as we know them today.

There was a cultural reason for this shift from a military-financed semiconductor industry to a consumer-driven personal computing industry. The concept of personal computing was born in the counterculture of the 1960s[17]. Its birthplace, California, was home to many rebels, from the first motorcycle clubs to artists, hippies, student leaders, LSD advocates, gay activists, the Black Panthers, and computer scientists. In 1969, the Vietnam War was at its height and Richard Nixon became president. It was around that time when some of those rebels loudly voiced the idea of empowering individuals against organizations and decided to act on that idea to change America forever. The pioneers of personal computing had but one goal in this adventure: augmenting individuals with technology so as to free them from organizations, be they public (the government) or private (IBM).

Another factor in the shift to personal computing was the difficulty that incumbent tech companies had in repositioning themselves within the computing industry. With the shift from the *"vertical"* proprietary industry of mainframes and minicomputers to the open, *"horizontal"* industry of personal computing (to quote Intel's CEO Andy Grove[18]), incumbents such as Digital Equipment Corporation and even the mighty IBM were imprisoned by the extraordinary economic rents being generated from their existing customer base. Thus, in a typical version of Clayton Christensen's *"innovator's dilemma"*[19], they were unable to participate in the new world despite their having very relevant technology[20]. This left the entire, rapidly expanding territory of personal computing almost entirely free for entrepreneurs to explore.

A third reason for the shift was financial. To found their ventures,

SCIENCE & ENTREPRENEURSHIP

1- EVERYONE IN THEIR OWN BUBBLE

2- THE MARKET FOR TECHNOLOGY

3- THE CORPORATE RESEARCH LAB

6- LARGE TECH
COMPANIES
(ALLIED WITH
THE MULTITUDE)

5- VC-BACKED
STARTUPS

4- STATE-SPONSORED
INNOVATION

entrepreneurs in the personal computing industry needed money. The military wasn't interested in providing it, since personal computers couldn't help them win the Cold War against the Soviet Union (or so they thought). Fortunately, a new breed of financier was beginning to make a difference: venture capitalists. You can't understand personal computing and the techno-economic transition it brought about if you don't keep in mind that it was all about radical entrepreneurs sealing an alliance with returns-hungry venture capitalists.

It was an alliance that worked beyond anyone's wildest dreams— and it led to the military market for semiconductors and computers becoming *"a marginally relevant niche"* (as stated by William H. Janeway[21]). Now with the spread of computers, laptops, smartphones and other connected devices, billions of individuals are equipped with ever-increasing, ubiquitous computing power. Through the Internet and various platforms, they are connected with others and harness the power of networks. This unprecedented connectedness as well as rising, distributed computing power have radically changed our very conceptions of corporate strategy and innovation. In the twentieth century economy, innovation was undertaken to occasionally break certain constraints. In the age of ubiquitous computing and networks, *innovation is a core everyday business practice.*

Indeed the digital economy is characterized by its ever-growing competitive pressure. Startups never stop entering the market: the cost of founding them is dropping and venture capital is rising as an asset class to fund them. Direct competitors can regain the initiative at any moment, as technology makes it possible to propagate new processes and features within a large organization without much friction[22]. As a result, large tech companies are continuously trying to innovate, if only to sustain their returns on invested capital and consolidate their dominant position on their original market[23]. In the age of ubiquitous computing and networks, the cards can be quickly reshuffled, which creates an unprecedented incentive in favor of continuous innovation.

What's more, continuous innovation has become more sustainable as technology spares executives from innovating in the dark. As innovation is more data-driven[24], with the possibility of measuring its impact almost in real time, technology minimizes the related risk and helps align innovation efforts with a given strategy[25]. Indeed we are now witnessing the convergence of innovation (anything that breaks a constraint) and strategy (which is about the constraints you embrace).

In the age of the automobile and mass production, every large corporation was confronted with painful choices: between mass production and personalization; between faster growth and higher margins; and between efficiency and innovation, in which they usually chose the former[26]. But now, it looks like tech companies can skip those choices. They seem to keep on growing longer, reaching a larger scale while still improving the quality of their product[27]. This makes their user experience more and more exceptional and even, in some cases, increases their margins as they grow.

As the rules of the new strategic game become clearer, changes are happening in many dimensions—which is exactly what a great surge of development is about[28]. Infrastructures change: we still need roads and bridges, but other infrastructures, such as cloud computing platforms, GPS satellites[29] and the Internet itself, have become more critical. Products change: fewer manufactured goods, more digital applications and entertaining experiences. Organizations change: not the rigid, pyramidal bureaucracies that used to thrive in the Fordist economy, but more agile and stacked architectures that combine user communities, digital activities, and tangible assets within a constantly evolving business model[30]. The managerial culture changes, too: instead of being obsessed by supply-side economies of scale, efficiency gains, standardization, and quarterly returns[31], managers are now focused on providing an exceptional customized experience and generating increasing returns to scale.

Entrepreneurs are here to stay

Entrepreneurs always play a key role in the installation period of a technological revolution. They're the ones who seize technology as an opportunity to discover new models. This is why, according to Carlota Perez, *"all installation periods are led by finance and free markets as innovation focuses on setting up the new infrastructure, letting markets pick the new winners and modernizing the old economy*"[32]. In a transitioning economy, where Schumpeter's creative destruction is in full force, the ability to experiment is necessary to discover new business models, put in place appropriate regulations and enlarge businesses[33].

But in an age that imposes continuous innovation on even the most dominant firms[34], most signs suggest that entrepreneurs are about to play a more important role over the long term, even though the new economy is becoming dominated by large companies instead of small startups[35]. From its beginnings, the economy of computing and networks developed itself on top of decentralized infrastructures governed by simple standards of voluntary adoption (TCP/IP, HTTP) and an economic model that did not impose billing based on volume or time spent[36]. The innovation dynamic of the current economy comes from its initial characteristics: it is particularly adapted to the appearance of emerging trends, to successive iterations, to observation and real-time adjustments.

As a result, entrepreneurs are not a vanguard paving the way for more mature managers. Instead, they emerge as the new elite destined to permanently dominate. The age of the automobile and mass production was dominated by engineers and operational managers focused on efficiency. The Dark Ages of financialization were dominated by financial managers focused on quarterly returns. The new age of ubiquitous computing and networks will be dominated by entrepreneurs focused on high quality at scale. This is why it can be best described as the *"Entrepreneurial Age"*, one in which entrepreneurship, otherwise defined by Babak Nivi as *"the ability to serve a customer at the highest level of quality and scale, simultaneously,"*[37] becomes the basis for any organization's strategic positioning.

The advent of the Entrepreneurial Age is best revealed by the fact that more and more people want to become entrepreneurs[38]. This trend, which my partners and I are witnessing everyday in Europe, can be partially explained by the relative scarcity of full-time jobs and the frustration (even suffering) that these jobs can provoke in many workers. This is compounded by the crisis that is upending many legacy institutions. For younger generations, the future is marked by uncertainty. The continued existence of the Great Safety Net, and particularly pensions, is no longer assured. Purchasing housing in urban areas has become nearly impossible. Healthcare coverage is becoming less certain. An entire system seems to be disintegrating, and this leads some to break free and create their own career, rather than relying on a system that seems to be faltering.

Entrepreneurship is also enjoying an increased social status. Great entrepreneurs are admired by many, if not by all. Steve Jobs was mourned throughout the world upon his passing, whereas Mark Zuckerberg was put on the big screen with David Fincher's *The Social Network*. As a result, entrepreneurship is becoming more widespread and democratic. It is a new identity that is sought out by those looking to increase their status in a society marked by Simon Kuper's *"great middle-class identity crisis"*[39].

And it's easier than ever to create a startup. Open source software and the deployment of huge platforms for cloud computing such as Amazon Web Services have trivialized the technologies needed to launch a new business. Developments in programming allow one to avoid having to recruit large teams of software engineers. Today, an app can be created by just one or two people. The myth of the garage has become a reality: we can now bootstrap a company from practically zero.

Finally, capital is becoming a commodity. The current discussions between economists about the *"global savings glut"* reveal that there is too much capital to invest and too few opportunities to secure sizeable returns[40]. This may come as a surprise for entrepreneurs who rack their brains in vain trying to pitch investors who refuse to deploy capital. But the commoditization of capital is a well-documented trend, and one that explains why growing startups have less and less difficulty raising funds as they reveal their secrets and accelerate their growth on large, global markets. (Of course, this doesn't negate the fact that, as William H. Janeway eloquently reminds us (in a lesson we repeat often at The Family), *"The secret to corporate happiness is positive cash flow"*[41].)

All in all, in the Entrepreneurial Age, entrepreneurs are a force to be reckoned with. Some of them are already scaling up companies by harnessing the power of billions of users, triggering unprecedented increasing returns to scale. Whether they fully embrace it or not, entrepreneurs have become agents of change. The superior power that was once held by the state now appears to be surpassed by that of entrepreneurship fueled by ubiquitous computing and networks. And that power is up for grabs for anyone who wants to achieve long-term policy goals. As Tim O'Reilly says, it's now up to us to imagine new institutions and provide prosperity and economic security in the Entrepreneurial Age[42]. And to be effective, the new version of the Great Safety Net will need to truly serve *the multitude*.

Key takeaways

• *Entrepreneurship took different forms throughout the ages. Since the Industrial Revolution, we went from mechanical tinkering to in-house corporate research to today's VC-backed startups.*

• *As they harness the power of ubiquitous computing and networks, entrepreneurs are playing a radically new game. Continuous innovation is now the rule, not the exception.*

• *Entrepreneurs are here to stay. They're rising as the perennial, dominant figure of the new corporate world, leading us into the Entrepreneurial Age.*

ENTREPRENEURSHIP: THE PERFECT STORM

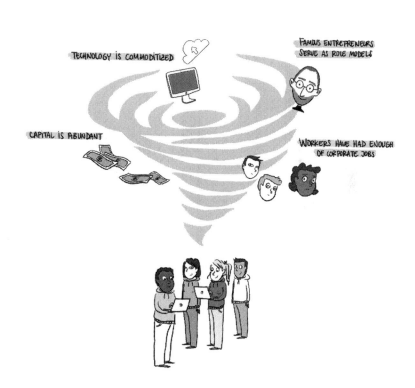

Chapter 5
Behind Entrepreneurs:
The Multitude

"Despite its supply-side economies of scale, General Motors never grew to take over the entire automobile market. Why was this market, like many industrial markets of the twentieth century, an oligopoly rather than a monopoly? Because traditional economies of scale based on manufacturing have generally been exhausted at scales well below total market dominance... In other words, positive feedback based on supply-side economies of scale ran into natural limits, at which point negative feedback took over."
—Carl Shapiro and Hal R. Varian[1]

How customers rose as the main force in the corporate contract

I was an entrepreneur once—from 2010 to 2012, to be precise. I can't say my startup broke any records; in reality, it never took off. But it was a comprehensive and rewarding experience, during which I tackled the same challenges as every other early stage entrepreneur: designing a product, raising funds, hiring developers, managing developers, marketing the product, selling it to customers, managing the company's finances, and other ungrateful tasks. At the very least I survived lots of ups and downs and learned many things that I never learned in my years working for the government.

My startup was rooted in Barack Obama's 2008 presidential campaign. My partners and I had observed how the Obama team had orchestrated relationships between voters who didn't know each other but had a lot in common. Our idea was that such a pattern could be replicated in many different situations: finding a job (a conversation with a former job seeker could help) or purchasing a product (maybe a customer who already purchased it and who resembles you has some useful insight). We did many things wrong, including constantly hesitating between addressing users directly or simply selling the software to merchants. But this period made me very sensitive to the idea that the age of ubiquitous computing and networks was all about interactions between individuals (and this was before Facebook became so important in so many people's daily lives, driving the point home for all of us).

Near the end of my stint as an entrepreneur, my friend Henri Verdier (now the chief information officer of the French government) and I wrote a book together: *L'Âge de la multitude*[2]. We designed it as both a testimonial of what the startup world was all about and a wake-up call for the old world of elected officials, civil servants, and corporate executives. The message was very simple: *"You need to take entrepreneurs seriously. The startups they're building in their garage just might end up becoming the largest corporations in the world."*

Henri had long worked in the publishing industry, so he knew a thing or two about marketing a book. What he said was pretty straightforward: *"Every successful book is built around a strong thesis"*. It's not enough to thoroughly cover a given field. You need to convey a strong and polarizing message. And so at first we had to work on what we called *"the single law that explains the digital economy"*. We were looking for a polarizing view of what technology was all about.

We came up with the following: *"The key to understanding the digital economy is that it redistributes power from the inside to the outside of organizations"*. A corollary to this law is that the businesses that succeed in the digital economy are the ones that realize how power has been redistributed outside of their organizations and learn to harness it anyway to fuel growth and generate profits.

But what exactly is the nature of that outside power? This question is the reason why we decided to use the concept of the *multitude*, which we borrowed from the Italian post-Marxist philosopher Antonio Negri[3]. For Henri and I, the multitude is defined as the billions of individuals that are now equipped with increasingly powerful computing devices and connected with one another through wide networks.

In that unprecedented state of connectedness, individuals change their behaviors and their relationships with organizations. In the past, they formed a mass, with organizations addressing them mainly through mass-oriented channels such as broadcasting, brands, and retail space. Now they form a multitude, in which individuals exchange and create their own information through networks. As a result, the entire field of business needs to be redesigned[4]. And the best place to start this effort is to reconsider the corporate world in an economy now dominated by the multitude.

My view is that the corporation is a legal fiction embodying a contract between several different parties that have conflicting interests: shareholders, employees, and customers. One of the factors that explains the balance of power between a company's many stakeholders is the competitive pressure on its end market. On certain markets, such as the food and grocery market, competition is so intense that it brings prices down at the expense of employees. Hence the infamous *"Wal-Mart Effect"*[5], under which affordability for consumers coincides with adverse conditions for workers[6] and suppliers (which are often small and medium businesses). On other markets, such as real estate or telecommunications, barriers to entry prevent newcomers from exerting competitive pressure on the incumbents. As a result, companies can focus on maximizing the producer's surplus at the expense of their customers.

Another factor that determines the balance in what I call the *"corporate contract"* is the surrounding institutional landscape. Institutions embody the social order and nudge corporations in terms of how they distribute the value they create and capture. The balance of power depends on the particular regulations that apply in the industry and the structure of its value chain. It changes from one country to another, because the rules and the business culture are different in the US, Germany, France, Japan, and China. And it shifts from one period to another, because institutions change with forces that are as potent as the market itself, among them war, politics, and culture. In many ways, the history of corporations can otherwise be told as the history of social and economic institutions.

Yet another determinant of the *"corporate contract"* is technology. In the age of the automobile and mass production, success depended on making workers more loyal and more productive. Hence trade unions succeeded at negotiating higher wages and better working conditions for their members, and technology was ultimately used in a way that was empowering for workers.

The Dark Ages of financialization, in turn, favored shareholders, who forced corporations to switch their focus from producing better goods and services to maximizing shareholder value—thus often using technology at the expense of stressed employees and frustrated customers. The more a corporation was dedicated to paying large, stable dividends to its shareholders, the more pressure there was on employees and the more value was extracted from entrapped customers thanks to technology.

Today, as we enter the Entrepreneurial Age, the contract between shareholders, employees, and customers must once again be rearranged. As they become the multitude, the customers—long the quiet party at the corporate table—are finally rising. After decades of silence and resignation due to their lack of bargaining power, consumers can finally obtain products of a higher quality at a cheaper price. And entrepreneurs are the ones that are now able to provide them with higher quality at scale.

Tech companies offer many signs corroborating this trend. Shareholders, for one, have to give up short-term gains as most tech companies don't make profits, let alone pay dividends[7]. Employees have to work under more duress, in some cases renouncing a steady job in favor of contracting[8].

Another even clearer sign is the behavior and discourses of tech executives, who are more obsessed with providing their customers with an exceptional experience than bonding with their employees or maximizing shareholder value. And this is notable, since as the most opportunistic player in the corporate equation, executives help reveal who among the corporate parties at the table has the most bargaining power. Indeed, to find where power lies in the corporate world, it suffices to check to see whose back corporates executives are protecting: the shareholders', the employees', or the customers'?

For most of the age of the automobile and mass production, corporate executives were former engineers, salespersons, and managers who had risen through the ranks of their companies. They shared a common practical culture with their employees. Sure they had to bargain with unions—and they disagreed with them more often than not. But executives mostly dealt with employees while all but taking shareholders and customers for granted.

Then in the Dark Ages of financialization, executives switched alliances. Instead of dealing mostly with employees and their unions, they primarily backed the interests of the company's share-holders[9]. CEOs started to emerge from a different background. Most were no longer engineers but rather MBAs with perfect credentials in corporate strategy and finance. Often they were promoted from the finance department, ascending from positions in which they had learned to master the subtle art of interacting with financial markets. They got used to being rewarded for their opportunistic repositioning with bonuses, stock options and other financial incentives. An upgraded vision of corporate governance contributed to consolidating this new version of the corporate contract and sealing the unprecedented alignment between shareholders and corporate executives[10].

There were exceptions, of course. In companies such as Walmart, which somehow kept the mindset of a family business even after it went public, a culture of relatively kind paternalism long contributed to preserving a strong bond between employees and management[11].

Particular countries also distinguished themselves by preserving a corporate contract decidedly less favorable to shareholders. This is the case in my home country of France, with the frequent involvement of the state in the business of large companies and the rise of a singular business elite initially trained within the government.

This is also the case in Germany, a country in which legendary hedge fund manager Julian Robertson was astonished to discover in 1989 that German managers *"were running the companies for the sake of the employees rather than the shareholders"* and that they *"could not care less about returns on equity"*[12]. The German indifference to short-term shareholder interest is a legacy of Ludwig Erhard's fateful decision in 1948 to bail out German business assets while wiping out paper money for private savers: it contributed to much of German industry still being owned by families rather than investment funds and other institutional investors[13]. And to this day, the German economy continues to stand out in this regard. Due to the large German banks' shareholding interest in corporations and the unique role of trade unions and industry associations, it keeps on imposing a long-term view of corporate management that goes against the short-term view that prevailed in the Anglo-Saxon world during the Dark Ages[14].

In the Entrepreneurial Age, it's now becoming common practice for corporate executives to insist on their dedication to customers. When Facebook did its initial public offering in 2012, Mark Zuckerberg wrote that *"we don't build services to make money; we make money to build better services"*[15]. In 2014, Uber CEO Travis Kalanick mentioned *"the ability to find things that people want and to use your creativity to target those"*[16]. Alibaba chief Jack Ma once famously declared that it was *"customers first, employees second, and investors third"*[17]. And of course, the playbook that all those executives follow started being written by Amazon's Jeff Bezos in 1997, when he boldly informed the public that Amazon was *"all about the long term"* and that he and his team would *"continue to focus relentlessly on (their) customers"*[18]. With all those words, tech companies seem to validate Roger L. Martin's idea of our entering the *"age of customer capitalism"*[19].

But do tech CEOs actually deliver? Many people see hypocrisy in those forceful declarations by Silicon Valley-style entrepreneurs. They point out that for decades many companies, however bad their customer service, have been touting taking care of their customers as the highest priority. Even worse, duplicity when it comes to serving the customers is especially evident at companies that, like tech companies, have been enjoying *increasing returns to scale*. Telecommunications companies and large banks, all blessed with powerful network effects, have a well-earned reputation for mistreating their customers and being hated by them in return[20].

Yet the situation is different for today's tech companies[21]. As the multitude, individuals can access a wider range of information, interact in real time[22], and really exert more bargaining power. Above all, the very nature of software makes it easier for corporations to enlist their customers in creating value[23]. It's true for early-stage startups, for which the support of their earliest customers is critical to success[24]. It's also true at a larger scale, when the more active role taken by customers makes them indispensable not only to the company's revenue but also to the sustainability of its supply chain. Customers taking such a great part in the supply chain is what makes

WHAT'S A CORPORATION?

THE CORPORATE CONTRACT DETERMINES HOW VALUE IS DISTRIBUTED BETWEEN THE PARTIES

FOR MUCH OF THE AGE OF THE AUTOMOBILE & MASS PRODUCTION, EMPLOYEES GRABBED MOST OF THE VALUE

IN THE DARK AGES OF FINANCIALIZATION, POWER SWITCHED IN FAVOR OF THE SHAREHOLDERS

NOW IN THE ENTREPRENEURIAL AGE, CUSTOMERS ARE TAKING THE UPPER HAND

the multitude so different from the faceless, nameless consumers of the past age of the automobile and mass production.

Production and consumption are increasingly blurred

In the twentieth-century economy, the individual lived in two distinct, parallel worlds. On the one hand, there was the world of production where the majority of individuals worked in exchange for a salary—the form of employment most adapted to the age of the automobile and mass production. On the other hand, there was the world of consumption where a number of institutions (all encompassed in the Great Safety Net[25]) provided households with the economic security and income stability that were necessary to sustain consumer demand.

Salaried labor was the link between the two worlds, the cornerstone that helped balance the economy. In exchange for the security it provided individuals, corporations could count on a reliable and loyal workforce. And because individuals could count on their monthly salaries, they were able to consume with the regularity necessary for corporations to plan production years in advance.

In the Entrepreneurial Age, the boundaries between production and consumption become blurred and eventually fade. Individuals are not workers in one world and consumers in the other. Rather they create value in their daily use of connected applications. Individuals will gladly lend a helping hand to those corporations who serve them well. They will freely share their advice on hotels and restaurants on TripAdvisor and they will let Google store their search requests in order to train PageRank and improve the experience of other users. They can even produce goods or services as amateurs and make the many resources they own available for trade—becoming hotel managers with Airbnb, drivers with BlaBlaCar, bankers with Lending Club, or energy producers with SolarCity[26].

Value creation by customers obviously did not wait for the Entrepreneurial Age. The economics of advertising is based in part on enrolling individuals in the value chain. Media corporations provide content in exchange for attention that they can in turn sell to advertisers. In service sectors, you can find situations when customers take charge of certain tasks in exchange for a cheaper price—such as when they serve themselves from supermarket shelves or when they set up their own Ikea furniture. There were also cases in which some customers participated in serving other customers, like with the Tupperware party business model for marketing and selling.

But today, customers take an even greater part in value creation. The Entrepreneurial Age provides individuals with terminals and connected objects previously reserved for businesses. It also makes it possible to secure transactions between parties that do not know each other thanks to authentication of the parties, adaptive design, reputation management, the installation of trust and the traceability of every aspect of user activity[27]. As a result, to quote Nilofer Merchant, *"across industries and worldwide markets, buyers are not parked at the end of a value chain, but often in the middle of its flow"*[28].

This is why the rise of the multitude changes the game of business. In the past, corporations saw customers as a mass of passive agents eager to consume standardized products without demanding a better experience. In the Entrepreneurial Age, the masses have turned into networks of connected users that consume while also being the essential resource that makes technology companies thrive. This is why the corporate contract has radically changed. The main balance of power is no longer between the shareholders and the employees, with the executives as an arbiter and the buyers as passive spectators[29]. The multitude has now become the strongest and most active party in the economy.

This paradigm shift was revealed as early as the 1990s. Craigslist and eBay were the first technology companies with a model based on interactions between users. This was theorized for the first time in a visionary text, 1999's *Cluetrain Manifesto*. It famously stated in its opening line that *"a powerful global conversation has begun. Through the Internet, people are discovering and inventing new ways to share relevant knowledge with blinding speed. As a direct result, markets are getting smarter—and getting smarter faster than most companies"*[30]. Its authors Rick Levine, Christopher Locke, Doc

Searls and David Weinberger had realized that the deployment of ubiquitous computing and networks would give individuals more power than organizations.

Since then, interactions between individuals have been multiplied and amplified through increased connectivity and ever-larger social networks. They shift the center of gravity of value creation. More often than not, firms are now simply the operators of applications allowing individuals to actively interact with each other, exchanging and sharing opinions, ideas, goods, services, capital.

This new approach to creating value has become a widespread phenomenon. Many individuals and organizations dedicate their time and resources to better understanding and promoting it. Its growth creates a tremendous amount of value for all their stakeholders: those who have resources to contribute; those who wish to use these resources; those who orchestrate the interactions between supply and demand and capture a part of the created value.

The Fordist economy was born thanks to the abundance of cheap oil. This led to the birth of the car industry, the improvement of mass production through assembly lines, and the building of the Great Safety Net of the past. Oil made urban sprawl possible, as it was needed to drive from the workplace to suburban areas and to perform critical features such as heating suburban homes. Oil also played a key role in many industries' supply chains and contributed to lengthening trade routes. We all realized the importance of abundant, cheap oil when it suddenly became scarce and expensive following the consecutive oil shocks in the 1970s. The economy was already faltering with the exhaustion of the mass production paradigm. Many of the main industries were reaching maturity, facing market saturation and a ceiling on productivity. The oil shocks did nothing but deepen the long and painful period of economic stagnation and mass unemployment that marked the 1980s.

In the following Dark Ages of financialization, oil still mattered but the essential resource became cheap labor, both in less developed locations where it became easier to outsource operations and in developed countries where a less favorable balance of power forced workers to renounce high wages, social benefits and overall economic security.

For a time microelectronics emerged as the digital equivalent of oil in the age of the automobile and mass production or cheap labor in the Dark Ages. Driven by the famous *"Moore's law"*, microelectronic components made it possible to produce ever cheaper and smaller computing devices[31]. But now Moore's law is entering a phase of exhaustion. We can finally see that the Entrepreneurial Age's essential resource is not the computing devices provided to individuals so much as it is *the individuals themselves.*

This is what the Entrepreneurial Age is about. In a techno-economic paradigm where individuals are more equipped and connected than ever, the multitude that they form has become a greater, autonomous power—one that companies must harness to fuel increasing returns to scale, best their competition and create even more value.

But joining with the multitude comes with a price. An alliance is necessarily balanced. Individuals do not lend their active, even enthusiastic support to corporations unless they can find aligned interests. The terms of this alliance are key to understanding what makes tech companies different and why they are bound to dominate the global economy in the Entrepreneurial Age.

What's a tech company, anyway?

The publishing of *L'Âge de la multitude* in 2012 caught the attention of the French government. As I went back to the public sector for a brief period, they asked me to write a report, alongside Pierre Collin (a respected tax judge in the French Conseil d'Etat), on taxation and the digital economy[32]. The engagement letter initially written by the ministers was long and polished. But the subtext was quite clear. Indeed you could sum it up in two direct questions: *"Why don't tech companies pay taxes?"* and *"What should we change so that they pay more?"*.

Working on corporate taxation in the digital economy was a rewarding experience. It introduced me to how the current transition redistributes wealth and power at a global scale. The "Collin & Colin" report was published in early 2013. It became an input for the work on corporate taxation by the Organization for Economic Co-operation and Development (OECD) and the G20. It also inspired widespread discussions in the global community of tax practitioners, landing Pierre and I on the *International Tax Review*'s list of the ten most influential individuals and organizations in the tax world in 2013. (Admittedly, I believe this distinction brought me fewer Twitter followers than did the defamation lawsuit I mentioned in the introduction!)

Considering what the government demanded, Pierre and I had started our work by reflecting on something basic: the definition of a tech company. And we realized defining a tech company is not as easy as it sounds. It is not simply a company that uses technology. Every modern corporation uses a lot of computers and is wired to networks, yet obviously not all corporations are tech companies.

Nor is a tech company just about a business model that presents increasing returns to scale (what developers, entrepreneurs and venture capitalists call *"scalability"*[33]). A telecommunications company also enjoys such returns, and yet such a company is quite different from Silicon Valley-style tech companies. It mostly sits back and makes a living off its rent while mistreating its customers, whereas tech companies such as Facebook, Uber, and Amazon seem to remain constantly on edge.

To be fair, Pierre and I were not the only ones feeling our way through the dark. With the emergence of new models relying on the power of the multitude, new words have emerged to qualify and better explain them. Jeff Howe calls it *"crowdsourcing"*[34]. Don Tapscott speaks of *"wikinomics"*[35]. Yochai Benkler evokes *"co-production"* and *"peer production"*[36]. Shoshana Zuboff coined the term *"distributed capitalism"*[37] whereas Clay Shirky stresses the importance of *"cognitive surplus"*[38]. Yann Moulier Boutang studies *"pollination"*[39]. And Trebor Scholz denounces the massive use of poorly paid *"digital labor"*[40]. In our book, Henri Verdier and I spoke of the *"Age of the Multitude"* in order to evoke the unprecedented power deployed by networked individuals[41]. Tim O'Reilly forged the term which has become most widely used thanks in large part to its simplicity: *"Web 2.0"*[42]. Yet all in all, no concept has truly stuck to describe the principle of a corporation harnessing the power of the multitude.

The coexistence of so many concepts shows just how far the notion of customers taking a more active part is from becoming mainstream. But the corporate contract as reshaped by the rise of the multitude has nevertheless become a source of inspiration for entrepreneurs. A better understanding of this new paradigm has propelled the growth of tech companies, leading them on a different path than that taken by the traditional corporate world.

Tech entrepreneurs succeed precisely because they realize the competitive advantages of working with the multitude rather than embracing a more traditional approach. From startup to startup, initial motives for inviting users into the supply chain are varied. Some entrepreneurs arrive there by idealism; others by cynicism; many, in fact, arrive by chance. Through many trials and errors, they end up discovering that allying with the multitude is the only sustainable way to offer the highest quality at a large scale[43]. What is the point of relying on a traditional business model if you can go faster and increase returns on invested capital by relying on the multitude?

The evolution of industry-wide value chains illustrates the emergence of the new breed of corporation. As the current techno-economic transition goes forward, the dominant companies are no longer those that operate factories in the middle of the value chain, but companies that design applications down the value chain, gaining the trust of the multitude and forging an alliance with it. The dominant tech companies are now operating consumer-oriented applications, frequently used by hundreds of millions—if not billions—of individuals at a global scale[44]. Factories still exist and add value, but they don't command as large a slice of the total value added as they did in the previous age. Even the emblematic car industry will soon be less dominated by car manufacturers than by the likes of Google, Uber and Tesla, whose main asset is a direct and trusted relationship with their end users through well-designed applications[45].

For a long time in the business world, the drive to become bigger was motivated by the pursuit of supply-side economies of scale[46]. As centuries of business have taught us, the bigger you are, the lower your marginal cost. Lowering unit costs is what economies of scale were all about. And yet economies of scale reach their limits soon enough. Commodities get scarcer, factories reach peak capacity, distribution routes get longer, and prospective customers become more difficult to convert. At that point scale ceases to be an advantage and turns into a liability. This is why most traditional companies fail to grow beyond a certain market share and most markets end up being dominated by oligopolies[47].

But tech companies behave differently as they add a key feature to traditional supply-side economies of scale: *network effects*. Most digital businesses connect their users with one another, enabling communication between them either directly (sharing content within our Facebook social graph) or indirectly (reading another user's review on an Amazon product page). Such connections turn users into nodes and trigger the needed network effects. When these are at work, the value created for each single user increases dynamically[48] (and up to a certain point[49]) as the number of users gets higher. As a result, the more a tech business grows, the cheaper it is to acquire new users and the easier it is to retain current users. These demand-side economies of scale, which are exponential up to a certain point, are critical when it comes to generating increasing returns to scale[50].

As tech companies get bigger, those various positive feedback loops sustain each other[51]. On the one hand, the stronger the network effects, the easier it is to achieve supply-side economies of scale in unprecedented proportions. For example, Amazon's network effects are the main reason why it keeps on growing and exerts an increased market power on its suppliers, forcing them to bring their prices down. Conversely, the higher the supply-side economies of scale, the more resources the company can invest in an improved customer experience that fuels even stronger network effects.

This virtuous circle of supply-side economies of scale and network effects explains why tech companies so easily challenge our understanding of corporate strategy. Their increasing returns to scale, a byproduct of the technology they masterfully exploit, is their true competitive advantage. With increasing returns, those companies' large scale is synonymous with acceleration instead of exhaustion.

Because of this rare characteristic, the Entrepreneurial Age is governed by the rule of *"winner-takes-most"*[52]. When several competitors fight to conquer one market, at some point one will come out on top, distancing themselves from the others and ultimately winning most of their market.

Because of their increasing returns to scale, we would traditionally presume that tech companies will all act like old networked business such as telecommunication companies and energy utilities: they'll cease efforts to innovate and begin preying on their customers.

But this is a key misunderstanding of what is at stake. Because their increasing returns to scale depend on the multitude, the network effects it generates and the data they collect from it, tech companies must maintain the trusted alliance with their customers at any cost. Tech companies can't try to hide like other corporations did in the past behind tangible infrastructures or regulatory barriers. Rather, they must innovate on a continuous basis, constantly improving their value proposition and meeting the evolving needs of every single customer connected to their network.

And so a tech company can be defined as a firm that features increasing returns to scale together with two other additional criteria. One is that it must provide its customers with an *exceptional experience* (high quality at scale), as serving customers well is the only way to inspire trust and retain those users that are so critical for sustaining network effects. The other is that a tech company must collect *user-generated data* on a regular and systematic basis—an additional positive feedback loop that enables it to constantly improve the experience and, again, sustain increasing returns to scale (notably through machine learning)[53].

In other words, a tech company is not defined as such simply because it uses technology. A tech company deserves the label because it uses ubiquitous computing and networks for what they do best: providing users with an exceptional experience, putting them to work through the collection of user-generated data, and using all of that to generate increasing returns up to a scale that was previously unimaginable.

Key takeaways

- *Using ubiquitous computing and networks, individuals now form the mighty multitude. As empowered customers, they're gaining the upper hand over both employees and shareholders.*

• *The reason why tech companies must cater to the multitude is that today's individuals aren't only passive consumers. Rather, they have become an essential force in creating value.*

• *To sustain increasing returns to scale, tech companies need to collect data from their customers, which requires trust. Therefore they must provide the multitude with an exceptional experience.*

WHAT'S A TECH COMPANY?

EXCEPTIONAL
EXPERIENCE

QUALITY
AT SCALE

ENGAGEMENT
& TRUST

INCREASING
RETURNS
TO SCALE

REGULAR &
SYSTEMATIC
MONITORING

NETWORK EFFECTS
& MACHINE LEARNING

Chapter 6
Consumer Power:
The Modern-Day Janus

"Diminishing returns hold sway in the traditional part of the economy—the processing industries. Increasing returns reign in the newer part—the knowledge-based industries. Modern economies have therefore bifurcated into two interrelated worlds of business corresponding to the two types of returns. The two worlds have different economics. They differ in behavior, style, and culture. They call for different management techniques, strategies, and codes of government regulation. They call for different understandings."
—W. Brian Arthur[1]

We're all undergoing the 'Wal-Mart Effect'

Amazon is my favorite example when it comes to explaining the Entrepreneurial Age. After more than 20 years of operations, it is one of the oldest tech companies around. And contrary to most of its peers, from the beginning it operated a business that included tangible assets (operating warehouses, delivering stuff) and lots of employees. Headquartered in Seattle, Amazon was reportedly despised in Silicon Valley for that very reason. Why would an entrepreneur bother founding a low-margin, difficult-to-scale retail venture when they could make tons of money in the ad-clicking business?

Today, Amazon has become one of the most fascinating tech companies out there. It even sets an inspiring example for traditional brick-and-mortar companies that are looking to become more digital. If Amazon can operate a business model that is both digital and tangible, why can't the US Postal Service, Ford, or American Airlines?

The problem I encounter while trying to communicate my passion for Amazon is that it also inspires mistrust and hostility. *"That is all very interesting, but why do they treat their employees so badly?"* is a frequent reaction. *"Where are the profits?"* is another. From union workers to corporate CFOs, everyone seems to have good reasons to hate Amazon or, at the very least, to refuse to draw lessons from its success. And this sentiment can be explained by the enduring shadow of one of Amazon's mighty predecessors: Walmart.

Walmart was long considered an exceptional company. It earned a lot of money, served its customers well, embodied proud American values[2], turned every member of the Walton family into a billionaire, created lots of jobs all around America, and even helped maintain inflation at record-low levels[3]. Yet in 2005, the reporter Charles Fishman published his best-selling book *The Wal-Mart Effect*[4]. In it he described in great detail how Walmart also contributed, at its unusually large scale, to the relocation of American businesses overseas, a lowered quality of manufactured goods consumed in the US, and the economic inequalities that are still today crippling the US economy.

No one could have foreseen those kinds of impacts back at the beginning. Sam Walton entered the retail store business in 1945. Then around 1950 he opened his own store in Rogers, Arkansas—certainly neither the city nor state that one would have predicted to be the home of global economic upheaval. Walmart's headquarters are still in Bentonville, Arkansas, even though the company quickly outgrew its roots: employing more than 1.5 million people, it is one of the largest corporate employers in the world.

Walmart also became one of the first big corporations to use computing and networks at a large scale[5]. The company collected vast amounts of data in its many stores. Then it used that information to make operations more efficient and push suppliers into constantly lowering their prices. Walmart ultimately grew so big, in no small part thanks to its advanced information system, that it transformed the American economy. Charles Fishman's *"Wal-Mart Effect"* involves both good and bad features: lower prices for consumers, but also lower wages for workers and an unbearable pressure on suppliers.

A large part of the Entrepreneurial Age's future can easily be predicted by those who know Walmart well. Tech companies resemble Walmart in many ways. They grow at an exponential pace. Customers are their priority, and the best tech CEOs make sure it stays that way. They obviously use technology extensively. And they have an ambivalent effect on the economy: as consumers, individuals enjoy the convenience, wide choice, lower prices, and ever-improved customer experience; but they also worry about tech companies' formidable economic power over the rest of economy—most particularly over themselves as they try to earn a living as workers. Questions abound: Isn't the tech industry too hard on workers[6]? Can society stand the pressure[7] of its exponential growth? Are tech CEOs bad? Should governments ally with incumbents to strike back against tech entrepreneurs? Should the power of consumers be restrained to alleviate the pressure on society as a whole?

Curbing consumer power would be a sharp reversal from the legacy of the past century. In the US consumer empowerment became an issue as early as 1906 with the shocking reporting by Upton Sinclair on the hygiene and working conditions in the meatpacking industry in Chicago, resulting in his landmark book *The Jungle*. It took an unexpected alliance between Sinclair and the progressive then-president Theodore Roosevelt to impose meat inspection as the law of the land and to enact the Pure Food and Drug Act, which became the cornerstone of hygiene enforcement in the food industry[8].

At the time, a distaste for trusts such as Standard Oil Co. already united farmers, laborers, the middle class, and entrepreneurial business owners[9]. This shared distrust was then turned into a powerful drive for advancing consumer empowerment with the unprecedented intervention of the federal government. This was all the more necessary because the age of the automobile and mass production led to complex products hitting consumer markets, not simply raw materials. With these products came frequent technical hazards, more complex value chains, distribution challenges, maintenance issues, and pricing uncertainties.

Antitrust, however, was not yet seen as a lever for consumer empowerment like regulations regarding hygiene and safety. The Progressive Era version of antitrust, that which led to the dismemberment of Standard Oil in 1911, was not meant to protect or promote individual consumers. Rather its goal was to empower small businesses against big corporations. Early in the twentieth century, future Supreme Court Justice Louis Brandeis came to embody the liberal approach to antitrust policy of that time—saying in one speech in defense of small businesses that *"if the Lord had intended things to be big, he would have made man bigger—in brains and character"*, and in another that *"thoughtless or weak, [the consumer] yields to the temptation of trifling immediate gain, and, selling his birthright for a mess of pottage, becomes himself an instrument of monopoly"* [10].

As a result, consumers had to wait until after World War II for antitrust law to be adjusted in their favor. The new focus on consumers was promoted by advocates such as Ralph Nader. It was made more critical by the vertical disintegration of the firm that gave birth to longer value chains. The conservative revolution played a role, too. Under the influence of legal scholars such as Robert Bork and Richard Posner, conservatives settled for an antitrust policy focused on the consumer because it effectively led to lighter regulations on corporations up the value chain. Businesses were left alone to fight amongst themselves so long as they didn't hurt the end consumer in broad daylight.

Bipartisan consensus led to accelerating progress, with detailed consumer-empowering regulations in industries as diverse as food[11], healthcare, cars[12], banking, insurance[13], taxis[14], and so on. The efforts to maximize the consumer surplus didn't succeed in every industry: think about housing[15], healthcare[16], or higher education[17], for instance. But overall the trend toward empowering consumers created a lot of value. In some cases, such as Walmart's, consumer pressure led to lower prices. In other industries, consumer-friendly regulations and greater competitive pressure rewarded the most innovative firms and contributed to improving the quality of products and sustaining ever-higher productivity gains. The case could finally be made, among others by Philippe Aghion, that consumer empowerment and the resulting competitive pressure favored innovation, prosperity, and economic security[18].

But this era is over. Now consumers have coalesced into the powerful multitude. Their empowerment can more and more be seen as a threat for society. Just like Walmart, tech companies such as Amazon and many others prove that in the Entrepreneurial Age, a multitude hungry for quality at scale beats workers and society most of the time, inflicting a continuous pressure on income from labor and corporate margins. This is much to the displeasure of those who wonder if technology really solves more problems than it creates[19]. They express reservations echoing Franklin Foer, who once wrote in the *New Republic*[20] that *"if we don't engage the new reality of monopoly with the spirit of argumentation and experimentation that carried Brandeis, we'll drift toward an unsustainable future."*

Today, Walmart is still a formidable player, but it's suffering. The way it used to treat its employees has backfired. The pressure it exerts on suppliers has alarmed trade organizations, politicians, and the press. To try and solve these problems, Walmart decided to drop its *"Lower Prices"* tagline[21] in favor of the more society-friendly *"Save Money, Live Better"*. Even more unexpectedly, it has decided to raise the wages of its many employees, thus contributing to a national debate around the minimum wage[22].

Yet just as Walmart tries to solve problems coming from the excessive power it provides to consumers, the Entrepreneurial Age is reinforcing the power of those consumers even more, creating the need to once again rebalance the corporate contract, especially when it comes to empowering workers against customers. What Amazon and other tech companies reveal is that in the new age, Internet users want to pay ever cheaper prices in exchange for ever better products. As the multitude, they also play a critical role in creating value within the supply chain. To be successful, corporations have no choice but to reward those customers with an unprecedented consumer surplus. As a result, shareholders have to give up short-term profits, suppliers have to trim down their operating margins, and already worn out workers seem to be plunged into a new precariat.

We need to realize that the 'Greater Wal-Mart Effect' brought about by Amazon, Uber and other tech companies is a key feature of the Entrepreneurial Age. In the past, large IT-driven players such as Walmart were able to bargain for their customers by relying on the power of critical mass. Nowadays, by harnessing the power of ubiquitous computing and networks and designing business models including what Tim O'Reilly calls an *"architecture of participation"*[23], tech companies invite the powerful multitude to climb up their value chain, take control of resources and contribute to creating even more value. But in doing so, they have contributed to carving

another of the Entrepreneurial Age's faces: the fundamental instability of multitude-driven consumer markets.

Instability is the new normal

Like every technological revolution, that of ubiquitous computing
and networks was born in a bubble—one that burst almost 20 years
ago. Its shadow still looms over the heads of entrepreneurs. Often it
inspires the old *"here we go again"* refrain whenever valuations go
higher or the fall of one overhyped tech company like Theranos or
Juicero leads to headlines discrediting all the others.

Not everyone in the startup world has clear memories of the
"dotcom bubble". Most entrepreneurs are actually too young to have
experienced it in their professional life. Conversely, many veterans
worked before, during and right after the bubble, to the point where
their vision has been irremediably distorted by how easy it was for
them to make money with less-than-average dotcom companies.
Should you value the advice of someone who sold their obscure
e-commerce startup in June 1999 for eight figures? The answer is
no—you should ignore them and focus on your business.

As for myself, I have a vivid memory of the late '90s tech bubble
as I was a student in computer science at the time. The tech-related
craze on financial markets was giving a lift to everyone on campus. It
provided me and my fellow students with the firm impression that
we were in the place to be, and that whatever we would do after
graduating, it would be part of a great adventure!

But then, poof. Right when my classmates and I were about to
enter the labor market, it was suddenly all over with startups and tech
companies. Overnight our options dropped down to joining a manu-
facturer, a telco, or an IT services business. Most of us were under-
standably bored by such perspectives. Some even decided to switch
careers. As part of that group, I chose to focus on political science
and public administration and soon joined the French government.
It was from there—or so I thought—that I could make a difference

after all. Little did I know that this bubble was only the first of a long series, for the Entrepreneurial Age is unstable in its very essence.

To be fair, instability has always been the flaw of large markets, especially consumer markets in which the number of participants is the highest. In the early twentieth century, the unprecedented instability of larger consumer markets in the nascent Fordist economy almost led capitalism to its death. Whenever consumer demand went down, businesses had to close factories and fire their workers, fueling unemployment, poverty, and anger in the process. If they did keep their employees on the payroll, the risk was producing too much and only delaying hardship instead of preventing it. As written by Nelson Lichtenstein about the US consumer-oriented industries in the 1920s, *"in 1928 and 1929 sales lagged, inventories rose, factories cut their output, and unemployment rose. Even before Wall Street's crash in October 1929, many executives thought their market saturated"*[24].

As explained in Chapter 2, most of the Great Safety Net 1.0 was designed to prevent such instability from recurring. It achieved its goals, albeit in very different manners, in the consecutive phases since World War II, first during the high economic growth of the post-war boom and then during the Great Moderation that the Western world entered when it finally managed to defeat the stagflation of the 1970s. What was left of the Great Safety Net 1.0 even played a key role in alleviating the consequences of the 2008 financial crisis. In France, a broader safety net and higher minimum wage relative to cost of living made it possible to provide economic security to the majority of households. Even if jobs were destroyed following the crisis, those who were still employed even saw their real wages going up in the aftermath of the crisis! Corporate margins took a big hit, but with consumer demand stabilized, France managed to make its way out of the crisis with less suffering than in the US or the UK.

However, in the Entrepreneurial Age, instability is of an even greater magnitude. In a world dominated by multitude-driven increasing returns to scale, companies are forced to aggressively race against each other in the so-called 'battle zone', out of which only one will emerge. Victory often depends on contingent factors, but the winner usually kicks most its main competitors out of the market, until the next race begins with a new wave of upstart competitors

HOW WIDESPREAD INSTABILITY LED TO THE GREAT DEPRESSION

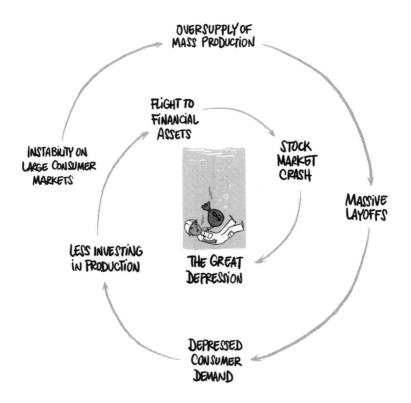

OVERSUPPLY OF MASS PRODUCTION

FLIGHT TO FINANCIAL ASSETS

INSTABILITY ON LARGE CONSUMER MARKETS

STOCK MARKET CRASH

MASSIVE LAYOFFS

LESS INVESTING IN PRODUCTION

THE GREAT DEPRESSION

DEPRESSED CONSUMER DEMAND

entering the field. With the utter fragility of strategic positions on markets where the multitude has the upper hand, the Entrepreneurial Age generates, as pointed out by economist W. Brian Arthur, *"not equilibrium but instability"*[25].

This is in no way restricted to certain segments of the economy. The high level of instability seen in the UK following the financial crisis, culminating in the Brexit vote and leading toward an unpredictable future, is a glimpse of what can happen in a global economy primarily powered by digital technology. After all, the financial services industry that forms the core of the British economy has been a pioneer in deploying and taking advantage of ubiquitous computing and networks at a large scale.

Because of the widespread instability, it's not enough for a business to be the market leader or the most profitable company. Rather the stake is to take the vast majority of the market[26], at (almost) any cost. Those who generate superior increasing returns to scale can crush competition and realize a sizable return on investment over the long term. Conversely, those who put the strategic emphasis on obsolete goals such as lower unit costs or short-term shareholder returns will end up critically weaker in this new competitive regime. The reason why tech companies pull no punches is precisely because winning most of their market is literally a question of their business's life and death.

Recurring bubbles simply reflect these fundamental economics. In the presence of increasing returns to scale, companies are not competing with more or less equal players to form a lasting oligopoly. Rather, they are engaged in a violent battle for total market domination. The result is that there is usually only one winner (and its happy investors) and many losers (and their very sad investors). No wonder why investors are willing to invest at any price the moment they sense that they may have picked a winner. The competition to be part of the best deals is so fierce that it pushes valuations sky-high. The dynamics of the Entrepreneurial Age look like a perpetual race with financial bubbles as temporary side effects.

In the presence of increasing returns to scale, raising a lot of money is not only a way to finance operations. It is also a signal to all stakeholders (shareholders, customers, employees, analysts) that a company is on track to become the leader and grab most of the market. This is why tech companies advertise their funding rounds so noisily[27]. When customers or prospects, who are mostly regular people, hear that one company raised a lot of money, they don't reflect on irrational exuberance. Instead, they're comforted in the feeling that this company seems to be the market leader and that, as a result, the quality is likely better and comes at a cheaper price[28] than that provided by lesser challengers.

A positive aspect of frequent bubbles in the Entrepreneurial Age is that they foster continuous competition. The absence of a bubble would mean that entrenched positions are impregnable. Instead, the abundance of capital enables new entrants and existing challengers to raise a lot of money and attempt to take over a dominant position at the expense of the market leader. Thus bubbles are healthy from an antitrust point of view. Without them, nobody would enter existing markets to challenge the dominant position of giant tech companies. Investors' irrational exuberance, exacerbated by increasing returns to scale, is part of sustaining a high level of competition on the market (and of redistributing wealth from shareholders to employees, customers, and suppliers).

Entrepreneurial ecosystems reflect the importance of being able to compete in today's races. A healthy ecosystem is designed to concentrate enough capital in a given area. As a result, the ecosystem is able to fund the occasional, improbable outlier that will then conquer a large global market. Eventually, massive amounts of capital concentrate in a few tech companies that have the potential to become global players. And so massive capital influx, far from being an anomaly, is in fact the mark of a strong ecosystem. It means local startups attract a lot of capital and the balance between supply and demand shifts to the advantage of the most ambitious entrepreneurs[29].

At the end of the day, what Carlota Perez dubs *"major technology bubbles"* are a good thing because they fuel innovation. It's only when investors renounce their rationality and stop demanding short-term returns on their investments that they are capable of pouring money into long-shot projects that end up transforming the economy for the better. As once written by J. Bradford Delong, *"the irrational exuberance of the late 1800s made the railroads a money-losing industry—and a wealth-creating industry. The more money investors lost through overbuilding, the lower freight rates became, and the more railroads belched out wealth for everybody else*"[30]. The likes of Amazon and Google do much the same by empowering networks of individuals and businesses, constructing pathways through which they can develop activities in ways that were unthinkable just a few decades ago.

The capital deployed by tech companies is spent differently than the capital that fueled the big corporations of the age of the automobile and mass production. For dominant corporations in the Entrepreneurial Age, the multitude, instead of oil, is the essential resource that they must harness. The Internet is the infrastructure they need to master if they want to succeed. They operate more digital applications than factories and distribution platforms. Production is about providing an exceptional experience at a large scale rather than mass producing standardized goods. Their organization has to be agile and innovative rather than hierarchical and optimized. Their managers must obsess over increasing returns to scale rather than lowering unit cost of production. Finally, they must see their customers as a multitude instead of as a mass.

It all leads to confusion about the economic nature of the multitude: are individuals consumers or resources? In fact, they're both, and that's why the new common sense is all about catering to the turbulent multitude. Because it's a factor of production and a consuming force at the same time, the multitude maintains an ever tighter grip on both extremities of business value chains—which, by the way, is a real challenge for neoclassical growth theory and its input/output approach to analyzing production. No wonder companies exert such pressure on workers and markets are now ridden with instability as the demanding multitude comes and goes.

All in all, what matters is not what happens during the recurrent bubbles, but what comes next. The price to pay for widespread instability is that some investors regularly lose money because they didn't pick the winner, whereas many employees eventually lose their jobs because they happened to work for the losers. In this context, the stakes are clear: the economy can keep growing only if it has the institutions to foster resilience in the presence of this instability fueled by the multitude. It's critical that both impoverished investors and jobless employees are able to rebound throughout the booms and busts of an economy driven by increasing returns to scale.

This is precisely what makes the strength of an ecosystem such as

EVERYTHING CHANGES

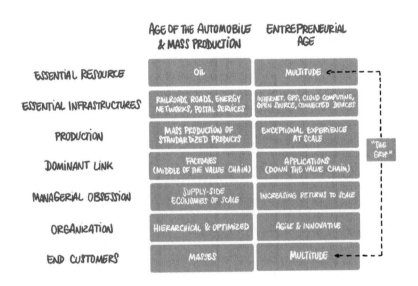

	AGE OF THE AUTOMOBILE & MASS PRODUCTION	ENTREPRENEURIAL AGE
ESSENTIAL RESOURCE	OIL	MULTITUDE
ESSENTIAL INFRASTRUCTURES	RAILROADS, ROADS, ENERGY NETWORKS, POSTAL SERVICES	INTERNET, GPS, CLOUD COMPUTING, OPEN SOURCE, CONNECTED DEVICES
PRODUCTION	MASS PRODUCTION OF STANDARDIZED PRODUCTS	EXCEPTIONAL EXPERIENCE AT SCALE
DOMINANT LINK	FACTORIES (MIDDLE OF THE VALUE CHAIN)	APPLICATIONS (DOWN THE VALUE CHAIN)
MANAGERIAL OBSESSION	SUPPLY-SIDE ECONOMIES OF SCALE	INCREASING RETURNS TO SCALE
ORGANIZATION	HIERARCHICAL & OPTIMIZED	AGILE & INNOVATIVE
END CUSTOMERS	MASSES	MULTITUDE

"THE GRIP"

Silicon Valley. After the dotcom bubble burst, most in the Bay Area chose resilience and continued to found startups, to invest in them, and to seek jobs in the tech industry. Meanwhile, other parts of the world were traumatized and relinquished all interest in the nascent digital economy. That post-bubble behavior explains most of Silicon Valley's competitive edge over other ecosystems.

What is true for the relatively privileged players in Silicon Valley must now be extended to society as a whole. Instability is the new normal at many different levels. In the Entrepreneurial Age, a larger proportion of businesses are struggling to find a profitable business model. Employees may still have long-term contracts, but with employers whose life span is getting shorter and shorter. Workers are employed by companies that either need to take critical risks to conquer a dominant position on the market, or for dominant companies that are in danger of being toppled by challengers at every turn. Even for the winners of the day, a temporarily dominant position on the market doesn't equal lifelong economic security for the workers.

And for individuals, this unprecedented sense of instability exists at every level of the income ladder. Obviously those at the bottom have genuine and pressing difficulties in making ends meet. But as pointed out by Rachel Sherman, the affluent, too, dread instability because *"their single-earner families [are] dependent on work in finance... earnings fluctuate and jobs are impermanent"*[31].

And so today's consumer power is a modern-day Janus. Looking in one direction, it allows consumers to benefit from lower prices and better products in many areas of their lives. But it also looks in the opposite direction as consumers exert pressure and trigger instability on themselves in their guise as workers. As such, consumers fuel an untenable situation, whereby the very thing that they love is the same thing that is destroying them.

With the 'Greater Wal-Mart Effect' and the widespread, pervasive instability characteristic of the Entrepreneurial Age, we shouldn't let individuals drown in the great ocean of evermore critical risks. Instead, if we ever want to live through another Golden Age, we now ought to build an upgraded version of the Great Safety Net and provide greater prosperity and economic security to both households and businesses— what we could call a *Greater Safety Net*, or a 'Great Safety Net 2.0'.

BETWEEN A ROCK & A SHAKY PLACE

PRESSURE ON WAGES & INCREASING LIVING COSTS
= DECREASING PURCHASING POWER

INADEQUATE SAFETY NET & UNFORESEEN CIRCUMSTANCES
= INCREASING INSTABILITY

Getting from Great to Greater

Like most of us working in the startup world and venture capital, I see technology as an opportunity to create more wealth and make things better. But I also realize that everything I've concentrated on during the past two decades has put me on the winning side of technological change.

I studied at some of my country's top institutions, which provided me a choice between prestigious government jobs and lucrative positions in the private sector. I had the means to make the most of technology in my day-to-day life, where things have become seamless and often less expensive. And ever since I've been working in the startup world (which was still an odd choice in France in 2010), technology has only risen in importance and visibility. All in all, I'm among those who are benefiting from the current paradigm shift. But this is clearly not the case for everyone in the middle class.

On the consumption side, technology provides a better life and more opportunities, with startups and entrepreneurs harnessing the power of technology to make the world a better place. On the production side, the rise of technology has reinforced the sense of perpetual crisis given the startups that are primarily seen as threats for incumbents, the instability that goes with increasing returns to scale, and the 'Greater Wal-Mart Effect'. Here, technology disrupts the world and displaces its inhabitants rather than making things better. Clearly the impact of technology is not the same if you're part of Richard Florida's *"creative class"* or if you have a mid-level assembly or desk job in an aging organization.

As we're going deeper into the Entrepreneurial Age, technology has become a constant challenge and a matter of life and death for traditional employers. Most of them are unable to take the risks required to make the most of computing and networks. To remain competitive without innovating, they have to cut costs continuously, thus increasing the pressure on what is now the weakest link in their supply chain—the workforce[32].

This echoes Clayton Christensen's argument[33] as to how corporate finance has made it harder for old corporations to comply with the fast pace of innovation[34]. Disruptive innovation, the one you need to implement to remain competitive over the long term, employs a lot of capital and creates many jobs. But corporate executives usually favor efficiency innovation, whose main consequences are the freeing of invested capital (hence the record-high corporate dividends[35] in the recent period) and massive job destruction. The fact that those executives prefer rent-seeking over risk-taking explains a significant part of the widening economic inequality gap and increased economic insecurity[36]. Yet workers in traditional industries will often point to tech startups as the main culprits for their problems, rather than the feeble and incompetent management of incumbents in traditional industries.

It's not that technology is absent from older organizations. Most of them have long since deployed information systems and equipped their workers with computing devices. Rather the problem is that using technology to achieve higher efficiency does not solve strategic problems as much as it makes work more alienating and inspires resentment in workers. Tech companies willing to ally with the multitude have made a priority out of making life simpler and more seamless for their users. But there is also an entire generation of older tech companies (what Peter Thiel calls the *"Rust Belt of the tech industry"*[37]) that have made it their mission to serve legacy organizations with ill-designed apps and closed systems. It certainly doesn't serve the cause of technology well.

The rapidly approaching spectre of automation is adding to the fear. The twentieth century created lots of jobs, whether in manufacturing or services, that consisted in executing routine tasks within an integrated supply chain under the principles of scientific management. Now technology makes it easy to replace humans with machines that execute those same routine tasks. And it's no wonder this hurts: for decades, those routine jobs were extremely attractive. People didn't need to be highly educated to perform them and they nonetheless came with good wages and the economic security underpinned by the Great Safety Net. In other words, those jobs gave rise to the middle class and the very idea of working families (father at a factory, mother either at home or at an office or retail store nearby). And now they are precisely the jobs that are being replaced by technology—or, potentially even worse, simply made redundant, inspiring workers to see their daily labor as what David Graeber calls a *"bullshit job"*[38].

In many ways, the transition to the Entrepreneurial Age is amplifying and accelerating a preexisting trend. Robots have been present in factories for decades, gradually replacing workers at various levels of the income ladder. Predominantly routine jobs have been affected the most. They're the easiest to replace with technology and they're also the easiest to relocate overseas, as technology (and free trade agreements) made it incredibly easy to build factories in cheap-labor countries and ship manufactured goods over much longer distances. This has been a concern for decades, but clearly the exponential power of technology has made the fear of it more vivid—and personal—than ever.

Things are becoming somewhat more urgent because less educated workers are far from being the only ones affected by technology-driven displacement. The acceleration brought about by the current techno-economic transition is leading to the replacement process affecting more than just manual routine tasks, and educated professionals are now being replaced with software. The common point for intellectual professions currently being eaten by software[39] is the mastery of vast amounts of knowledge. Thanks to advancing artificial intelligence, this knowledge can be mastered by autonomous software, leaving to humans only the personal service / caring side of the job: think about IBM's Watson (healthcare)[40], Watson-based Ross (legal)[41] or high-frequency trading (finance).

A less understood way in which technology contributes to destroying jobs is that it makes it possible to replace workers with a multitude of users whose contributions are coordinated by networks. Through these networks, many tasks previously executed by paid workers are passed over to the multitude itself. This happens either individually (I can type on a computer myself, a task rendered so simple thanks to software that no secretarial jobs are needed anymore) or at the aggregate level (entire professions are gradually overthrown by contributing users: travel guide writers vs. TripAdvisor, encyclopedia writers vs. Wikipedia, journalists vs. Medium). Professionals are replaced with user communities working for free[42] on relatively small individual tasks.

On top of that, we have difficulties in translating the higher productivity and quality brought about by the Entrepreneurial Age into better working conditions for those who retain a job. As technology makes progress, most jobs can now be held by less skilled workers[43]. As observed by Tim O'Reilly, technology can augment people and enable them to do things that were previously impossible[44]. But it also makes it possible to do the same things with less skilled workers. Like Uber, technology can even do both: employing less skilled workers (Uber drivers don't know the city map by heart like old fashioned taxi drivers) while delivering higher quality than the incumbents[45] to ever more demanding customers.

This 'downward augmentation' is a promising perspective when it comes to creating jobs for less educated people in an economy driven by technology[46]—and a radically new way of looking at software and robots in the context of Schumpeterian job destruction. But it's also bad news for most workers, as Marx's *"reserve army of labor"* is now larger than ever. In the Entrepreneurial Age, corporations have an infinite pool of low-skilled job-seekers that they can tap into to replace those who have the nerve to organize and demand better working conditions. And this can only make the 'Greater Wal-Mart Effect' even worse.

All in all, technology isn't changing the world in a day. Instead, creative destruction is triggering gradual yet massive transitional unemployment due to a radical shift on the job market. On the supply side, the new economy is taking over without yet creating enough jobs to compensate for the amount of destruction. On the demand side, it is proving difficult to attract middle class workers into the new, more tech-driven segments of the job market. If the Dark Ages seem to be lasting so long, it's because such a techno-economic transition takes time and inflicts quite a lot of pain on the workforce that finds itself caught between two eras.

What's more, with the instability that is characteristic of the Entrepreneurial Age, demand is less steady than ever. The exponential pressure exerted on workers by consumers allied with large tech companies (the 'Greater Wal-Mart Effect') brings wages lower and lower, which in turn causes consumers to seek out more savings. It's a vicious cycle in which individuals are both perpetrators and victims. Even the financial system doesn't work anymore since it was

WHEN TECHNOLOGY DESTROYS WESTERN JOBS

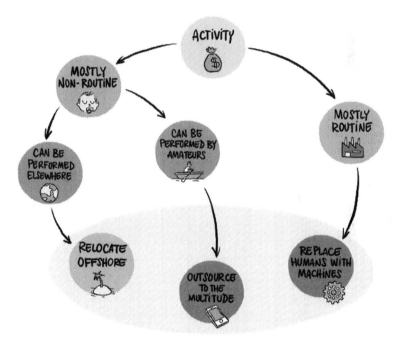

designed for a society of salaried workers employed by big, resilient corporations. Once jobs are more precarious and corporations are more prone to failure, the financial system is proving incapable of fulfilling the financing needs of either households or businesses of the Entrepreneurial Age.

This is the challenge we need to tackle today: revisiting every function that was once performed by the Great Safety Net back when it worked so well. We need to imagine institutions to once again serve the three goals that we should all be obsessed with: making consumer demand steadier, increasing household income, and providing access to affordable credit.

It's not about restoring things as they were in the 1950s and 1960s. It's not about implementing the principles of neoliberalism that led us to the 2008 financial crisis. Rather we have to imagine a radically new mix of social insurance programs, financial innovation, and worker empowerment mechanisms to better manage risks and increase prosperity and economic security for all. This is what the Great Safety Net 2.0 is all about—a way out of the Dark Ages and a virtuous macro mechanism to fulfill the promise of the Entrepreneurial Age.

Key takeaways

- *Consumers gaining power as the multitude is not good news for everyone. Like once happened with the infamous "Wal-Mart Effect", it inflicts an ever-growing pressure on workers.*

- *As the Entrepreneurial Age is driven by increasing returns to scale, it displays instability at levels far beyond what was observed at the dawn of the age of the automobile and mass production.*

- *It's time we imagine a Greater Safety Net, or 'Great Safety Net 2.0', to hedge both households and businesses against these new adverse features of the Entrepreneurial Age.*

Part 3
The Collapse
of the Cathedrals

Chapter 7
The Safety Net
in an Open World

*"Sometimes simple and bold ideas help us see more clearly a
complex reality that requires nuanced approaches. I have an
"impossibility theorem" for the global economy that is like that.
It says that democracy, national sovereignty and global economic
integration are mutually incompatible: we can combine any two of
the three, but never have all three simultaneously and in full."*
—Dani Rodrik[1]

Software is opening the world

One of the most striking articles I read in 2016 was written by
Rex Storgatz for the *Wired* edition of *Backchannel*[2]. The piece is about
a paradox observed in the small, isolated town of Napoleon in North
Dakota. As remarked by the author, nothing has changed in the appearance of the place where he once spent his childhood and teenage years:
the population is the same, the number of jobs is the same, the same
stores are up and running. Yet as he digs deeper and talks with teen-
agers who live there, he discovers that their lives have almost nothing in
common with what he experienced twenty years before. For him, living
in Napoleon equaled being cut off from the world. But today, there's
something new that considerably broadens the perspective of Napoleon's residents. As remarked by Storgatz, the town *"would be trapped in
the amber of time, in a big glass case, if not for one thing:* Access to information."

Until the 1960s, the main force at work in modern societies were
local communities. In the absence of mass media and with the national
government still a loose organization gathering people from different
areas and various backgrounds, action on the ground was key to delivering economic security and prosperity. Those local systems were more

than simply living in the same area. Their primary function was to provide people with a sense of community. At the local scale, people gathered and bonded working in the fields and in the factories, walking around the local marketplace where they went for groceries and communing at church where they congregated on Sundays.

Those tight-knit communities played an even more crucial role because the Great Safety Net didn't exist back then. To find a job and cope during difficult times, individuals needed to belong to that community, which led them to participate in the political process. In the case of the infamous political machines in the US, people literally sold their vote (and that of their community) in exchange for favors and material support. Patronage was the lever candidates had to operate in order to bond with individual voters and their community. Geographic proximity formed the basis for mitigating risks at the local level[3].

At a larger scale, entire territorial systems were controlled by powerful intermediaries. Their mission, on behalf of their constituents, was to bargain with power players at the national level. In exchange for delivering votes for their party, these local leaders obtained public money to facilitate patronage of their constituents. And like in the case of segregation in the Deep South of the US, they also ensured that there would be no intrusion from the national level in their own local businesses, sustaining fragmentation and regional differences in the process.

The way to aggregate the various local systems at the national level was to form loose electoral coalitions that pulled together different constituencies around tailor-made coalition-building policies. In the US, one such coalition existed with the first populist movement in the late nineteenth century: it was driven especially by the farmers' response to the overwhelming power of the railroads and it led to their forming an alliance with the urban working class, long before industrial trade unions were even a thing.

The New Deal, which led to building the American version of the Great Safety Net, was another opportunistic coalition[4]. In November 1947, the 'Clifford Memo', a document laying out the strategy to be followed by President Truman the following year, reminded its readers that *"the Democratic Party is an unhappy alliance of Southern conservatives, Western progressives and Big City labor... The success or failure of the Democratic leadership can be precisely measured by its ability to lead enough members of these three misfit groups to the polls on the first Tuesday after the first Monday of November, 1948"*[5].

The mass media shift from the 1950s onward definitively weakened those local political systems. Even in 1947, the aforementioned 'Clifford Memo' already detailed how *"the old 'party organization' control [was] gone forever. Better education, the rise of the mass pressure group, the economic depression of the 30s, the growth of government functions—all these have contributed to the downfall of the organization...They have been supplanted in large measure by the pressure groups"*[6]. As soon as the Great Safety Net of the Fordist age was in place and delivering results, the sense of community became national rather than local.

Today, the unprecedented connectivity experienced in places such as Napoleon is something that we should factor in as we try to better understand the nature of community in the Entrepreneurial Age. Ubiquitous computing and networks enable many things that didn't exist in the past: you can now learn anything from YouTube, Facebook, and Medium; you can exchange information with people anywhere in the world with the help of Twitter, WhatsApp, and Google Translate; you can form new networks of remote, yet like-minded individuals who will pool their knowledge and power to achieve new goals and form new organizations.

Thus the redistribution of power from the inside to the outside of organizations and the rise of the multitude are changing the game. Openness in the Entrepreneurial Age is quite different from globalization in the Dark Ages of financialization. The global world of the 1980s, 1990s and 2000s was dominated by giant, bureaucratic corporations. As it constrained nation states, the level at which people tended to congregate in those times, globalization was a direct threat for people's sense of community.

But today things are different. The open world of the Entrepreneurial Age is dominated by networks of individuals equipped with ever more powerful computing devices. Not only do people travel more, they're also more connected with one another across the borders that still divide the physical world. It doesn't mean that local communities or nation states are now obsolete. But from the point of view of individuals, they don't matter as much as they used to. In this new world, people don't need to live close to one another to feel a sense of community.

Indeed connections within the multitude are more and more difficult for nation states to capture. A growing part of the population is mobile at the global level, with young (and less young) people now used to working in different countries and adapting to local customs. Gone are the days when Western people working abroad were so-called 'expatriates', still relying on their home state and institutions when it came to employment, banking, social insurance, and various other ties. Today, more individuals, however privileged, are effectively behaving like emigrants. They leave things behind and convert to the way of life and institutional framework of their place of residence. Alongside the travelling professional class that still consumes stereotypical products and experiences from one large city to another[7], there's another fringe of the creative class that dives deeper into foreign countries, weakening their attachments to the one they were born in.

In some aspects, the digital economy is still trapped within borders: Netflix still streams different movies and series depending on where you watch it; Uber has to comply with heterogeneous regulations from the US to the UK to Germany to Italy; European citizens have the *"right to be forgotten"* whereas in the US the First Amendment makes it most difficult to suppress online speech; most US tech companies have failed to gain a foothold on the Chinese market, which is mostly owned by Chinese ventures.

But in many other dimensions, we can all sense how the growing power of ubiquitous computing and networks is being translated into the tangible world. In the Entrepreneurial Age, cross-border trade is less easily measured; the changing geography of value creation casts doubts on traditional macroeconomic indicators such as GDP; our very understanding of well-being and growth is radically changing. As underlined by W. Brian Arthur, *"we have entered a different phase for the economy, a new era where production matters less and what matters more is access to that production: distribution, in other words—who gets what and how they get it"*[8].

In this context, there are many reasons to think that the current Entrepreneurial Age could see a retreat of the nation state and a rebirth of sub-national and trans-national systems. Many signs are pleading for that to be the case: the fragmentation of society, with individuals increasingly trapped in filter bubbles and connected mostly to people who share similar views; the rise of individuals as an active multitude rather than a mass falling prey to the influence of large organizations; the many practical purposes of individuals as they gather in online communities to form a network; the possibility of tying those online communities together by harnessing the power of technology to advance a political agenda.

In this new world rendered more open by ubiquitous computing and networks, the current fascination for the model of the city state[9] is understandable. For Silicon Valley, the idea of empowering cities flatters the taste for changing the world by founding new ventures—a preference for 'exit' as opposed to 'voice', as pointed out by Balaji S. Srinivasan[10]. This is a sentiment that is only being amplified by the repulsion inspired by Donald Trump[11].

For others, having cities gain their autonomy would be a way to affirm a clearer direction when it comes to imagining a new socio-in-stitutional framework for the new age[12]. For those with faith in public policy, the city emerges as the main level for experimentation[13] in a world where the the state has shrunk from its role as a positive agent of change. That's because most social innovations in history were first implemented at the local level, either by the authorities, by activists, or by individuals themselves: this was notably true for the European mutualist movement in the nineteenth century, which anticipated the Great Safety Net through many experiments within local communities. Later in the US, Supreme Court Justice Louis Brandeis dubbed the states the *"laboratories of democracy"* to stress how much the US federal system provided room for experimenting with new policies at the local level[14].

And so in a way, this temptation of the city-state can be explained by the flowering of the Entrepreneurial Age[15]. Many countries are relying on that model to harness the power of technology-driven networks. One example is China, which is a large country whose national economic strategy originated in special administrative regions such as Shenzhen and the Pudong district in Shanghai. Now the Belt and Road Initiative is providing China with an infrastruc-ture to expand its power along the new digital trade routes of the day. Another example is Israel, which more resembles a city-state.

There the government-sponsored Yozma program has contributed to forging strong links between the Israeli entrepreneurial ecosystem and the US venture capital industry, thus helping Israel make the most of a more digital world. A third example is Estonia, an even smaller country whose famous e-Residency program enables anyone in the world to access the pioneering, digital, seamless infrastructure that is e-Estonia and use the nascent ecosystem of business services that is growing on top of that revolutionary platform.

But I believe that there's another historical precedent that more closely matches the Entrepreneurial Age than even the city-state. And it is a model that can provide significant insights on how nations can best position themselves for future prosperity and economic security.

The thalassocracies

Although I live in Europe, my first trip to Venice, one of the most famous destinations in the world, was only in 2013, when I was 35 years old. It was a rewarding experience because I had already read a lot about the place. I remember having my mind blown by Giacomo Casanova's legendary memoir *The Story of My Life*, which I read one summer during my years as a student. I'm also a fan of a Hugo Pratt comic series, in which the hero Corto Maltese, a rogue sailor, crisscrosses the world from Central Asia to Argentina to Manchuria to Switzerland in the early twentieth century. One episode is set in Venice, Pratt's home town, and tells the complicated story of freemasons hunting a legendary treasure during the rise of Italian fascism[16].

Apart from the extraordinary sights, what's stunning in Venice is the vibrancy that surrounds you, as is common in such very old places. Even though history is not actually written on the walls, you can feel, simply by walking along them, the depth, complexity, and violence of a multi-secular historical legacy. Terrible things happened there. And massive amounts of wealth were accumulated as well.

Back when it was an independent republic, Venice dominated the

Mediterranean Sea and the trade routes for silk and spices through the Bosphorus to the vast plains of Central Asia[17]. To assert power so far beyond its tiny territory, the *Stato da Màr* needed a unique strategic positioning. The Arsenal, an industrial facility for manufacturing munitions and galleys, became a platform for experimenting with assembly-line methods of production, anticipating the Industrial Revolution by several centuries[18]. It was also in Venice that modern patent law was first enforced, with a 1474 statute designed to make sure that *"most clever minds... would exert their minds, invent and make things that would be of no small utility and benefit to"* the Republic[19]. Throughout the centuries, the strength of Venice's institutions provided the tiny republic with the sense of urgency and cohesiveness necessary to take bold risks and affirm its power—from hacking the Fourth Crusade in order to encourage the sacking of Constantinople in 1204 to negotiating a trade monopoly with the Great Khans of Mongolia from 1267 forward.

The Venetian Republic is an illustration of a rare model of power: the *thalassocracy*, or a state with primarily maritime realms and the means to defend and expand them. History provides us with only a few examples of that combination of political, military, and economic resources, from the Republic of Venice to the Portuguese empire in the fifteenth and sixteenth centuries to Victorian Britain following the repeal of the Navigation Acts that had previously restricted colonial trade to England[20]. As noted by historian Fernand Braudel, long-distance maritime trade was the epitome of pre-industrial capitalism[21]. And oddly enough, there are many parallels to be drawn between the thalassocracies of the past and the current Entrepreneurial Age.

A first trait of thalassocracy is that it's not about the resources you own, but about the resources you exploit by way of superior strategy. Old thalassocracies didn't own the sea as much as they used it as a means of communication and exchange. As put by French scholar Hervé Coutau-Bégarie, this presupposed *"a large and efficient merchant fleet, ports capable of receiving and distributing continuous flows of goods...but also a system of credit superior to that of the competitors, insurance, information control"*[22] as well as the military seapower necessary to ensure continuity of trade.

Likewise in the Entrepreneurial Age, tech companies don't own

VENICE : THE "STATO DA MÀR"

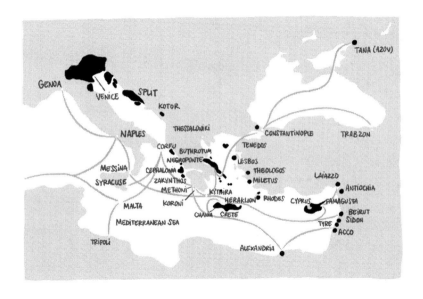

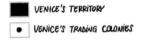

VENICE'S TERRITORY

VENICE'S TRADING COLONIES

the multitude to which their users belong, yet they exploit it as a strategic resource thanks to the superior design of their applications, the regular and systematic monitoring of their users' activity, and the increasing returns to scale they derive from networks. It's not about mastering the sea through superior maritime power but rather about mastering the multitude by way of trust inspired in billions of individuals all around the world.

Another trait of a thalassocracy is that, as always with strategic positioning, trade-offs are essential[23]. Most old thalassocracies mastered the sea because they didn't have much land to defend. Conversely, most countries with vast swaths of land had a hard time competing on the sea, because they lacked the focus and cohesiveness that made it possible for maritime powers to concentrate and occasionally give all they had to defend their realm. This is what the Republic of Venice achieved when its Genoan nemesis almost destroyed it during the War of Chioggia from 1378 to 1381[24]. As for Britain, it took the 1846 abrogation of the infamous Corn Laws to convert it to international trade at the expense of its domestic agriculture. Only in the following Victorian era was British maritime power radically reoriented toward global commerce and mastery of the sea[25].

In the Entrepreneurial Age, it takes focus and clear strategic positioning for certain countries such as the US, China, Israel[26] and Estonia[27] to prosper in an economy driven by the multitude. Meanwhile other countries are still competing in a lesser league because they remain trapped in their focus on legacy industries such as tourism and agriculture in France, finance in the UK, and manufacturing in Germany. You can't succeed on the sea if land remains your primary focus.

A third trait of a thalassocracy is that the state cannot succeed alone. Mastering a resource as unruly as the sea eventually requires the assistance of a thriving ecosystem of entrepreneurs and financiers with whom the state must share the profits of trade. In Britain and the Netherlands, conquering new trade routes was an opportunity to organize and enrich a new class of merchants. Conversely, countries in which the state retained a tight monopoly over trade, such as France and Spain, failed to establish lasting commercial and financial empires at a large scale[28].

The same can be observed in the Entrepreneurial Age. The US

owes its power mostly to the strategic moves by the US government to lay the ground on which US tech companies are now able
to thrive[29]. Infrastructures such as the Internet and GPS, ruled by
principles such as (the now-temporarily defunct) net neutrality,
are the contemporary equivalents of the settlements and trading
posts established by old thalassocratic regimes to secure their trade
routes[30]. Like the modern law of the sea was inspired by the British
to consolidate the superiority of their fleet and maritime posts[31], the
current rules governing the Internet, such as the limited liability of
Internet service providers, were set up by the US government with
the goal of enabling a level of innovation at which only US technology companies could compete[32]. Finally, it should come as no
surprise that contemporary entrepreneurs are supported by financiers, the venture capitalists, whose model was precisely inspired by
the financing of risky maritime expeditions in the past[33].

All in all, old thalassocracies help us understand what it means
for a national economy to prosper in the Entrepreneurial Age. With
borders now closing in every part of the world, most big countries
are somewhat blinded by their own size, with their larger domestic
market and diversified industries providing them with the illusion that they can go it alone in a divided world. Meanwhile, other
countries are working hard on their strategic positioning to try and
make the most of the new landscape. With a characteristic sense of
urgency and cohesiveness, tiny states and dense cities, but also very
large countries such as China, appear more prone to understanding
the shifts in the global economy and taking action[34]. Drawing lessons
from history, they convert to the practice of old maritime empires and
try to master the Internet like the Republic of Venice once mastered
the sea.

And so the model of the thalassocracy emerges as the most useful
precedent to understand the current challenges related to the
competitiveness of nations. In the Entrepreneurial Age, what matters
is less the enclosed land than the wider sea; less asset ownership
than the mastery of non-appropriable resources (the sea yesterday,
the multitude today); and less the crown than the entrepreneurs
and financiers that the state brings along in its effort to conquer and
secure new trade routes.

To go beyond simply understanding and move into making

the most of a more open world, nations would be well served by following the thalassocracy model: instead of retreating within national borders, conquer the many strategic resources that are there to be taken, beginning with the multitude itself; instead of catering to both the old and the new economy, focus on the opportunities brought about by the Entrepreneurial Age; instead of relying on the state only, enroll a class of entrepreneurs and financiers; instead of looking inward, affirm an agenda of economic security and prosperity and imagine a global order to foster it. Like with the Republic of Venice, it's about exploiting the global resources necessary to grow in power and prosperity while building and maintaining strong, inclusive institutions at home. Alas for the moment that is not the path being taken by most traditional twentieth-century powers.

A more open world calls for greater economic security

Globalization is old news nowadays. When I grew up, tech companies were not the enemy yet—they barely even existed. But people were already hating multinational corporations that were relocating their supply-chain in cheap-labor countries. And the 2016 presidential campaign in the US has only revived this old fear of international trade as a danger to our way of life.

There's a paradox here. For most of the twentieth century, free trade was not seen as a danger for the Great Safety Net. On the contrary, promoting free trade long went along with shared prosperity and economic security for both households and businesses. In some cases, those advocating a stronger safety net were promoting international trade with a clear conscience of how much it contributed to providing their constituents with good jobs and sustained prosperity. But much of the time, the key reason was found in the mere necessity of forming an alliance with business leaders. In exchange for more economic security for workers, the corporate world demanded that a practical government should support them in their conquest of foreign markets and ensure access to cheap supplies wherever they could find them[35].

US history lets us understand the complicated path through which a part of the political spectrum unexpectedly came up in favor of both free trade and more economic security. In the nineteenth century, the new Republican Party had inherited the interventionist ideas of Alexander Hamilton and Henry Clay: protective tariffs plus direct subsidies for local investments in canals, turnpikes, and then railways. As for the Democrats, they were largely Southern but also allied with the big urban financial centers at a time when finance was principally oriented towards foreign trade, and hence they were all for *laissez-faire* (except, of course, when it came to enforcing the Fugitive Slave Act).

As a result, the issue of free trade figured prominently in the challenges that led to the Civil War. The southern slave states, ruled by the Democratic Party, wanted to increase international trade to the benefit of their largely cotton-exporting economy as well as that of the financial industry. The northern states still preferred a protectionist regime, one that nourished their still-developing industrial concerns. After the Civil War, the Northern Republicans, who ruled at the federal level for most of this period, retreated from interventionist economic policies but stuck to protectionism and installed a series of tariffs. The Democrats, out of federal power for long stretches, were only able to promote free trade again beginning in 1932 with the election of Franklin D. Roosevelt.

Under the administration of FDR's successor Harry Truman, in the early months of 1947 George Kennan and William Clayton laid out the groundwork for what would later become the Marshall Plan. They insisted on imposing the principle of free trade between European nations as a counterparty for massive American aid. Progress would then be made for decades within the framework of the Marshall Plan and the Bretton Woods compromise. In this favorable context of stable exchange rates and international cooperation, Western governments were standing on two legs: one which lowered tariffs to stimulate growth, and one which put in place the Great Safety Net to protect individuals against the more critical risks that were inevitably found in a more open economy.

In the US, the New Deal was the end of tariffs, but it also put in place the rudiments of a modern welfare state. It was an agreement with big business as well as a never-before-seen base for unions that could now better defend workers' interests. This was a winning combination. Thanks to free trade, America's corporations created and captured more and more wealth throughout the world. And thanks to the Great Safety Net at home, that prosperity turned into more economic security and distributing wealth to the many rather than holding it entirely in the hands of the few.

The origins of today's anti-trade mood go back to 1971, the year that marked the end of the Bretton Woods international monetary system. Advised by the likes of John Connally, then Secretary of the Treasury, Richard Nixon decided to suspend the convertibility of the dollar into gold[36]. The outcome of what came to be known as the 'Nixon Shock', a direct reaction to speculative market pressure against the dollar, was the end of stability in exchange rates, increasing uncertainty when it came to international trade.

Until that period, you could be forgiven for thinking that free trade was the key to widespread prosperity and never-ending expansion. But from the 1970s forward, global competition reached a new level of intensity[37]. Many countries, making the most of US support within the Marshall Plan and lower trade barriers, were busy completing their catching-up process. As they reached levels of performance closer to that of the US economy, global markets became more competitive. US car manufacturers found their match in Japanese competitors producing smaller, more energy-efficient cars. European countries also took initiatives in leveling up their competition with dominant American firms: this was when the Airbus consortium started its long journey to toppling Boeing in aeronautics. The post-World War II global covenant had initially enabled all countries to actively support their national champions. But domestic industrial policy was only tolerated as long as cross-border competition didn't pass a certain threshold of intensity. With the post-war boom slowing down, competition between firms turned into an entirely different game.

In that context of tension on more competitive markets, the enforcement of free trade had to become more intrusive. It was not enough for more developed countries to guarantee lesser competitors access to their domestic markets. As once laggard firms became tougher matches, suddenly it became necessary to check if their improved competitiveness could be explained by entrepreneurial prowess or rather by various forms of state support. It all called for reaffirming the principle of free trade by other means, notably trade agreements and reinforced constraints on domestic policies. Within a more competitive post-Bretton Woods global market, advocating for free trade became synonymous with constraining nation states as to what policies they were implementing at home.

The more intrusive international approach to free trade explains the current backlash. More advanced countries are no longer allowed to enforce their long-term superiority by way of industrial policy. Less advanced ones, like China or Mexico, are under scrutiny because their efforts to catch up have been so successful. In this context of rising tension, the backlash against free trade is taking shape on both ends of the political spectrum.

On the left, it is fueled by the fact that free trade seemingly goes directly against what is left of the Great Safety Net. It is not only about tariffs anymore, but also about labor law, taxation, public procurement, social insurance, and even public health: domestic policies in every one of these fields are constrained by international trade. In reaction, opposition to free trade is mounting. This can be seen in the US with the rise of left-wing leaders such as Bernie Sanders[38]. In Europe, a clear signal is the growth of left-wing euroscepticism: the reason why Denmark, Sweden and the Netherlands, for instance, have grown suspicious towards the European Union is partly because public opinion in those countries now see the EU as a threat to their generous welfare state[39].

On the right, anti-free trade positions sometimes come as a surprise. Pro-business conservatives are usually considered fierce supporters of *laissez-faire*, and neoliberalism was about using free trade as a lever to break down the political consensus in favor of state intervention. In effect, however, curbing international trade was always consistent with right-wing positions. For old-school European conservatives, trade barriers were always a way to preserve the vestiges of an old feudal order. And in the US, George W. Bush's 2002 steel tariff[40] showed that the Republican Party was never far from reconnecting with its anti-trade positions of the nineteenth century—even though it proved a politically risky move at the time[41]. Indeed in 2018, being against free trade has become a sure winner on the right. It flatters the rent-seeking ethos of entrenched and stagnant corporate interests. And it helps conservative politicians convince disgruntled working class voters to support them at the polls.

All in all, a key reason for this widespread temptation for protectionism is that the two legs of free trade and the Great Safety Net have long since lost their balance. When Bill Clinton was elected president in 1992, he signed the North American Free Trade Agreement (NAFTA), but he failed to put in place a system of universal healthcare. More recently, Barack Obama held to the free trade principles of his party, but his social projects were blocked or seriously damaged by resistance from Congress[42]. In Europe, leaders have complied with the demands made in the name of free trade through international institutions such as the European Union and the World Trade Organization. Yet they also contributed to weakening what was left of the Great Safety Net through self-imposed austerity measures[43].

Without social progress at home, the pro-free trade stand is no longer associated with prosperity and economic security. Rather, it is perceived as exposing workers to instability, lowered purchasing power and accelerating unemployment in sectors of the economy that are no longer competitive on the global stage. Thus the image of most politicians is burned to a crisp. Instead of being the supporters of a prosperous and secure economy, they're seen as inextricably linked to a *laissez-faire* attitude, lower taxes for the rich and powerful, and resignation to a further widening of inequalities. By promoting free trade without reinforcing the Great Safety Net, today's leaders ignore their voters' quest for greater economic security[44].

In reality, the social fabric depends less on open borders than on the combination of free trade and economy security. Some countries, like Hong Kong, Chile or (to a certain extent) the post-Thatcher United Kingdom, combine a knack for free trade with a very thin safety net for workers. This usually makes for an open and prosperous economy, with many opportunities to be seized by those who embrace an entrepreneurial attitude. Yet it also brings about a high level of economic insecurity and market instability that occasionally fuels a deep and violent crisis.

The conservative anti-trade vision, one that would close borders and further dismantle the Great Safety Net, is even worse: as can now be seen in Trump's America, it favors an economy driven by the powerful, who will increase their rent-seeking activities through tariffs and predatory behavior, all at the expense of the non-wealthy.

THE TRADE / SAFETY NET MATRIX

	TRADE BARRIERS	FREE TRADE
BROAD SAFETY NET	DECAY & SCARCITY	SECURITY & PROSPERITY
NARROW SAFETY NET	PREDATION & INEQUALITY	INSTABILITY & PRECARITY

The third option, proposed by left-wing opponents to free trade, is a world of both protectionism and a preserved Great Safety Net. But this is also not ideal as it is difficult to finance the related policies (notably social insurance) in a country that closes itself off from the rest of the world and becomes the victim of scarcity, as has been recently seen in Venezuela[45].

The best option, indeed, is the combination that links an openness to free trade with covering individuals against the adverse consequences of exposure to the violent winds of the global market. As Dani Rodrik remarked in 1998, *"government spending plays a risk-reducing role in economies exposed to significant amount of external risk"*, which explains the *"positive correlation between an economy's exposure to international trade and the size of its government"*[46].

Alas most governments are now trapped in what Rodrik has otherwise called the *"political trilemma of the world economy"*[47]: they have to trade off between the domestic safety net and their principled support of free trade as the main source of economic growth. If they choose free trade, they must be resigned to more economic insecurity. If they choose protectionism to restore the possibility of state intervention, they have to pay the price of scarcity and the inevitable tensions, rent-seeking and inequalities that it brings with it[48].

An open world is a more prosperous world, but it is also a world in which both individuals and businesses must be better protected against critical risks. In the thalassocratic paradigm, instead of folding in on themselves, countries must continue to defend free trade but with its complement: a Great Safety Net 2.0 that is in sync with today's economy. This calls for a better understanding of globalization in the Entrepreneurial Age and of how we can make the most of it while providing individuals with economic security. If we aim at pursuing individual empowerment in a more open world, we have to account for how value is created in the Entrepreneurial Age, what new jobs it will bring about, and what critical risks businesses and individuals are now exposed to.

Key takeaways

- *The Entrepreneurial Age calls for lowering trade barriers. The economy cannot prosper if tech companies are unable to generate increasing returns at the largest scale possible.*

- *A historical parallel can be drawn with the old thalassocracies, tiny states such as Venice or Portugal that prospered not by controlling land but by mastering trade routes through the sea.*

- *The absence of trade barriers exposes national economies to even more pressure and instability. Thus the necessary corollary to software opening the world is a broader safety net for all.*

Chapter 8
From the Old
to the New Working
Class

"When the working class shifted from 'making stuff' to 'serving people', it brought with it lots of historical baggage. The long-standing 'others' in our society — women and people of color — became a much larger share of the non-college-educated workforce. And their marginalised status in our society carried over into the working class, making it easier to overlook and devalue their work."
—Tamara Draut[1]

The old working class has been left behind

I was as stunned as anyone when Donald Trump won the 2016 US presidential election. Not that I hadn't seen that something strange was happening. During the entire Republican primary I was convinced that Trump had a real shot at becoming the nominee: he was the only one with a direct, powerful connection with enthusiastic voters. I was also well aware of the weaknesses of Hillary Clinton, a candidate who I saw as belonging to a bygone era of Democratic politics, that of centrist moderation and reverence for wealthy donors[2].

What I didn't expect was that Trump would owe his victory to a few industrial states in the Rust Belt that all used to be Democratic strongholds. He won Pennsylvania, the historic steel capital of the country, as well as manufacturing-rich Ohio and Wisconsin. He even narrowly took Michigan, home of the Union of Automobile Workers and the automobile industry centered around Detroit. That was all on top of crushing Hillary Clinton in coal-mining West Virginia—a state that was reliably Democratic until the 2000 presidential election, but that has turned conservative ever since[3].

This impressive string of victories sounds like a summary of our entire industrial history: the coal mines of the age of steam and railways; the large mills of the age of steel and heavy engineering; the assembly lines of the age of the automobile and mass production. It is also a testament to the sad political shape of the Democratic Party. Democrats used to own those states because their values were all about defending and empowering their residents. That these voters have turned their back on them is a clear signal, among others, of the deep and painful transitional crisis that the economy entered decades ago.

Indeed it's hard to deny the crisis and its impact in those states. While people are still there, most of their jobs have disappeared. The exhaustion of industrial activities has impoverished those regions and demoralized their inhabitants. Having lost their jobs and with their purchasing power eroded, workers end up rejecting immigration and free trade. Their politics change as they're attracted to populism rather than issue-oriented ideologies. As Alan Greenspan declared in 2016, "*populism is not a philosophy or a concept, like socialism or capitalism, for example. Rather it is a cry of pain, where people are saying: Do something. Help!*"[4].

In the nineteenth century, most industrial activity and factories were located in large cities. One reason was the proximity to essential infrastructures. The point of factories was to produce goods, and those goods had to be transported and distributed through the rudimentary logistics systems of the time. For factory owners, access to those depended on being located close to rivers and canals, train stations, port facilities. The further you were from those infrastructures, the costlier it was to distribute goods to customers.

Cities were also where workers lived. Back then it was difficult to move around due to the lack of adequate transportation. Laborers didn't have their own cars, so there were few options. Either both the factory and the workers had to be located in urban areas where they could rely on the public transportation system, or workers had to live near the factory, and so some factory owners built homes for their employees away from the city. In any case, with factories came clustering: it was easier to operate a factory in a populated area; in turn, the factory attracted even more population. Once it was up and running, the surrounding area would only become more urban.

But then factories left the larger cities. With the strengthening of the Great Safety Net 1.0, the new age provided workers with the possibility of buying their own house, which led to the massive relocation of the urban industrial workforce into less expensive suburban areas. Individual cars powered by cheap oil facilitated traveling from home to factory and back without the need for public transportation. Cheap land previously priced for agricultural use was converted to residential use. All of this could only happen once, but it facilitated a smooth transition to the emerging middle class way of life.

Transportation of goods also underwent a revolution. Early in the twentieth century, cheap oil already made it possible to rely on trucking to transport whatever came out of factories, thus facilitating their relocation to less urban areas. Later in the 1950s, the invention of the shipping container radically changed the logistics system on which manufacturers depended to distribute their products[5]. With less dependence on the large workforce needed to handle goods in traditional logistics facilities, it became possible to redraw trade routes away from the cities.

Getting rid of urban factories was also a matter of clean air. As happened with the London smog of 1952[6], the concentration of factories in dense areas inflicted hazardous pollution on urban populations. As city inhabitants rose in sophistication and purchasing power, they started to exert pressure on their elected officials to obtain the removal of factories for reasons of public health. Indeed today factories are still the main reason why there's such pollution in large Chinese cities, whose density makes it harder to disperse toxic emissions. But as China is undergoing rapid economic development, it's only a matter of time before industrial facilities leave the cities to be relocated further from where people live.

Finally, the constant flow of new inhabitants into cities led to ever more expensive real estate. Thus the factories relocated simply to escape the higher fixed costs that came with having an industrial facility occupying prime urban real estate. At first, industrial ventures had clustered in Chicago, Pittsburgh, and Detroit because only such large cities could provide the necessary labor, financial capital, infrastructures, and managerial talent. But later in the twentieth century, factories were disseminated across vaster territories to increase the scale of their operations and reduce the unit costs of production.

With factories relocating away from large cities, attracting them became a new game in which smaller cities had an opportunity to compete. As observed by Paul Krugman, the prosperity of smaller cities can be seen as an enigma in today's world. After all, their traditional function was to serve *"as central places serving a mainly rural population engaged in agriculture and other natural resource-based activities"*[7]. But when agriculture ceased to be a massive job provider, some of those cities managed to rebound by welcoming industrial activities in search of a new home.

In some cases, it was through random events that smaller cities were put on a path to becoming industrial clusters. In others, there was determined action by local officials to woo factory owners and convince them to settle there. Prompted by anti-labor business leaders opposing the New Deal[8], certain US states enacted so-called 'right-to-work' laws to prevent workers from organizing and then attracted factories using this argument. It was a setback as far as workers' rights were concerned, and a direct consequence of the Taft-Hartley Act of 1948. But it also meant opening factories in less industrial regions, thus spreading the wealth that came with the techno-economic paradigm of the day. As we are reminded by Emily Badger, that was a time when the largest industrial firms, with their headquarters still located in large cities, drew on raw materials and manufactured goods from all around the country[9].

Factories created quite a lot of value for local communities. In the age of the automobile and mass production, they were the dominant link of industrial value chains, capturing a large chunk of the total value added in any given industry. And at a time when large corporations were not yet restructured into over-optimized global value chains, having a factory in town meant much of that value spilled over locally: lots of local jobs, both qualified and less qualified; indirect wealth creation through the massive development of adjacent businesses that served both workers and the factory itself; additional tax revenue that made it possible to invest in local infrastructures and better public services.

The model was so successful in fact that we're not used to the idea of a clustered economy anymore. We grew up in a world in which it was assumed that every city, however small, would have its factories, and then its retail shops, and many other service businesses.

But now not only have most factories been lost due to globalization and the techno-economic transition; those that remain (or are coming back due a trend known as *"reshoring"*[10]) do not generate as much local value. They're part of global value chains in which factories are not the dominant link anymore, as most assets, functions, and risks are located elsewhere. And the jobs those new factories provide are of a lesser quality than in the past—if they provide jobs at all. As Ben Casselman, of *FiveThirtyEight*, wrote on the eve of Donald Trump's election, *"today's manufacturing jobs aren't necessarily the high-paying, stable jobs that we tend to remember"*[11].

With suburban factories now a shadow of their former selves, we're not even sure that there's another way of spreading wealth geographically. The Entrepreneurial Age seems to reward large cities and nothing else, and old jobs have been radically displaced as a result. As factories are now empty, the occupied working class is now employed primarily in services—services that are more and more concentrated in cities. Hence, as Richard Florida puts it, the city has become the *"new factory floor"*[12].

The new factory floor

I've spent most of my life in large European cities—except for a few years in my childhood when we lived in a residential suburb (but not for long, because my mother hated it), and then when I was a computer science student on a campus near the sea. Only recently did I realize how different these European cities are from those in the US.

Apart from a few exceptions such as New York, Boston, and San Francisco, American downtowns have historically been largely inhabited by the poor and lower middle-class, whereas in Europe living in the city center is an expensive mark of social accomplishment. US cities are also designed to make room for cars, whereas our European cities are older and denser, providing little room for traffic and thus having to offer better public transportation. Finally, European cities have long been rather safe, whereas the decrease of crime in US *"inner cities"* (as Donald Trump likes to call them) is fairly recent[13].

It's true that American cities grew up in unique historical circumstances. The Cold War saw a push to decentralize the territory, pushing the populace away from urban centers to counter the potential effects of a nuclear war[14]. Franklin D. Roosevelt himself felt, in no small part due to his youth spent in upstate New York, that cities were unstable and subject to booms and busts, and thus should be countered with population growth away from urban centers[15].

Throughout the country, development was also guided by zoning laws that strictly separated industrial and residential spaces. This practice, known as Euclidean zoning, is quite foreign in European cities that have been mixed-use for centuries[16]. Finally, there is the racial component of US history. From the 1930s onward, mortgage lending was aimed primarily at the white population, leading to a dream of suburban homeownership that pulled investment away from what came to be seen as poor, black inner cities. The federal government encouraged this trend with the redlining practiced by the Federal Housing Administration, which gave cover to residential segregation practiced by private players[17].

And so today, with the unprecedented rise of a more urban economy, the US is becoming a bit more European. Its cities are safer, with a displacement of crime towards less urban spheres— including the cybersphere[18]. They're investing in public transportation[19] and innovative solutions such as ride-hailing and ride-sharing[20] to make it easier for people not to own cars. They're also confronting the challenges of higher density, fueled by sky-rocketing real-estate prices, heated discussions on zoning and construction permits[21], and fewer housing options for working families. And so the US is now discovering the specific problems that affect the working class in large cities. As the transition to the Entrepreneurial Age makes the economy ever more urban and emphasizes proximity services, it's high time we reflect on solutions to these problems.

I use *"proximity services"* to refer to all sectors in which the work routine is constantly broken by frequent and direct interactions with customers—be it in retail, hospitality, education, healthcare, personal care, or last-mile logistics. Because these sectors never become truly routine, the tasks performed by their workers are difficult to standardize and optimize through scientific management—at least not in a way that is satisfactory for both workers and customers (remember the "*Wal-Mart Effect*", a consequence of ill-advised Taylorism applied to retail, which led to a vicious circle of demotivated employees and lowered quality of service[22]). In turn, the impossibility of applying the recipes of Taylorism implies that those particular tasks, and the sectors in which they are performed, were never integrated into the Fordist model of the large corporation.

As a result, most proximity service sectors have remained overlooked exceptions to the norm, never fitting into the socio-institutional framework of the age of the automobile and mass production. What Richard Florida calls the "*service class*"[23] has always been there, serving us all every day. But since it didn't fit with the dominant representation—that of a stable nine-to-five job in a big Fordist corporation—we never cared much for those sectors and the conditions of those working in them. It didn't help that all the work falling in the domestic or care categories has long gone unmeasured and unrewarded, because it used to be largely performed for free by women in the private sphere. And in the US specifically, domestic work has also long gone overlooked because it was first slave work and then work performed by the descendants of slaves[24].

The reason why we should focus more on proximity services now is that in the Entrepreneurial Age they are the industry with the biggest potential for creating future jobs. The rise of ubiquitous computing and networks will lead to the disappearance of many routine jobs in services as well as in factories. But at the same time less routine jobs, those whose tasks cannot be performed without interacting with customers, are on the rise in a familiar process of Schumpeterian "*creative destruction*". Since jobs in proximity services rely primarily on human interactions, they are harder to automate—like they were harder to Taylorize—and almost impossible to relocate overseas.

As a consequence, workers are being redeployed from the suburban industrial class of the twentieth century to the urban service class of the twenty-first century. Tamara Draut's book *Sleeping Giant* describes the growing strength of that new American working class that doesn't fall within our representations of work. Unlike factory workers or those occupying desk jobs in large corporations, who fought for and obtained higher wages, better working conditions and more political representation, this new working class has never been able to achieve much progress. Throughout the age of the automobile and mass production, proximity service workers have had to make do with low wages, unattractive working conditions, and unaffordable housing[25].

The government took over certain proximity sectors, for without its intervention there simply wouldn't have been enough supply in densely populated areas. Thus a part of the service class eventually managed to climb up the social ladder by joining the public sector, with the rather higher wages and economic security that came with working for the government. These luckier proximity workers include the likes of teachers (education), nurses (healthcare), police officers (law and order), drivers (logistics and transportation), fire-fighters (public safety), and trash collectors (waste management).

Other proximity sectors populated by the service class were deemed not critical or distorted enough for the government to take over, including retail, food, hospitality, private security, cleaning and maintenance, logistics, and a large part of child care and elderly care. Because the government didn't take charge and Taylorism couldn't be effectively applied by the private sector (at least not without terrible side effects), those sectors didn't generate productivity gains and subsequently saw little progress in working conditions. They still inflict long and unconventional hours, low wages, harsh management, no collective bargaining, and long commutes. And this explains why proximity services are still populated with workers with the least bargaining power. As opposed to the old working class, which was generally white and rather concentrated in the now Trump-voting Rust Belt states, the new working class includes more women, people of color and immigrants[26] (including undocumented ones), all living and working in European-style large cities.

This realization provides us with a hint of the current institutional challenges. The rise of the new working class is accelerating, and the problems that it encounters are only getting worse. The current transition contributes to the clustering of everything (people, wealth, businesses) in large cities[27]. Entrepreneurs best succeed in dense cities where it's easier to emulate fellow innovators, access critical resources and rebound following failure. And then there's what economist Enrico Moretti calls the *"multiplier effect"*[28]: absent frictions and obstacles such as a cluttered housing market, the urban service class in proximity services grows at the same pace as the *"creative class"*—the highly qualified and entrepreneurial workers that dominate the Entrepreneurial Age.

Alas we can't simply replicate what once worked for factory workers. Indeed the industrial working class and the proximity-service working class have little in common. One is peri-urban (living near factories), the other is urban (living near the customers they serve). One is still unionized[29], the other never has been. One pulls together while working next to one another on the assembly line, the other is dispersed and lacks opportunities to bond with other employees in the same sector. One is visible in our understanding of work (working class pride, overalls, picket lines), the other is right in front of us and yet invisible. One is relatively homogeneous in sociological terms (because of union-enforced agreements which unified status and pay[30] and geographic clustering in suburbs around factories), the other is much more diverse (from taxi drivers to Tamil and Guatemalan cooks, from receptionists and fast-food employees to bicycle delivery workers, from nurses to waiters, from child care specialists to policemen, from security guards to cleaning persons in the hotel industry). And so the way we once provided economic security and prosperity to the suburban industrial class is simply not replicable for the urban service class.

But things are changing. On the political side, Democrats are in the process of completing a radical electoral shift between the old working class and the new working class—not unlike the painful shifts made when they drifted away from the farmers, craftsmen and small business owners of the nineteenth century to embrace the cause of laborers in the new industrial world of the twentieth century[31].

The new working class was already at the heart of the coalition that brought Barack Obama to power in 2008 and 2012. His consecutive wins prove that this urban service class now has a certain weight in the electoral process, with the ability to make or break elections. Its members form a *"silent majority"*[32], dominated by women[33], that generally prefers Democrats. And it's now consolidating as young people flee unemployment-ridden manufacturing areas to settle in larger cities[34]—the reason why Hillary Clinton handily won Illinois in 2016, which includes the large city of Chicago, while losing the neighboring, less urban Rust Belt.

The reshuffling is not without adverse consequences, as the unprecedented urban concentration of the new working class contributes to polarizing the electorate between city and country—a phenomenon that Richard Florida dubs *"the most disruptive transformation in history"*[35]. It is also made more difficult because the Democrats' new urban focus leads them to shifting too much into courting the economic elite that is as concentrated in large cities as the service class[36].

Things are also changing on the social side. As part of emergent collective initiatives known as 'alt-labor', workers are attempting to secure bargaining power *vis-à-vis* both employers and customers—who, again, are now the most powerful party at the corporate table. Recent victories on the minimum wage front in the US[37], although limited in terms of effective purchasing power[38], were obtained through an alliance between workers and consumers. For the first time in history, service workers seem to be gaining some influence over improving their working conditions, for instance through the National Domestic Workers Alliance. Likewise, freelance workers, the upper segment of the new urban working class, are exploring new ways of organizing with the pioneering effort of Sara Horowitz's Freelancers Union[39].

Will these prove to be hollow victories or do they foreshadow the terms of a Great Safety Net 2.0 tailored for the Entrepreneurial Age? If the city is to be the new factory floor, then we have to go through our entire social history again, with the service class organizing and bargaining with employers, the government, and customers to conquer economic security and a decent way of life. Because it's a radically different world, it calls for radical imagination—something all the more difficult because the old working class still dominates our representation of the corporate world and because it proves very hard to create good jobs in proximity services.

The problem with proximity services

There are multiple reasons why most people find it so difficult to switch from one working class to the other. A frequent argument is that skills are different in the two worlds, so people have to train for the new jobs and learn how to become better at performing the non-routine tasks that dominate work in the urban economy (essentially, learning to be better and more caring service providers[40]). And whatever their skills, older workers find it difficult to enter a new economy: it's a different culture, and starting at the bottom means a loss of revenue[41]. This is all a challenge on the front of workforce development—one that is currently better tackled in a country such as Germany, with vocational training in the education system, than in the other countries such as the US and France where execution of such training is poor and funding is inadequate[42].

What's more, the new jobs for less educated workers are found more in large cities than in suburban areas. They come with harder work, long hours, seasonal hiring, off-peak hours, long commutes, and a lack of recognition. It's not that workers from legacy industries are lazy. But there's a mismatch in expectations: most simply don't see themselves doing such jobs. They prefer to stay far away from large cities as they dread harsher conditions in terms of wages, hours, housing, and transportation[43]. Why jump into the new economy if jobs there lack social recognition, strong unions, decent wages, and social benefits?

None of this even addresses the stigma for male workers that comes with entering a traditionally female-dominated field[44]. Most have not been trained, culturally speaking, for jobs that are less about making things and more about caring for people. Would a coal worker from West Virginia switch to elderly care in Pittsburgh or Washington, DC? For someone with a previous career on an assembly line or behind a desk, becoming a nurse, a child carer or even a delivery person simply doesn't match their representation of what work is about.

During periods of transition, there has always been a mismatch between what workers expect and what employers offer. Every techno-economic paradigm produces jobs that didn't exist before or multiplies jobs that weren't valued in the past. Historically, because those jobs initially come without economic security and good wages women and immigrants tend to be the only ones ready to take them. In doing so they enable innovative ventures to take off and grow at a larger scale. In time, broad progress eventually makes it possible to improve the quality of jobs for the next generation of workers.

Indeed mass migration and then women joining the workforce are two reasons why the US economy has been unusually prosperous since the middle of the nineteenth century. During every techno-economic transition since then—to the age of steel and heavy engineering, to the age of the automobile and mass production, and to the age of ubiquitous computing and networks—, the US surmounted the difficulties of succeeding in a techno-economic transition by welcoming new participants into the workforce: women who had previously stayed at home and immigrants from other countries, especially those with less education who would take the lousy jobs brought about by the transition.

When the US economy transitioned to the age of the automobile and mass production, most of the new jobs on assembly lines weren't taken by American workers, but rather by laborers who had recently immigrated from Germany, Poland, Ireland, and Italy (or were the children of immigrants from those countries). Those diligent workers willing to take any job were critical to succeeding in the transition. Had the US locked down its borders before the Immigration Act of 1924, it probably wouldn't have become the prosperous center of gravity of those new ages[45].

The same is true in today's China. Though it isn't particularly welcoming to immigrants from other countries, immigration is nonetheless a massive phenomenon within China, a huge country with disparate levels of development between the coastal cities and the hinterland. The online commerce and urban logistics boom there wouldn't be possible without the many work-hungry, less educated workers made available by massive internal migration. But it's not easy, as regulatory restrictions to workers' mobility turn migrating from poor Yunnan to prosperous Shanghai or Hangzhou into a chal-

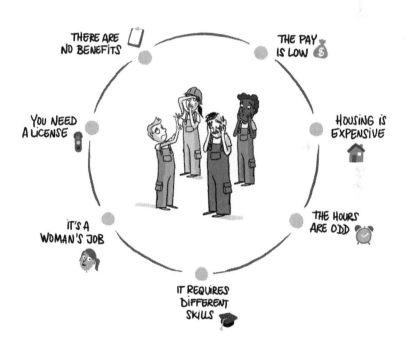

lenge comparable to emigrating from Africa to Western Europe and looking for a job—any job.

Our effort at imagining a Great Safety Net 2.0 for the Entrepreneurial Age must be focused on today's very different context. Women are now part of the workforce, hence they no longer constitute a reserve army able to fulfill the new jobs of the day. As for less educated immigrants, the closing of borders in the West makes it impossible for them to help us succeed in the current techno-economic transition. Unlike during the previous great surges of development, we in the West don't have a pool of workers entering the workforce with a readiness to fill the radically new jobs of the day.

On top of that, many new jobs are simply unsustainable (if not plainly illegal) due to regulations rendered obsolete by technology but that endure nonetheless[46]. The taxi industry has become an infamous example of corporatist resistance against the creation of new jobs. We could all renounce our personal car and be driven around through ride-hailing and ride-sharing platforms which would create many jobs and radically change urban mobility. But how do you create those jobs when confronted with the obsolete regulations that we inherit from the past and fierce resistance of the taxi industry? There are many cases, across many industries, in which the corporatism of existing professions slows down job creation in proximity services[47].

Beyond industrial regulations, what's left of the Great Safety Net 1.0 also contributes to slowing down job creation in the Entrepreneurial Age. Continental Europe is the best illustration of how many jobs in proximity services are not created because of the lack of a favorable institutional context. In the US and the UK, there are many workers in market-operated proximity services. But their condition is so miserable that generous tips (and food stamps[48]) are barely enough for them to make ends meet. In continental Europe the market has been led down a very different path: due to the higher minimum wage and more worker-friendly regulations, all of which are part of the Great Safety Net 1.0, low-skilled workers in proximity services are much scarcer than in the US or London.

The result can be felt in the day-to-day experience of using proximity services in large European cities: higher prices, longer lines, and a high propensity to seek help through illegal channels (such as hiring a nanny, often an immigrant, without a formal contract and with all earnings paid in cash). Coming from France, I quickly noticed the differences in 2015 when I moved to London. There, market-operated proximity services (that is, restaurants, delivery, cleaning services, child care, and ride-hailing) are relatively cheap as compared to continental cities such as Paris, Munich, and Amsterdam.

The conclusion, I must say, is *not* that we should lower the minimum wage and remove all regulations. Rather the different landscapes seen in the US and continental Europe reveal the extent to which everyone's Great Safety Net 1.0 is ill-fitted for the Entrepreneurial Age—and how much institutions from the past always stand in the way during the transition toward a new techno-economic paradigm.

Because the US has been weakening its own Great Safety Net at a faster pace, it creates more jobs in proximity services. Alas these are too lousy for the coal miners from West Virginia or the factory workers from Michigan to take them. Many positions remain unfilled because too few workers are able or willing to settle in the large cities where those jobs are, as reflected by the extremely low unemployment rate in cities such as San Francisco[49]. And so the hastened transition in the US doesn't mean it can afford to not build the Great Safety Net 2.0 for the Entrepreneurial Age. On the contrary, if it fails to do so, it is certain that the lack of economic security will harm prosperity and cause the US to lag behind. Inequalities will rise, standards of living will plummet, agitation will grow, and illiberal politics will continue in their corruption of democracy[50].

As for the stronger Great Safety Net 1.0 in continental Europe, it makes the labor transition more difficult yet no less necessary, as the technological trends of the Entrepreneurial Age do not stop at national borders. Continental Europe isn't creating enough jobs in proximity services, which is leading to a higher unemployment rate, a lesser quality of life for those inhabiting large cities, and fewer opportunities for those living elsewhere. Many potential jobs matching a demand for better proximity services are simply never created. And many business leaders and policymakers don't even realize that those jobs could exist if only we had a better version of the Great Safety Net.

Everyone—the US, the UK, continental Europe—needs a Great Safety Net 2.0 tailored for the new working class. This is what it is all about: creating many jobs in proximity services while improving the condition of workers in the related sectors and making the services they perform more affordable. Participating in this segment of the job market must come with enough purchasing power, economic security, and a sense of social recognition. Jobs in proximity services must become more attractive not only for those who have nothing and enter the job market for the first time, but also for workers that are already part of the workforce. Unlocking that potential is key for the Western world to maintain a high rate of economic development. The urban service class must become the new middle class.

It's difficult to say whether the US or continental Europe is best positioned to achieve such a goal. In the US, the Dark Ages of financialization have been a powerful drug. They have blinded many of the elite to the fact that new institutions are needed to make the most of the Entrepreneurial Age. Meanwhile in continental Europe, having maintained more of the Great Safety Net 1.0 makes for more economic security—but it also makes the current transition feel more radical and thus more difficult.

That being said, my bet is that Europe's lagging behind in dismantling the Great Safety Net 1.0 reflects a deeper attachment to economic security, which could eventually lead to more swiftly building the Great Safety Net 2.0. The only problem, as seen in Chapter 3, is that Europe lacks the economic power to do so. Conversely, the US is already enjoying returns on their earlier actions (notably under the form of more jobs in proximity services). Alas it can give them the illusion that they've already succeeded and thus don't need to run the second half of the race—namely the harder, imaginative, counter-intuitive institutional work required to resume the economic security and prosperity of the past.

Key takeaways

    • *The displacement of the old working class has many explanations: globalization, financialization, automation, but also the concentration of economic activities (and most jobs) in large cities.*

• *Cities as the new factory floor aggravate problems that were previously overlooked. Improving the condition of the new urban working class is the main social challenge of the day.*

• *Imagining the Great Safety Net 2.0 is critical for creating good jobs in proximity services. It's not about deregulation but about replacing old mechanisms that don't fit today's world.*

Chapter 9
The Lost Art
of State Intervention

"Liberalism has spent the better part of the past century attempting to prove that it could competently and responsibly extend the state into new reaches of American life. With the rollout of the Affordable Care Act, the administration has badly injured that cause, confirming the worst slurs against the federal government. It has stifled bad news and fudged promises; it has failed to translate complex mechanisms of policy into plain English; it can't even launch a damn website."
—Franklin Foer[1]

The state as the solution to many problems

I was once drawn to working for the government because I wanted to make a difference in the world. It helped that in France becoming a senior civil servant is still the opportunistic dream of many ambitious students. Entering such spheres is the French equivalent to joining the 'Oxbridge' establishment in the UK or receiving an Ivy League education in the US. The state *grand corps* I joined, the *Inspection générale des finances*, is an exclusive society of about 250 living souls which in the last few decades has given France two presidents (including Emmanuel Macron, who was once a colleague of mine), several prime ministers, and many top executives in France's largest corporations. But there was also a more altruistic reason for my choosing that path: in the past century, government came to be seen as a mighty force you needed to harness in order to solve critical problems.

The history of how the state emerged as a positive agent of change is often unappreciated. In 2004, the late Michael C. Janeway, former executive editor of the *Boston Globe*, published *The Fall of the House of Roosevelt*, a book tracing US politics from the New Deal through Lyndon B. Johnson's presidency[2]. In one way, his work was an intimate portrait of his parents, Eliot and Elizabeth Janeway, who played a role throughout this period. But it was also a wider picture of the complex games played around Franklin D. Roosevelt and his successors by an improbable entourage of men (yes, all men) who were neither politicians nor businessmen, but middlemen: Tommy Corcoran, the corporate lawyer who became the ultimate Washington power broker; William O. Douglas, the Yale professor turned Supreme Court Justice; Abe Fortas, another lawyer who then became Lyndon B. Johnson's closest confidant.

All were part of a tight network that turned the New Deal into reality. They spread ideas, aligned the interests of conflicting parties, and became masters in the art of wielding power to advocate their big idea: the state taking over from the market. As written by Janeway, *"these 'president's men'... executed a broad-based professionalization of policy making marked by strong departures in theory and practice—such as in governmental intervention in the economy"*[3]. Far from being the people overtaking the elite, the New Deal was in fact the elite coming together, from politics to academia to business, and making the case that government should take a more active role in social and economic matters.

In a world still impregnated by the nineteenth-century ideology of *laissez-faire*, this was not easily done. Indeed in the context of the crisis of the 1930s, state intervention was not imposed to comply with principle. Rather it was prompted by a national emergency. Because they were the first of their kind to do business on large consumer markets, the industrial corporations of the time were confronted with unprecedented market instability, a macroeconomic setback that led them (and the entire economy) into the Great Depression. It fell upon the state to save them: only the government could face the critical risks that came with the nascent age of the automobile and mass production[4].

Another trend that contributed to favoring state intervention was a growing demand for fairness and social justice. As the labor movement intensified calls for worker empowerment and economic security, the private sector alone was unable to deliver such outcomes. Market imperfections made it impossible for a *laissez-faire* approach to hedge people against risks such as old age, sickness, and unemployment. Either those risks were too critical, with the probability or magnitude of a loss higher than average, or the market to cover them was ridden with imperfections, such as moral hazard or adverse selection. Thus such risks were better covered at the scale of an entire country rather than on a local or individual basis. As market-based solutions and even small-scale mutualist schemes fell short, only the state could deploy adequate programs and fulfill the needs of a complex and diverse society.

As governments experimented with a more interventionist approach worldwide, an intellectual and practical framework was provided and consolidated by figures as diverse as Teddy Roosevelt and Louis Brandeis (the father figures of the Progressive Era[5]), Woodrow Wilson (the founder of administration as a science[6]), John Maynard Keynes (who made the scientific case for public spending as a preferred way to sustain the economy), and the military (where advanced progress in operations research and large-scale management served as models for large government organizations).

For a time, there was no agreement regarding the need for state intervention to overcome large-scale problems. Consensus was only built over time and reinforced by rallying the reluctant majority to the principle of the government's taking over. It was not Franklin D. Roosevelt, the popular wartime president, who inspired that consensus, but the equally popular post-war Dwight Eisenhower who, despite belonging to the opposite party, decided against dismantling Roosevelt's legacy[7]. Likewise, in the workplace it wasn't the victory of state-assisted unions over industrial employers that clinched victory, but rather the employers' reluctant (and temporary) discovery that submitting to the rule of the Great Safety Net was in fact good for business since it led to stabler consumer demand, better morale, improved quality, and higher productivity[8].

In sum, consensus emerged as the state succeeded in implementing the policies needed in the new age. All over the world, a call for radical imagination led to governments laying out a new social contract more in line with the age of the automobile and mass production. In some countries such as France and Germany, success was facilitated by the pre-existence of an effective command-and-control bureaucracy. In other countries such as the US, deep-rooted skepticism toward the state forced liberals such as Roosevelt's men to demonstrate the value added by delivering results.

But opponents of state intervention didn't lay down their arms. Fueled by ideological fervor, the fear of communism, and in-depth works by prominent economists, the ideological warfare against state intervention began again right after World War II in the form of neoliberalism[9]. It gained steam because of major societal changes. The rising aspiration for individual emancipation culminated in 1968, when counterculture activists denounced bureaucratic authority as an enemy of imagination. The shift in favor of a more individualistic perspective—as was also seen with the birth of personal computing—eventually muddied the view of the state as a provider of economic opportunity and an agent of social justice and led to discrediting state intervention.

The fact is that public policy is complex, even frustrating. In most fields where state intervention is needed, it is not enough to levy taxes on some and pay a monetary benefit to others. In many cases, the state also has to supplement the market with government-sponsored entities such as hospitals, job agencies, child care facilities, retirement homes, social centers, utilities, independent authorities. And all those must be overseen by a gigantic, centralized bureaucracy—at least so far.

How bureaucracy reached the point of irrelevance

For a time, I enjoyed working for the government. It provided unrivaled proximity to power and I was confronted with intricate, stimulating policy problems. But in the end, like many of my peers, I felt a sense of disappointment. You have to believe in grand possibilities to endure the pain and difficulty of the selection process to join the French civil service at a senior level. Only once inside do people open their eyes and realize it's more complicated than expected: the state's bureaucratic structure, the lack of imagination, the obsession with the short term, the resistance to change, the scarcity of resources, the frightening pusillanimity of politicians.

This explains why many young people, after having worked for the French government for the inaugural years of their careers, leave to join the private sector. For them, something has been lost along the way. There was a time when you could make a difference by working for the government. Now it appears the action is taking place else-where, far from the stuffy spheres of government. And the agony of an exhausted state bureaucracy explains a lot of that feeling.

The quintessential state bureaucracy is the British National Health Service (NHS), which operates both the single-payer insurance system and most hospitals and medical practices in the UK. The advantage of such a system is fairness: it guarantees everyone access to affordable and professional care no matter their location or income level. The problem is that in today's context characterized by tax revolt, hatred of government, and fiscal austerity, the quality of the experience provided by the NHS has declined, with longer waiting lines and less customized care. Ultimately it has fallen into a vicious circle in which everybody loses, patients as well as professionals.

For a long time, the problems associated with bureaucracies such as the NHS were tolerated for the sake of operational effectiveness at a large scale. While it was far from perfect, the state was able to act at a larger scale than non-governmental entities. Hence quality could be sacrificed for the benefit of scale and affordability. In health-care systems, waiting lines and one-size-fits-all were accepted as the only way to access and afford competent doctors and expensive treatments. In postal services, the mother of all public services, the rigidity of the postman's daily rounds was traded against the service's availability all the way out into the country's remotest areas.

But the economic crisis that started creeping forward in the 1970s affected the strength of state intervention. The Bretton-Woods monetary system went down in flames; the consecutive oil shocks broke the balance of many markets; the unprecedented phenomenon of stagflation led to higher unemployment and skyrocketing interest rates. This period also marked the time when many developed coun-tries caught up to the US. Under increased competitive pressure, corporations started working on their strategic positioning[10], cutting costs, and pushing in favor of a more globalized economy.

As a larger version of the big corporations of the time, the state experienced its own setbacks during that period: fiscal revenue went down; new policy challenges erupted; individuals demanded support in a time of crisis. But the responses in the public and private sectors were different. Corporations were aided by a new breed of consultants who helped them level up their operations for the Dark Ages of financialization[11]. Meanwhile, the state was ultimately seized by neoliberal politicians who saw the government merely as a problem and had no interest in improving its performance. As a result, that performance kept on going down. Neither quality nor affordability could be achieved anymore, at least in the eyes of ever more demanding citizens. The consensus was finally broken.

Thus state intervention came to be discredited by a value proposition that was no longer aligned with individual aspirations. The *laissez-faire* approach was never attractive: it deprived the poor and even the middle class of access to affordable essential services. But the interventionist counter-offer ended up looking not that attractive, either: with heavy bureaucracy, quality was now bound to go down, prompting the rich to escape the system altogether while everyone else had to deal with a frustrating, one-size-fits-all, paperwork-ridden experience (leaving aside the pain of the occasional incompetencies, inefficiencies, and even corruption that can develop in large bureaucracies).

It took a new generation of liberal politicians to try and rehabilitate state intervention. US Democrats had been the first struck by the conservative revolution, losing badly against Republicans from 1968 onwards. In reaction, some among them decided to strike back with the goal of reaching out to middle class voters and making the case for a new kind of state intervention.

The federal nature of the US made things easier there. Following the shock of the Watergate scandal in 1974, many young Democrats, among them Michael Dukakis (the Democratic presidential candidate in 1988) and Bill Clinton, launched political careers at the state level. As young governors, they seized the opportunity to use their states as *"laboratories of democracy"*[12], exploring new ways to design and implement state-led public policies. The whole idea was to restore the fairness and effectiveness of state intervention, all while falling in line with the more demanding requests of middle class voters.

The race to reinvent government accelerated in the 1990s. Several trends were at play. Transformative leaders, such as Bill Clinton in the US and Tony Blair in the UK, won national elections at about the same time. Austerity in the face of rising interest rates forced every government to reduce public spending and reform interventionist policies. Above all, a progressive intellectual framework finally emerged to support the idea of reinventing the government and restoring the power of state intervention. It went under the name of *new public management*[13], and it was all about improving the way government was organized and functioned[14].

One lever for that was experimentation. Like the New Dealers of the past, the progressives of the 1990s decided that experimenting at a small scale was key to discovering new models in an adverse political environment. It was promising in principle, but experimentation was limited by the new political and economic context. The scarcity of resources and the tax revolts of the 1970s[15] made it difficult for the state to undertake new programs and cover new risks at a large scale. What's more, the absence of a major economic crisis deprived progressive governments of the urge to take radical action. Some experiments did advance, particularly in the fields of zero-based budgeting, performance management, delivery of public services, and public-private partnerships[16]. But few led to convincing results at a national scale. In the end, a highly resilient bureaucracy neutralized innovative efforts and state intervention was scaled back down to business as usual.

Another lever was accountability. As the governor of Arkansas, Bill Clinton was confronted early on with an impossible equation whereby his constituents wanted more public spending, but they hated any politician that raised taxes to finance that spending. Clinton experienced the bitter results: after becoming governor in 1978, he lost his reelection bid in 1980 because of his tax hikes.

Yet instead of renouncing the attempt to improve public services in Arkansas (one of the least developed states in America), he chose to focus on education and offered taxpayers what became known as a *"New Covenant"*: he would raise taxes to invest in Arkansas's failing school system; in exchange, he would hold teachers accountable using performance indicators. After his defeat in 1980, Clinton went on to win the governorship again in 1982 and every subsequent

election until he ran for and won the US presidency in 1992. Education policy in Arkansas became a landmark example of what liberals
needed to do: state intervention had to be based on accountability
and improved performance. Voters were willing to pay more taxes;
what they demanded was value for their money[17].

Problems arose when the virtuous principle of accountability was
extended beyond public agencies and civil servants and onto the
private citizens who happened to be recipients of taxpayer money.
Following the same reasoning, the idea was that in exchange for
social benefits, welfare recipients should prove that they were doing
everything possible to find their way out of poverty. What happened
afterwards—namely, the widespread discrediting of welfare policy
in the eyes of middle class voters—revealed the weakness of the
accountability approach. Most liberals were advocating accountability because they held public service to high standards. But
nurturing the idea that individuals further down the social ladder
may be undeserving of benefits effectively contributed to weakening
the idea of state intervention. Accountability proved to be a double-
edged sword.

The main problem, however, was of the symbolic sort. The state
has always complied with the dominant organizational model of
the twentieth century: that of a cathedral, a large, monolithic, resilient organization. During most of the twentieth century, this form
inspired consensus since the cathedral was a techno-economic
optimum at the time. In the age of the automobile and mass production, it was the surest way to maximize long-term returns on invested
capital and deliver an affordable service at the largest scale possible.
All the major players in the private sector were cathedrals, too, with
corporate executives scientifically managing a giant bureaucracy
dedicated to maximizing economies of scale—all without much innovation. You couldn't criticize the state for being a gigantic bureaucracy when all big corporations were bureaucracies, too!

Thus it didn't matter that for much of the twentieth century, the
cathedral of state didn't work so well. Nobody, even in the mighty
business world, could come up with an alternative: other models
simply didn't exist for them. The entire world of large organizations
was dominated by malfunctioning and suboptimal cathedrals[18]. The
state had no choice but to comply with that model—even if, like

every other large organization, it was trying to turn it into a better, more effective cathedral.

What changed with the transition to the Entrepreneurial Age is that the idea of the cathedral as an optimum is no longer valid. A new breed of technology-driven, entrepreneurial venture is proving that in the Entrepreneurial Age you can provide a more affordable service with a higher quality at a larger scale without being a cathedral. As the state remains a cathedral, it is losing the symbolic legitimacy that once came with embracing that form.

This is the challenge that we need to tackle today. Can we imagine a new art of state intervention for the Entrepreneurial Age, with a new organizational form? Or should we look beyond the state and turn to the mightiest forces of the day: entrepreneurs and the multitude[19]?

Reviving the state

Reinventing state intervention for the Entrepreneurial Age is not an easy task. As a cathedral, the state experiences the usual problems of large organizations, including sluggishness (particularly when the economy is moving faster) and inefficiency. It is ill-fitted to be relevant, let alone add value, in the age of ubiquitous computing and networks. While it managed to solve many problems in the past, the state has now become an obstacle to solving the problems of the twenty-first century.

Obviously the state could transform itself, from a Fordist cathedral to an organization designed to deliver performance in the Entrepreneurial Age. The problem is that like many big, dominant corporations, it experiences a version of Clayton Christensen's *"innovator's dilemma"*[20]. One reason is the rule of law, which in many cases prevents innovation and experimentation at the margins since it's difficult to go through a trial-and-error innovation process if every step in that process has to be enacted by law. Another reason is that the state's growth in the twentieth century has turned it into a corpo-

THE STATE YESTERDAY:
A CATHEDRAL AMONG OTHERS

THE STATE TODAY:
THE LAST CATHEDRAL STANDING

ratist power in and of itself. As civil servants become more numerous (currently up to 20% of the employed workforce in countries such as France), they also become an electoral constituency on whose support politicians rely. Elected officials are now dependent on civil servants as an electoral force—and civil servants, as stakeholders, tend to push against change instead of favoring it.

The wake of the financial crisis didn't make things easier. Here in Europe, austerity has been the main answer to tightening economic conditions. It has seen European states renounce their traditional mission of countering cyclical downturns with higher spending or lower taxes. It has also deprived them of the means to invest in their own reinvention, precisely during an accelerating paradigm shift which should have seen the state undertake unprecedented efforts at imagining and building new institutions. Instead, backwards-looking European leaders have decided to tighten the bolts even more, often seizing the crisis as an opportunity to implement the same old neoliberal reforms that were better designed for the 1990s than for the 2010s.

The US could have put itself in a better position as it didn't embrace austerity as overarching policy. Rather it chose to implement fiscal spending and quantitative easing, embracing the traditional Keynesian response to a sharp downturn and even making inroads into institutional innovation by implementing Obamacare. Indeed, early on during the Obama administration there were signs that perhaps the US was undergoing what Michael Grunwald dubbed a *"New New Deal"*[21].

Almost one century ago, economic security and prosperity were restored thanks to decisive initiatives in building what became the Great Safety Net 1.0. For a time, the Obama administration appeared as if it was about to replicate that feat. There was the American Recovery and Reinvestment Act of 2009 that prompted a vast effort of public investment in cutting-edge technology, then the JOBS Act of 2010 that upgraded the financing of new and innovative businesses, as well as the Dodd-Frank Act to strengthen regulation of the financial industry. And of course there was the Affordable Care Act, also of 2010, which aimed at providing all Americans with affordable healthcare insurance. All those legislative achievements were reminders of the sweeping ambition that came with the Second New Deal of 1935.

However, a series of circumstances made things difficult. The Democrats lost their majority in both houses of Congress only two years after Obama's election. With the rise of the Tea Party, the aftermath of the financial crisis led to a surge of rebellion against the very principle of providing Americans with universal healthcare insurance. Instead of bringing the US together, Obama, much like Bill Clinton a decade earlier, unwillingly contributed to polarizing it even more. He didn't lead the Republican Party to rally toward a new consensus, but instead saw it drift even further to the right, all the way to nominating Donald Trump for President in 2016. And so the cause of restoring the legitimacy of state intervention to provide economic security and prosperity seems to be more desperate than ever.

Making matters even worse, the state is too often captured by special interests that simply don't want it to change, preferring to use it to preserve the status quo. In the US, influencing the state and submitting it to special interests is a discipline that dates back to the 1970s, when the conservative revolution was accompanied by the development of the lobbying sector on K Street in Washington, DC[22]. It has now gained even more strength with the ability of entrenched interests to finance the campaigns of candidates dedicated to their cause. In their book *The Captured Economy*, Brink Lindsey and Steven Teles document the influence of industry interest groups in great detail and analyze how this distortion of the democratic process contributes to widening the inequality gap[23]. Can we still trust the state when it is captured by special interests to such an extent?

But just as we see with the most successful entrepreneurs, the state could regain its effectiveness by sealing an alliance with the most potent party of the day, the multitude. Building this alliance starts by providing the multitude with what they want: fairness and quality at scale. And the problem is that instead of improving, the quality of public services has gradually decreased due to the long economic crisis of the Dark Ages, the neoliberal response to the crisis, and a general lack of imagination. It's not only that the fiscal context is adverse to improving the quality of state-provided services. It's also that government leaders, whether elected officials or civil servants, remain mentally trapped in a paradigm in which quality always has to be sacrificed for the sake of affordability at scale.

Furthermore, customer expectations regarding quality are in fact relative, depending on the level of quality individuals experience in other parts of their lives. If you're accustomed to being mistreated by rude salespeople in every bank, store and call center, you might look fondly upon the altruistic, slightly quaint sense of dedication found in most civil servants. The problem is that we now live in a world in which ever-increasing quality and personalization have become the norm[24] thanks to the shift to the Entrepreneurial Age. As entrepreneurs now manage to serve individuals *"at the highest level of quality and scale, simultaneously"*[25], scale is not an excuse for less-than-average quality anymore. This impacts large, exhausted corporations that have failed to transform themselves during the current techno-economic transition. It also impacts the state itself.

As the performance of state-provided services goes down, the day-to-day frustration the state imposes contributes to fueling anger and populism[26]. Thus citizens are eventually moving against the state because they don't want to pay taxes without receiving any benefits; because they (in some cases, rightfully) see the state as unfair; because the level of quality they expect is increasing over time. When they're so well served, on a daily basis, by tech companies such as Amazon, Uber, and Deliveroo, citizens have a hard time understanding why the state is incapable of providing that same high level of quality. As Franklin Foer, then the editor of *The New Republic*, wrote in 2013, *"the onus was (once) on liberals to prove the concept of government. And while their ideas for what the state could accomplish were often quite vague, they made confident claims about their capacity to implement them"*[27]. As of today, state intervention is a lost art. If the state is to remain a positive agent of change, it must rediscover that art and reinvent it for the new age.

This won't be easy. Many people, myself included, think that the state in its current shape is incapable of delivering on radical imagination. We are still misled by the power the state accumulated in the past age of the automobile and mass production. But as my colleague Younès Rharbaoui once wrote, *"government is a process that only works backwards by validating what exists"*[28]. The state can be useful when the time comes to accelerate and reach a larger scale. But before the state can act, the field must be marked by a first generation of pioneers. Innovators and activists are the only ones capable of doing the hard work at the early stage, namely spotting the new economic and social challenges of the day and discovering the basics of the new mechanisms that can effectively tackle them. The state can then take inspiration from what works and design the policy framework to make it more sustainable at a much larger scale.

Indeed most of today's government programs found their roots in local, entrepreneurial efforts. The first attempts to implement social insurance were not made by the state, but by individuals that took part in fraternal societies and the mutualist movement and organized their own pooling of risks at a small scale. In the US, fraternal societies were among the most successful associations in the nineteenth century because, as put by historian David T. Beito, *"in contrast to the hierarchical methods of public and private charity, fraternal aid rested on an ethical principle of reciprocity"*. In France, the fraternal benefit societies that pooled risks within certain communities or professions succeeded the *Ancien Régime* corporations that were abolished by the revolutionaries in 1791. The same bottom-up approach was seen in the US with the rise of cooperative banking, mutual savings banks, and credit unions.

The reason why the state had to take over was that back then the self-organizing efforts of individuals could not extend up to the point of covering the entire population. A large part of the fraternal benefit societies' success was due to the strong bonds their members forged by living in the same area or belonging to the same profession, being workers from the same factory or industry who pooled their resources to cover risks such as occupational accidents, old age and illness; regional farmers did the same to cover the risk of crop loss. That sense of community proved difficult to replicate at the scale of entire nations in a fast-spreading Fordist economy with limited networking capacities.

But today things are different. One path to reinventing government through a more entrepreneurial approach has been brought forward by Tim O'Reilly, who coined the notion of *"government as a platform"*[29]. The vision is inspired by the strategy of the most successful tech companies. The likes of Amazon, Facebook, and Apple do not only operate applications designed for end users. They also operate platforms that provide resources and enable other companies to design their own applications and serve specific segments of the market. In O'Reilly's compelling vision, government should no longer be a cathedral, but an infrastructure and a marketplace on which a multitude of suppliers are invited to seize state-provided resources to design better public services for ever-more demanding citizens.

Like new public management in the 1990s, government as a platform remains an attractive idea in theory. It has been rendered somewhat more concrete by initiatives such as Code for America in the US[30], Estonia's impressive government-deployed platform[31], and the work of government chief information officers such as Italy's Diego Piacentini, a former senior vice-president of Amazon[32], and my friend and co-author Henri Verdier in France[33]. In practice, however, the implementation of O'Reilly's vision has so far proved too difficult in the face of fierce resistance from many parties, a lack of interest from politicians across all segments of the political spectrum, and mere indifference on the part of the citizens themselves. It seems that in such spheres, we're still lacking what makes new ventures successful in the Entrepreneurial Age: the support of the multitude.

Another approach is that of Mariana Mazzucato. In a highly praised book published in 2013, *The Entrepreneurial State*[34], she makes the case for once again empowering the state as a player in the field of innovation. Like at the time of the New Deal, the state must lead in experimenting, exploring new approaches, and discovering the socio-institutional framework of the new age. Now at the head of the Institute for Innovation and Public Purpose (IIPP) at University College London (UCL), Mazzucato promotes a mix of antitrust policy, government support for certain companies and industries, and entrepreneurship by the state itself so as to make the economy more prosperous and more secure. In other words, an industrial policy for the Entrepreneurial Age.

I have mixed feelings about the very concept of industrial policy. For one, I'm not certain the state still has the capacity to work in the general interest. We're not at the end of the nineteenth century, when the state was still small and could be shaped from the ground up. Today is also different from the 1950s and 1960s, when the Cold War focused Western leaders on the goal of ensuring technological domination over the Soviet Union. Now the state is simply lagging behind and is widely influenced by corporate interests that have learned to harness its power to serve their goals instead of the public's.

Furthermore, as argued by Rainer Kattel, who's working with Mariana Mazzucato at the IIPP, it takes a certain organizational form to support innovation in the economy[35]. And based on my experiences as a senior civil servant, I highly doubt that the current form of the state allows it to impose what Carlota Perez calls a *"direction for innovation"*—one that would lead us all to a Golden Age of ubiquitous computing and networks.

I believe that in truth the current techno-economic transition does not call for more or less state intervention. Rather it should lead us to redraw the map denoting the respective perimeters of the market and the state. There are areas in our economy, such as housing, where the rise of technology calls for more, not less state intervention. Conversely, there are other areas, such as urban transportation, where new technology-driven models end up correcting imperfections that long rigged the functioning of the market[36]; with those imperfections now gone, state intervention becomes a nuisance rather than a value-creating institution.

Redrawing the map must evaluate the areas where state intervention in a world of ubiquitous computing and networks will be beneficial and where it will be detrimental. In the next part, I want to take a look at what I believe to be the most pressing of those areas. I'll also discuss how a more entrepreneurial approach, from both the state and the private sector, can lead to imagining and building the Great Safety Net 2.0.

Key takeaways

• *The idea that the state is best positioned to solve problems is hardly clear. However, that case was successfully made in the wake of the Great Depression and it led to the post-war boom.*

• *State intervention entered a period of crisis from the 1970s onward. Initiatives in reinventing government mostly failed and so today's state is ill-fitted for the Entrepreneurial Age.*

• *Now we must revisit both the form and the missions of the state.*

If the state is to once again become a positive agent of change, it must seal an alliance with entrepreneurs.

Part 4
A Greater Safety Net

Chapter 10
Always Be Rebounding

"In The Persian Wars, Herodotus describes a feared people known as the Scythians, who maintained a horticultural-nomadic society unlike the sedentary empires in the "cradle of civilization."...With no fixed cities or territories, this "wandering horde" could never really be located...The fear inspired by the Scythians was quite justified, since they were often on the military offensive, although no one knew where until the time of their instant appearance, or until traces of their power were discovered...They wandered, taking territory and tribute as needed, in whatever area they found themselves. In so doing, they constructed an invisible empire that dominated "Asia" for twenty-seven years, and extended as far south as Egypt."
– Critical Art Ensemble[1]

Education is no longer the magic bullet

One of the first books that inspired my interest in technological change was Robert Reich's *The Work of Nations*[2]. In this work first published in 1991, the future US Secretary of Labor envisioned the current polarization of the job market. Reich identified three groups of workers: *"routine producers"* (the predominant category of the old working class), *"in-person servers"* (what Richard Florida calls the *"service class"*), and *"symbolic analysts"*, who manipulate symbols for large profits (e.g. the *"creative class"*). Needless to say this book had an impact on my career. I remember that after reading it in 1993 (in French), I *really* wanted to become a symbolic analyst!

Obviously Reich's influence went way beyond just me. Alongside other authors such as Anthony Giddens[3] and Jeremy Rifkin[4], he was instrumental in crafting the message of a new generation of progressive leaders that the era of the steady, lifelong job was over. In a more global and unstable world, lifelong education was the new key to providing workers with economic security. In the US, that vision was at the heart of Bill Clinton's promoting a fundamental upheaval in the American economy. As written in 2001 in the *Washington Post*, *"tuition tax credits to encourage lifelong learning [were] the entitlement of Clinton's era"*[5]. In Europe, the *"Lisbon Strategy"* was adopted in 2000 with the aim of turning the European Union into *"the most competitive knowledge-based economy in the world"*.

Alas Western voters, both in Europe and the US, have never been convinced that the problems brought about by globalization and the techno-economic transition would be solved by education alone. In the absence of a suitable system of lifelong training with large-scale, proven results, disillusionment has taken hold among voters. Great declarations on education, career shifts, and equal opportunities end up inspiring indifference, even irritation. Elected officials themselves are unable to put their discourse into perspective and fail to explain the channels through which lifelong learning can deliver value. What they usually come up with are chosen statistics and international rankings, almost entirely unrelated to the personally lived experience of their constituents.

Some, like French president Emmanuel Macron, think that the good idea of lifelong education has failed only because it was implemented too pusillanimously. Others, including Paul Krugman[6] (and myself), think that the case for lifelong training has been blown out of proportion, overshadowing the many other problems that explain workers' difficulties in rebounding in the Entrepreneurial Age.

The mark of the Entrepreneurial Age is greater instability at every level. It leads to permanent fluctuations in households' sources of income. Today's workers alternate overlapping periods of training, wage-earning, starting a business, looking for a job, working as a freelancer. With this intermittent working life, the income structure of households evolves at a much faster rate, not without transitional periods that present many challenges for individuals.

The impact of such instability is multiplied by the changing structure of working families. With the higher frequency of divorce and the fact that both parents working has become the new normal, the probability that a family is facing adverse economic events is now much higher than in the past. And so economic insecurity has been on the rise while lifelong education has been systematically touted as the magic bullet to counter it.

It's true that with such instability on the job market we need more lifelong education. But while the need for acquiring new skills is becoming more widespread, learning resources are also more and more commoditized. In the past, when most of the workers' education happened early in life, not having the right skills to find a job was a critical risk. If a worker missed out on an education when they were young, there was little way to save them from long-term unemployment later in life. Today, however, not having the right skills for the economy of the day is a much more common situation. Know-how becomes obsolete faster with the ever-accelerating progress of technology. The decreased longevity of firms[7] pushes the workforce into more frequent professional switching[8]. These trends combine to make training more common all along one's working life, including for Robert Reich's *"symbolic analysts"*.

More lifelong education doesn't mean that initial training has become useless. Quite the contrary actually: early education is becoming critical as we need to provide young workers with the tools, methods, and state of mind that they need to approach a life of constant occupational change. But that's very different from the training provided by today's education system. Most schools and universities tout the practicality of what they teach. Yet initial learning should in fact be less about practice and more about abstract frameworks. What matters when you're young is fundamental, imperishable knowledge such as reading, writing, counting, reasoning, learning history, and practicing foreign languages. It's also about the people you get to know. In an economy dominated by networks, the group formed by people you're connected with early in your life becomes a key personal asset that creates value over the long term.

Technology only accelerates this redistribution of goals between initial training and lifelong training. For instance, the work environment is increasingly augmented by software that constantly adapts and informs workers about the quality of their work. Thus technology makes it easier to train workers on the spot and to adapt their workplace and assignments to their specific skills[9].

What's more, the pool of trainers is broadening beyond the narrow segment of professional educators to all experts and practitioners who have something to share about their knowledge or their craft. With this ever larger pool, training resources have become commonplace. Most of them are even freely available on Wikipedia, Facebook, Medium, Quora, and YouTube—all platforms where networked learning communities are here to provide answers to any question regarding any skill. As a result, the approach to education during one's career becomes more short-termist. Experienced workers invest less in general training with the expectation of a decades-long return than in practical training for immediate application. In the Entrepreneurial Age, learning new skills and embracing a new occupation is becoming cheaper and easier than ever.

The problem is that this changing landscape in skills and education is not translating into greater economic security or lower unemployment rates. And so if the ease of learning new skills is not enough to counter growing technology-driven unemployment, there must be other barriers to switching careers. And we need to lower these if we ever want to provide individuals with a greater ability to rebound.

Occupational licensing for amateurs

One barrier against moving from one occupation to another is vestigial regulations from a previous age. In theory, technology contributes to better matching supply and demand on the job market. It provides workers with adequate training resources and helps beginners find work in their new chosen occupation. In particular, technology-driven platforms make it easier for unemployed people to embrace a new occupation, find their first gigs, and hone their skills through hands-on work with an early run of employers or customers. Thus far from creating more problems and destroying even more jobs, technology should lead to minimizing transitional unemployment as we go further in the current paradigm shift.

In practice, however, there are many jobs that could be created but simply aren't because *the law forbids it*. And the main culprit is the constant rise of occupational licensing. As observed by *The Economist*, "*in 1950 one in 20 employed Americans required a licence to work. By 2017 that had risen to more than one in five*". This includes most legal, medical, and financial professions, but also occupations such as hair stylists, bartenders, and makeup artists[10].

In most cases, the existence of occupational licensing reflects the government's past willingness to guarantee consumers a certain level of quality. But today, its rise is also a reaction to the harshness of the Entrepreneurial Age. Technology augments less skilled workers and makes it possible for them to deliver higher quality services at a larger scale. Thus corporations now have an infinite pool of less educated job-seekers that they can tap into to fill positions in many occupations. Marx's "*reserve army of labor*" being wider than ever leads to a vicious circle: because they can be replaced in an instant, workers don't have bargaining power; and because the jobs remain lousy, they don't attract the most demanding workers.

The traditional approach to improving workers' bargaining power would be to impose the set of institutions that in the twentieth century became the Great Safety Net 1.0: social insurance, a financial system designed to boost working families, and collective bargaining. But those institutions are now in retreat—to say nothing of their never having existed for the new urban working class. This is why workers at many skill levels[11] have held onto occupational licensing as the last resort to maintain their standard of living[12]. Many professions have organized themselves not to enlarge their ranks or embrace radical innovation, but rather to defend the status quo, preserve supply scarcity, and live off their rent.

The problem is that legally imposed scarcity of supply is not sustainable in the Entrepreneurial Age. If there are not enough professionals to match the occasional (and predictable) peaks in demand at a reasonable price, there are two possible outcomes. Either the prices occasionally go way up dynamically, as with Uber's surge pricing or, more likely, the prices are fixed at a high level by default, which leaves many consumers perpetually unserved (usually those with fewer means, as is the case on the US healthcare market). The taxi industry is a case in point; it constantly raises prices due to ever more expensive medallions[13]; at the same time it leaves entire neighborhoods unserved[14].

In the Entrepreneurial Age, that kind of suboptimal imposed scarcity is ill-advised. Most licensing mechanisms were imagined long before the emergence of new business models made possible by technology. As they don't account for the new possibility of higher quality at a larger scale, they end up pitting workers against the more powerful consumers. And in an age in which the multitude is the most potent party in the economy, pitting workers against consumers tends to end badly for the former[15].

It's no wonder why Uber and Lyft had such a rapid rise in competing against the taxi industry[16]. They opened a breach through which amateur workers could burst onto the market and contribute to providing higher quality at a larger scale. Thanks to those companies, being driven around by a chauffeur suddenly ceased to be the privilege of rich tourists or businesspeople. Now it was made affordable for a larger segment of the market, solving real problems in many people's daily lives. And the same conflict between legacy regulations and the rising multitude exists in many other sectors, albeit to a lesser magnitude.

Amateurs are frightening competition for professionals[17]. They have lower capital costs because there are certain assets that they don't need to invest in to do a good job (like an office or...an occupational license). They also have other sources of revenue, so they're willing to cut the prices down since it isn't like their entire income depends on that activity. By the way, amateurs also voluntarily lower prices precisely because they see themselves as amateurs and they don't feel legitimate enough to command higher prices. Finally, some (not all) amateurs actually do a better job than professionals because they do it with heart and a spirit of craftsmanship. These many competitive advantages all lead to a common response, with licensed professionals often deeming amateurs *"unfair competition"*.

Yet supporting amateurs trying to embrace a new occupation should be the norm in an economy where the ability to rebound is the worker's most critical need. In the past, we had to switch from one occupation to another with a clean cut between the two. In the Entrepreneurial Age, the norm should be that we go on with our current job while giving a new occupation a try. It should be a smooth transition between two overlapping experiences rather than an abrupt switch from one job to another.

To encourage this new approach we should explore the idea of how amateurs could become allies of licensed professionals instead of foes. In my view, technology is showing us ways in which it will be possible to put a ceiling on the number of workers while satisfying consumer demand even in the most extreme circumstances. The stake is to prevent rent-seeking and ensure that demand is always served at the highest quality and the largest scale. The goal should be to impose occupational licensing to professionals in exchange for certain benefits...while simultaneously using amateurs as a backup.

In this approach, professionals would reach out to the consumers to better understand their needs and make sure that these are met within a legal framework that satisfies everyone's interests. If an additional workforce is needed to match certain peaks in demand or serve particular segments of the market, the solution is there: inviting amateurs so that they focus on those slots and segments where demand cannot be met by the professionals alone[18]. If contained on this part of the market, amateur supply can reinforce the professional workforce instead of weakening its bargaining power. The reserve army of labor that is normally such a threat can thus become the workers' most potent asset.

Indeed in this framework, instead of being the enemy, amateurs could serve many goals matching the professionals' interests. First, they would backup the professionals to help keep the consumers happy, actually increasing these consumers' propensity to pay a higher price. Second, by sharing data they would help professional workers gain better, real-time knowledge of the market, making it possible to build a strong alliance between workers and consumers over the long term. Third, amateurs would form a pool from which new professionals could be hired, based on their record as amateur workers, their appetite for becoming professionals, and their support of the values underlying the profession's social contract. In an even more sophisticated version, professional unions could form cooperatives, like a farmers' co-op, to invest in supplementing sharing economy platforms, thus grabbing a share of the value added on the amateur segment of the market.

Many industries have become battlefields because the transition to the Entrepreneurial Age has pitted licensed professionals against startups allied with the multitude and harnessing the power of amateurs workers. But professionals shouldn't be waging a war against such a coalition[19]. Winning it would come with too high a cost for society in the form of destroyed value, unserved needs, and ultimately a rebellion by the multitude.

Instead, licensed workers should forge an alliance with amateurs participating in the market through platforms. This is the way in which we should imagine a new kind of occupational licensing for the Entrepreneurial Age: not one that empowers occupied workers at the expense of consumers and outsiders seeking to give their profession a try, but one that fits an economy in which career shifts are the new normal and satisfying the mighty customer is the one nonnegotiable rule.

Affordable housing for hunters and settlers

One of my most rewarding intellectual experiences in recent years has been reading a 2014 article by then-*TechCrunch* journalist Kim-Mai Cutler on the housing crisis in San Francisco—an article with a particularly entertaining title: "How Burrowing Owls Led to Vomiting Anarchists"[20]. Cutler's piece narrated the origins and implications of the housing crisis in the Bay Area. It demonstrated in the most convincing way how housing is both a factor in rising inequalities and a contributor to many jobs not being created.

There are two reasons why I'm now relentless in praising Cutler. One is her inspiring personal story (and talent at telling it)[21]. The other is that her chosen topics of urban planning and housing explain a great deal about why individuals have difficulties rebounding in the Entrepreneurial Age. In my eyes, Kim-Mai Cutler is a pioneer (and one who merits many more followers) in crossing institutional and policy ideas with a deep understanding of technology. In fact, ever since I read her article, I've been reflecting on how we can imagine a new housing market for the Entrepreneurial Age.

It's not that urban housing as a pressing social issue is a new problem. For most of the nineteenth century, the workforce flocking to urban industrial areas was a strain on tense real estate markets and the construction sector. Most of those leaving the countryside for the city were escaping raw poverty, but they still had to settle in what were effectively slums. For working families who could find better accommodations, it was not unusual to welcome a lodger in the spare room to make ends meet[22].

In other cases, employers themselves had to shelter their workers, like was the case for the large department store described in Emile Zola's *Au Bonheur des Dames*. Already at that time real estate was spotted as one of the key factors in rising economic insecurity for most of the population. As the self-taught economist and activist Henry George declared about unequal land ownership in 1892, *"some get an infinitely better and easier living... others find it hard to get a living at all"*[23].

Later in the twentieth century, making housing more affordable was a key outcome of the Great Safety Net 1.0. It was achieved mostly thanks to affordable cars fueled by cheap oil. But there was also the contribution of many institutional innovations: the rise of salaried work; the deployment of social insurance mechanisms; a banking system serving the needs of working families; the stronger bargaining power of trade unions. Equipped with cars and backed by the Great Safety Net 1.0, many Western families in the age of the automobile and mass production could finally achieve what was once the privilege of rich people: settle in their own house, even one surrounded by a piece of land. Obviously not all could afford the dream of suburban homeownership. But the backup plan of subsidized social housing made it possible to accommodate most of those who didn't earn enough, faced discrimination, or simply had no choice but to live in denser urban areas.

The benefit of the Great Safety Net 1.0 didn't mean that housing in the twentieth century was never subjected to the occasional crisis. Dense, prosperous cities have always struggled to provide affordable housing to most households, as can be seen in the cases of New York City, London, Paris, or the even more extreme cases of Tokyo and Hong Kong. It has also been documented that urban sprawl, although it contributed to serving the needs of the middle class, was accompanied by environmental damage, longer commutes, and racial segregation—sometimes, as is the case in the US, even supported by the government and the banking system[24].

There have been cases in which governments have been particularly successful in tackling the housing challenge. Germany, for instance, has long made the radical choice of promoting renting at the expense of ownership, making housing more affordable in the process. The rate of possessing property there is one of the lowest among OECD countries: less than 46% in 2011[25], compared to now almost 63% in the US and 65% in the UK.

The continuous existence of a quality, affordable rental market in Germany can be explained by various factors. Laxer zoning regulations favor a satisfactory housing supply. Tenant-friendly rules provide for price moderation and protections for those who comply with their lease. The structure of the more decentralized German banking sector results in a more cautious approach to mortgage lending, which discourages many households from pursuing home-ownership. Most importantly, the German approach must be understood in the broader context of homeownership not being the sole source of economic security for German households. Their Great Safety Net works well enough to distract individuals from an obsession with owning real estate.

Housing challenges are increasing now that the global economy is once again clustering in cities, as it did in the nineteenth century. A balanced housing market demands that wealth, jobs, and houses coexist in the same geographic areas. Absent that coexistence, market imbalances pave the way for a variety of economic, social and political problems. One resulting issue is that it is difficult to create jobs in proximity services because those who would do them cannot afford to live where they're needed[26]. Housing problems also crowd out inhabitants such as artists and entrepreneurs who contribute value as members of the creative class but don't have the financial security to find proper housing[27]. Above all, a tense housing market widens the inequality gap between those living in cities and those who are trapped far away from them and can't move because they simply can't afford the upfront cost[28].

Indeed housing has become a major factor in today's increasing economic insecurity. In the Entrepreneurial Age, a booming urban economy is bound to experience a crunch when rising real estate

Housing's Sweet Spot

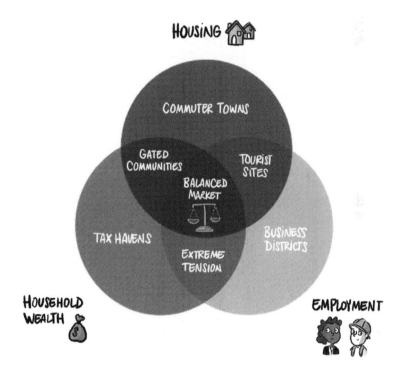

HOUSING

COMMUTER TOWNS

GATED COMMUNITIES

TOURIST SITES

BALANCED MARKET

TAX HAVENS

EXTREME TENSION

BUSINESS DISTRICTS

HOUSEHOLD WEALTH

EMPLOYMENT

prices make living in the city unaffordable for most. No wonder why Kim-Mai Cutler struck a chord writing about it. Among many social topics, she chose to focus on the very one which I think resonates the most with individuals and workers all around the world, from Shanghai to Paris to San Francisco. Imagining a new approach to the housing market has become urgent.

Harnessing the power of regulations to make housing more affordable is a particularly daunting task. Real estate is highly dependent on the state of other parts of the economy such as the financial system, local transportation, and proximity services. Interference by the government is often met by fierce resistance from many players with conflicting interests—and those who have patrimonial or business interests tend to have the upper hand on those who are desperately pushing for lower prices. Above all, any regulatory move on the housing market can only bear fruits over the very long term, usually while simultaneously revealing many unintended, adverse effects. This is a reason why radical change on the urban planning and housing fronts has usually happened under quasi-authoritarian rule and at a great social cost, like was the case with Robert Moses in New York[29] or the Baron Haussmann in nineteenth-century Paris.

Most current debates are not very helpful. Yes, we need to build more and make large cities denser[30]. We should also explore mechanisms to slow down increasing rents. Charity and public housing still have a role to play in alleviating the pressure for those in the most dire situations. And why not, as suggested by Social Capital's Chamath Palihapitiya, explore the idea of an Equality Fund to redistribute wealth from successful local tech companies in order to finance affordable housing on the real estate markets they're contributing to drying up[31]. But all those ideas sound like they don't account for the magnitude of the current paradigm shift. The usual systems of subsidizing construction or imposing rent control are, to say the least, rudimentary in relation to the scale and variety of housing needs in the Entrepreneurial Age.

As for me, it took me a while but I recently came up with what I think is the right framework to reflect on housing in the Entrepreneurial Age. I think most of today's problems exist because, as Clayton Christensen once put it, *"we have the categories wrong"*[32].

We're used to visualizing the housing market in terms of owners vs. tenants, or rich vs. poor, or housing vs. hotels vs. retail vs. office space. Those categories preside over most government interventions on the housing market, notably through zoning rules and household subsidies. But in the age of digital nomads, coworking, coliving, and short-term renting of personal residences, we can see that those categories are no longer sufficient.

My thinking is that in the Entrepreneurial Age the housing market should be analyzed through a categorization scheme that simply separates two groups. On the one hand are what my wife, Laetitia Vitaud, calls the *hunters*: people who spend a relatively short amount of time in a particular area because they're hunting for money (as workers), knowledge (as students), or experiences (as tourists). On the other hand are the *settlers*, those who need to have a fixed place of residence for the longer term, one that is attached to a steady job, their kids' school, or simply their taste for a particular neighborhood that they eventually decide to call home.

Each group is indispensable for the prosperity of a given geographic area. Hunters bring the energy, diligence, new ideas, and money that help large cities thrive. Settlers provide the *"eyes on the street"*[33], the density of proximity services, and the underlying trust (the *"ties on the street"*) that make the local culture richer and more welcoming. What's more, the two groups have many things that they like to share. Settlers can serve hunters, for example by hosting them through platforms such as Airbnb, while hunters can give settlers new connections to the world beyond their neighborhood.

In the past age of the automobile and mass production, the default way of life was that of the settlers. The majority of workers had a job for the long term, which delineated an optimal area in which they should locate a permanent residence. They could then decide on the school their children would attend and buy a home that complied with this set of constraints.

Hunters, on the other hand, were the minority. Their way of life was not regarded kindly. Hunting was tolerated as long as it was a passing phase. You could only be a hunter as a student, then for the first years of your professional life, and then occasionally as a tourist visiting other places.

Some people chose to hunt over the course of their entire lives because they had the money to hop from one 5-star hotel to another. But many others kept on hunting simply because they didn't have a choice. This was notably the case for many low-skilled immigrants, and their condition was miserable as a result: submission to predatory landlords; the impossibility of reassuring an employer or a bank; being constantly away from their family. This terrible fate of most perpetual hunters explains why settling was the preferred way of life in the age of the automobile and mass production.

The Great Safety Net 1.0 was thus designed to convert hunters to the settling way of life, because only the latter was in line with the techno-economic paradigm of the day. Then during the Dark Ages of financialization even more households felt a need to buy since homeownership became the main source of economic security, with urban real estate appreciation clearly outpacing wage gains (as it is bound to continue doing if we remain in our current environment).

But as for the Great Safety Net 2.0, that of the Entrepreneurial Age, it should have the opposite goal: to help settlers reverse back to the hunting way of life that provides them with the best jobs and the most opportunities. That's because in the Entrepreneurial Age, the urban world has been turned upside down. Nowadays our working life has become a constant hunting trip, with the many switches, overlaps, and unexpected events that you can count on in such an experience. And those who thrive and win in the Entrepreneurial Age are precisely individuals who embrace hunting as a way of life.

Technology is easily harnessed to help people become better hunters, as shown by businesses such as WeWork (which can provide an office desk in many cities), TransferWise (for seamless cross-border money transfers), Airbnb (to find shelter wherever you travel), and obviously Facebook (which has the power to connect you with almost anyone in the world). Technology is also a way to solve the loneliness problem that used to affect hunters in the past. Now they can hunt as a pack, connected through the networks that turn lone individuals into the powerful multitude.

Settling, however, is here to stay. Many hunters, however successful, will eventually be subject to constraints that will lead them to settle. One such situation appears when people get married. Having a spouse

Hunters & Settlers

THE CORPORATE WORLD USED TO BE AT THE CENTER
SURROUNDED BY SETTLERS, WITH HUNTERS AT THE MARGIN

NOW IT'S THE MULTITUDE THAT'S CENTRAL, SURROUNDED
BY HUNTERS, WITH CORPORATIONS AND SETTLERS AT THE MARGIN

greatly multiplies your set of constraints. Your partner now counts on your steady income. And whenever you want to move and take up hunting again, it means that your spouse has to give up their current job if they want to come along. Then obviously the next set of constraints that reinforces the need for settling comes with having children.

One way to mitigate the risks that come with the need to settle would be drafting zoning rules that favor the constant mingling of hunters and settlers, rather than doing the opposite (as they currently do). There wouldn't be a crisis of suburban housing if suburban areas were attractive for hunters—which they aren't. Likewise, there wouldn't be a crisis of urban housing if it was easier to settle in such areas.

The stakes are high. New legal frameworks should make it possible to harness technology and achieve a radical upheaval of the way of life for both adventurous hunters and settling families at every level of the income ladder. If they fail to accommodate both populations, the danger is for every large city to be inhabited only by *very rich* hunters and *very old* settlers.

For hunters, housing should function more like the hospitality industry. Like hotels and Airbnb rentals, real estate professionals should approach hunters more as customers. They should provide them with the agility they need while being frequently in motion— all according to their preferences and their earning power. As a diverse group, hunters need lodgings of all sizes, targeted at the various ends of the market. Some would want a place of their own while others could want to share with others. They could opt for something impersonal or a place with character. They could be there on a part-time or full-time basis.

The convergence between housing and hospitality is already happening. Young professionals form a hunting vanguard, as they have a more nomadic life and frequently adopt alternative mechanisms such as co-tenancy, coliving, remote work, and even plain nomadism. But this trend hasn't yet translated into an upgraded regulatory framework for the entire housing market. We continue to regulate housing like it's only meant to provide permanent shelter for stable families. Meanwhile what hunters need is a well-furnished place where they can reside as long as they have a reason to be there, where they can have access to many relevant services, and that they can leave in an instant when they're called elsewhere.

A market like that is easier to regulate with the goal of affordability, because the interests of workers and employers are very much aligned. Hunters could get used to finding housing through dedicated, data-driven marketplaces targeted at professionals. Employers could also take charge by providing their employees, including less educated workers, with affordable housing—just like some employers did back in the nineteenth century (this practice, by the way, is still widespread in the public sector).

As for settlers, they have very different needs from the hunters. For them the goal should be to harness technology to recreate the spirit of community that was once found in villages. A village is people knowing and, above all, trusting each other. In turn, this trust enables the pooling of resources so as to cope with certain needs in a more customized and affordable way. For settlers, technology can be harnessed to make energy more affordable, to improve the quality of transportation, and to provide access to proximity services such as schooling, childcare[34], elderly care, cleaning, maintenance, and at-home delivery—all services that mitigate the adverse consequences of having to settle.

Embracing the new categories of hunters and settlers is in the interest of real estate operators. For them, it's a matter of diversifying their revenue model. Hunter housing is a high margin/high capital employed business because hunters expect quality and won't themselves invest in repairs or refurbishing. Meanwhile, settler housing is more of a positive cash flow/low investment business because the residents themselves tend to invest in maintaining the asset. And so from a financial point of view, providing housing for both categories in the same lot is a financial optimum.

Likewise, mixing hunters and settlers is in the interest of local governments. In 2016, Kim-Mai Cutler aimed at reviving Henry George's idea of a land tax. As she explained, *"if an owner wanted to develop their property to make it more useful or productive, George argued that they should have the right to keep the value from those efforts. But increases in the value of underlying land were created by — and ultimately belonged to — the public at large"*[35]. The idea is that in the more attractive areas, the higher land tax would generate public revenue to invest in more amenities, better infrastructures, and denser, more affordable housing. With a well-functioning land tax, attracting a diverse population composed of both hunters and settlers would be not only a matter of inclusiveness. For local governments, it would also be a matter of maximizing business revenue derived from local real estate, and getting hold of a slice of that revenue.

Ultimately we must imagine a new approach and encourage a more mission-driven housing market. Today's approach to urban planning and housing is upside down, as are many institutions designed in the age of the automobile and mass production. And so we should radically revisit our understanding of the categories on the housing market. Now there should be the land, and the land tax we should levy upon it. And there should be the things constructed on the land: buildings augmented by technology-powered networked services, with the goal of providing agility for hunters and a sense of community for settlers. We're still lacking a broad-based political coalition for such an approach. Thus it will take radical imagination, and a great deal of entrepreneurship, to make these ideas more tangible in the political debate as well as in people's daily lives.

Yes, there are social problems outside of big cities that will persist. But they will be dwarfed by the systemic issues of the Entrepreneurial Age, which take place in urban areas. In those cities, no single land tax, zoning reform or way of harnessing technology will be enough to provide affordable housing for the many in the thriving cities of the Entrepreneurial Age. As in the twentieth century, what is made possible by the new technology of the day (cars yesterday, computing and networks today) needs to be complemented by new institutions—those of the Great Safety Net 2.0.

Key takeaways

- *When it comes to work displacement, most of the attention in the past two decades has been focused on lifelong education. Yet although it's important, it is no magic bullet.*

• *In an age of constant career shifts, we must make it easier to enter regulated professions. It calls for reinventing occupational licensing based on an alliance between professionals and amateurs.*

• *Urban housing is the main problem when it comes to dealing with instability. It's time we redesign the housing market around the more relevant categories of settlers and hunters.*

Chapter 11
Institutions for Hunters

"We need to democratize finance and bring the advantages enjoyed by the clients of Wall Street to the customers of Wal-Mart. We need to extend finance beyond our major financial capitals to the rest of the world. We need to extend the domain of finance beyond that of physical capital to human capital, and to cover the risks that really matter in our lives. Fortunately, the principles of financial management can now be expanded to include society as a whole. And if we are to thrive as a society, finance must be for all of us—in deep and fundamental ways."
—Robert J. Shiller[1]

A new breed of consumer finance

My partners and I at The Family are constantly rooting for old incumbents to become more like tech companies. The reason is simple and very much in line with our mission of supporting entrepreneurs: startups cannot succeed in Europe until everyone in the business world is convinced that tech companies will win in the end in every industry. A healthy ecosystem requires that startups and entrepreneurship are taken very seriously by all participants.

Obviously, the financial services industry is one that has yet to convert fully to the new paradigm. And in the spirit of inspiring this industry to reposition in the Entrepreneurial Age, I often talk about innovating in finance in front of various audiences—corporate executives, entrepreneurs, policymakers. My key message is always that the revolution in finance is not about big data, machine learning, chatbots, or crypto protocols. Rather it is about the current paradigm shift and how the financial needs of businesses and households are changing as a result. The financial powerhouses of the Entrepreneurial Age won't be the firms using the most cutting-edge technology. Rather the winners will be those who design financial products more in line with what the Entrepreneurial Age is about.

Take the case of consumer finance. An entire system has been designed to finance the typical middle class household of the age of the automobile and mass production: a married couple of salaried workers with 2.2 children whose financing needs are related to owning a suburban home and one or two cars, and occasionally borrowing money through a credit card to cover peaks in their consumption. This decades-old mechanism involves central banks, retail banks, payment processors, state subsidies, and various government-sponsored enterprises designed to complement the market.

But the Entrepreneurial Age requires a different mechanism for consumer finance. Widespread instability and constant pressure on workers make households' financing needs different from what they used to be. How can an employed person ensure the continuity of their income when they found their own business? How can a self-employed person smooth out their income if their business is seasonal? How can a worker borrow money over the long term if they're subjected to the impoverishing 'Greater Wal-Mart Effect'? The value propositions of traditional players in consumer finance do not meet these needs which are only becoming more typical—the needs of hunters rather than of settlers.

Ballooning student loans in the US are a sign of the current system's inability to meet today's challenges. Investing heavily in initial training is relevant if the goal is to settle in one particular profession. But it is poor preparation for a career during which an individual will frequently switch jobs. In addition, entering one's working life burdened with debt means ruling out entrepreneurial ambitions from Day One. The gap between the level of student indebtedness in the US and uncertainty in their future careers explains the diminishing rate of young people starting up new businesses and the related exhaustion of the US prosperity engine. It also inspires the hypothesis of a student loan bubble.

Housing is another example of the exhaustion of legacy consumer finance. Today this field is dominated by the model of homeownership, which has become a strong marker of middle class status and a cornerstone of the Great Safety Net 1.0. It relies on foundational institutions such as Fannie Mae and Freddie Mac, which were founded following the Great Depression with the purpose of securing the financing of home mortgages and raising levels of homeownership.

But in the Entrepreneurial Age in which hunting becomes the norm and settling more of the exception, the stake is not merely to buy a flat or a house close to the factory or office where an individual will hold a job for years. Rather, as previously discussed, it is to be able to move in and out without any hassle and without the upfront costs and potential asset depreciations that come with frequently switching jobs and changing your domicile.

The problem is that banks have not developed products beyond granting home-buying credit to households with savings and a high probability of a stable, single-source income in the future. Despite their purportedly high knowledge of the risk profile of their customers, banks are unable to guarantee rent payments to a landlord or attribute a high credit score based on an individual's future earning power. The consumer finance we've inherited from the past has become irrelevant in an age marked by permanent instability and frequent career shifts.

Thus the financial system needs to deploy more capital in a new breed of consumer finance, one that is designed for hunters rather than for settlers. New value propositions should be to the Entrepreneurial Age what mortgages were to the age of the automobile and mass production. This means not a loan to buy your own house, but rather a loan to make it easier to switch careers in a world where economic security depends on one's capacity to rebound[2]. As of this writing, hundreds of startups (some obviously more successful than the others) are providing us with an overview of what consumer finance could look like in the future, from paying for higher education with a fraction of your salary once you're hired[3] to diversifying your assets beyond the home you're living in[4].

But there are many institutional prerequisites for these new approaches to succeed. First, we need to innovate in the manner in which we assess individual creditworthiness—and on that front ventures such as LendUp[5] or Marcus by Goldman Sachs (a consumer-facing subsidiary of Goldman Sachs)[6] are aiming to help. Second, we should bring the government along, like once happened with Fannie Mae and Freddie Mac, to be the guarantor of a new kind of financial product—not one focused on expensive higher education or suburban homeownership, but one that covers the needs of the fast-growing population of hunters in the Entrepreneurial Age.

The usual objection is that if we give individuals credit to take a sabbatical and make a career shift, most of them will squander it on useless things and end up more miserable as a result. But we need to realize that this imperfection already existed in the times when mortgages were the pillar of consumer finance. Some people used mortgages to make wise investments on dynamic real estate markets; others squandered them buying a house in poorly chosen locations where the value of their asset could only go down. The 2008 crisis itself is the result of the housing economy running amok and enabling people to invest in overvalued assets that neither they nor their bank could recover at face value.

What would be the equivalent of mortgage origination in the case of a career shift credit? I think that the abundance of data creates value that makes it easier for banks to reach better allocation decisions. Much like Amazon in retail and Facebook in design[7], banks need to learn to exploit data so as to turn everything, including failure, into value-creating information. Beyond that, the more comprehensive tracking and predicting of individual income thanks to technology will make it easier for banks to claim loan reimbursement over longer periods of time.

This could appear as a nightmarish vision of crushing lifelong indebtedness, much like exists with student loans today. But it's precisely where the government can make a truly beneficial difference once it realizes that this new approach to consumer credit should be an integral part of the Great Safety Net 2.0. As proved by mortgages in the past, there has never been a problem with many households borrowing lots of money over the long term. The real problem is the obsolescence of the old system: nowadays most households are borrowing money for obsolete or overpriced assets (such as a house in a sagging suburban area or too expensive a college education) or merely to compensate for the dissolving Great Safety Net of the past (Colin Crouch's *"Privatized Keynesianism"*[8], the policy of sustaining consumer demand through the rise of private debt rather than public spending).

For the state, the goal should be to approach consumer finance in a more entrepreneurial way, starting with the needs of the fast-growing population of hunters and reshuffling the cards between the various players—including between the state and the financial system.

Take the case of unemployment insurance. In the past, when settling on the job and housing markets was the norm, unemployment was the dreaded exception. And as that risk struck mostly those who lacked a proper education, there were problems in covering it: potential insurers would have been tempted to practice adverse selection and cover only the more educated, while those with enough education simply wouldn't have worried about purchasing such insurance. In that imperfect context (adverse selection against risky customers and lack of interest from the others), it was almost impossible for the market to sustainably cover the risks of career shifts. That's why the government had to take over by providing unemployment insurance with a mandate, a fair price, and a single-payer mechanism.

Today, however, intermittent unemployment is no longer the exception but more and more the norm. It is a state through which most individuals will frequently pass in their professional life. As it becomes a common transitional situation for more intermittent workers, it also spreads the risks over a much larger population. And so it makes more business sense for bankers and insurers to develop products to address those who are exposed to that risk, providing them with the means to learn a new craft, move into a new home, or simply take the time to regroup and prepare their rebound.

We can find inspiration in various historical precedents, including in the business world. At the beginning of the twentieth century, Henry Goldman (the son of Marcus, the 'Goldman' in Goldman Sachs) found a way to underwrite securities for a new breed of companies that didn't own tangible assets of substantial value: retailers and manufacturers of consumer goods. As recounted by Charles D. Ellis in *The Partnership*, his voluminous history of Goldman Sachs[9],

"The public securities markets, both debt and equity, had always been carefully based on the balance sheets and the capital assets of the corporations being financed—which is why railroads were such important clients. Henry Goldman showed his creativity in finance: he developed the pathbreaking concept that mercantile companies, such as wholesalers and retailers—having meager assets to serve as collateral for mortgage loans, the traditional foundation for any public financing of corporations—deserved and could obtain a market value

for their business franchise with consumers: their earning power."

Now is the time to reinvent consumer finance with the same spirit of creativity. We should learn to do for hunting individuals in the Entrepreneurial Age what Henry Goldman did for retailers a century ago: provide them with access to capital not based on what they own (the old paradigm of homeownership for settlers), but on what they might earn in the future (the new paradigm of assessing the future earning power of hunters).

As technology makes it easier to enter the banking market, we can count on entrepreneurs to radically shake up the financial system and imagine this new consumer finance for the Entrepreneurial Age. In the old days, being a commercial bank provided a firm with access to the infinite pool of household savings. But it came with a serious price tag. If they wanted to attract household savings, such banks had to operate a vast, dense, and costly network of local branches and comply with tight regulatory frameworks. This is why bankers who had a taste for inventing new things were forced to renounce large consumer markets and fall back on the narrower segment of investment banking—a part of the financial system that, for better or for worse[10], was much more welcoming to financial innovation.

Today, this trade-off between serving households and innovating in banking has all but disappeared for two reasons. First, it has become easier for innovative new entrants to comply with the industry's regulatory framework, notably because most of the old rules, particularly the separation between commercial banking and investment banking[11], have been dismantled and replaced by prudential rules that simply force banks to tie up capital in proportion with the assets they hold.

Second (and this is where technology truly makes a difference), operating on larger retail markets doesn't require physical branches anymore. This leads incumbents to close down many branches[12] (suppressing jobs in the process). But it also makes it easier for new entrants to serve customers through digital channels and to design new products that meet the needs of the day. We can see this in the innovations in retail banking brought about by Western startups as well as the widespread disruption of asset management orchestrated by WeChat and Alipay in China[13].

With adequate institutions, households can be better and better served by a financial system tailored for the Entrepreneurial Age rather than for the age of the automobile and mass production. It only needs a helping hand from the state and the complementary contribution of other pillars of the Great Safety Net, including social insurance.

Dealing a new hand in insurance

We are all exposed to risks in our daily life. And in some cases, they are critical enough that we hire insurers to do the job of covering them. The business of an insurer is to collect premiums in exchange for the promise to compensate its customers for a possible loss. A claim can lead to a payment linked to the temporary lack of income (*"I have to stop working due to illness"*) or the destruction of an asset (*"My house burned down"*). It can also lead to providing much-needed services operated by a third party or the insurance company itself.

The reason why governments are involved in insurance is because, as seen above with unemployment insurance, not all risks can be covered by the market in a fair and effective way. In fact, the market of risk coverage is widely affected by many imperfections. Moral hazard is one, as it leads to people taking more risks because someone else supposedly bears the cost of potential damage. Another imperfection is adverse selection. If given the choice, an insurer will refuse to cover those who present individual signs of wider risk exposure. It leads to a somewhat absurd situation: insurance is provided only to those who eventually don't need it.

The primary level of government intervention on the insurance market is when it makes it mandatory to buy a policy covering a certain risk. In the presence of a mandate, everyone is expected to find an insurer, pay premiums and be covered in case of damage. Car insurance is a well-known example. The existence of a mandate is a guarantee that if an accident occurs, any damage to the cars and their occupants can be paid for—even if, as is often the case, the damages exceed the capacity of the one who provoked the accident to pay them. Insurance mandates exist in real estate as well, notably to cover the risk of fire, and in certain professions subject to occupational licensing, such as law. The outcome of such a mandate is clear: it makes coverage universal and thus broadens the market considerably, attracting many insurers and (in theory) stimulating competition.

The reason why mandatory car insurance is not called social insurance is that insurers are allowed to practice selection. As a result, individuals with a long history of damages are forced to find specialized insurers covering only the riskiest drivers and to pay very high premiums to comply with the mandate.

However this selective approach is not acceptable for every risk. In the case of healthcare, for instance, all individuals will at some point be exposed to terrible situations of distress. The associated cost is so high that an insurer will typically refuse to cover a person who is already ill or likely to become so due to a pre-existing condition. And the problem is that if exclusion (or price-hiking) is an option for insurers, the market is flawed. Most insurers will prefer to exclude potential customers rather than incur the risk of having to pay in case of illness. This is the reason why a cornerstone of the Affordable Care Act of 2010 was to forbid insurers from refusing customers with pre-existing conditions.

In many ways, the mandate and the non-selection rule are two sides of the same coin. The mandate (which makes the insurance universal) provides insurers with the guarantee that everyone will seek to purchase insurance. The no-selection rule (which is an extended version of mutual insurance) unhitches the price from the individual risk profile and makes insurance affordable for everyone instead of only a few. Insurers can afford to not select customers only because the mandate is a guarantee that they'll have lots of them, collecting enough premiums to cover the losses of those more exposed to risk. Conversely, the mandate is effective because thanks to the non-selection rule everyone, whatever their risk profile, can afford to be insured against a given risk. In the presence of both a mandate and a non-selection rule, the insurance can rightly be called a social insurance.

The next stage of government intervention is when this social insurance function (or a part of it) is taken over by the state. This provides the whole system with one main advantage: cost reduction. When insurers competing on the market are replaced by a single payer, there are few marketing and distribution costs because there's only one payer and it's mandatory for everyone to be insured by it. And so single-payer systems (like those that exist in most European countries and in the US with Medicare) provide the great advantage of making social insurance more affordable.

Additionally, a single payer can also pressure or regulate providers to make sure the prices of services designed to mitigate losses are commensurate with the premiums paid by the customers. The downside of single-payer systems, obviously, is that the absence of market competition deprives customers of its virtuous effects on the innovation front. As an insurer, the state can lag behind when it comes to covering new risks or inventing new ways of covering old risks. This is especially true in the context of tax revolts and constant fiscal austerity such as we have seen in recent decades.

Finally, the ultimate stage in the world of social insurance is when the state takes over both insurance and providing services to those who've been confronted with a loss—as is the case with the British National Health Service (NHS), which is effectively both an insurer and a care provider. The state's vertical integration of the two functions makes it easier to make the whole system affordable both for its users and from a fiscal point of view. But as seen in Chapter 9, in the age of mass production this usually comes with a top-down bureaucratic approach, leading customers into a frustrating one-size-fits-all experience[14].

Now, why go through this tedious social insurance 101 discussion? Mostly it's because the techno-economic paradigm of the Entrepreneurial Age has a major impact on this whole architecture. State intervention in insurance was originally developed in certain sectors such as healthcare and agriculture to protect individuals against the most critical risks: professional hazard, old age and illness for employees; illness and crop loss for farmers. Because those risks were so critical, it was worth it to deploy the complex mechanism of pooling resources, imposing constraining rules such as a mandate and forbidding selection, and adequately compensating those confronted with a loss. But today technology makes it easier to incentivize the market towards an approach resembling social insurance, this time without the top-down, one-size-fits-all approach.

One contribution of technology is the possibility to induce network effects. Ubiquitous computing and networks make it easier to create relationships between the customers of a certain insurer, eventually turning them into a multitude. This enables peer pressure so as to prevent moral hazard and free riding, which is one of the major flaws on most insurance markets. It also contributes to virtuous group dynamics when promoting good prevention practices (not smoking is easier done together) or following a loss (groups of patients covered by the same insurer can stick together and help each other as they undergo demanding and painful treatment).

With more intensive monitoring of user-generated data, technology also provides insurers with the tools to implement better prevention at a much larger scale. It makes it possible to collect more data, which in turn makes it easier to target prevention measures. Data can be used both at the individual level (to know us better and influence our lifestyle in a virtuous way) and at the aggregate level (to assess statistical results and improve the capacity to predict both individual losses and the insurer's underwriting margin).

Hence technology provides private insurers with the unprecedented capacity of scaling up to the point of universal coverage in a more beneficial manner. Contrary to a traditional insurer, an entrepreneurial insurer needs as many people as possible, well-behaved or sick. In the presence of technology, a new customer, whatever their risk profile, contributes to maximizing returns on marginal input, which encourages the insurer to welcome as many customers as possible. This is just how Google Search performs better as its application is used by a growing community of individuals, even if most of them don't click on sponsored links and thus don't directly generate revenue for Google.

With the proper infrastructure and legal framework, the Entrepreneurial Age could therefore be conducive to an unprecedented universalization of insurance benefits. It doesn't mean that everyone will be served the same way. Rather, it means that there will be less incentive to practice adverse selection.

A traditional approach to health insurance invites selection based

THE PYRAMID OF SOCIAL INSURANCE

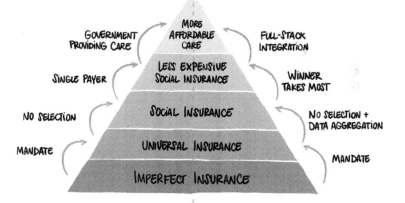

on signal, leading to a careful screening of pre-existing conditions and a widespread exclusion process. Conversely, a multitude-driven approach triggers different dynamics. Because each new customer contributes to increasing returns to scale, the insurer has an interest to be more welcoming to the many. In the new world of health insurance, a customer is not only a potential loss that you need to exclude or rob with high premiums so that they cover the cost of future compensation. It's a new node in a network that over time will create value for the entire community of insurees through aggregated data, behavioral influence, and peer-to-peer work. Overall, the bet is that *network effects beat selection effects most of the time*.

Up to now, social insurance systems have been designed and managed under the old rules of top-down bureaucracy. You needed to reach critical mass in order to make an average, standardized experience affordable for the masses. We all count on the health-care system to be treated when we need it. But we also hate it for the complexity and endless frictions of its user experience.

Many startups, notably in the US, are trying to change that. A first generation[15], among them Oscar[16], has been lifted by the regulatory disruption of Obamacare. But now that the Democrats have lost power, the new generation will have to be even more radical. Fortunately, it doesn't look as if the tech industry is avoiding that challenge. Q Bio, an Andreessen-Horowitz-backed startup, is aiming to reinvent preventive medicine in the age of ubiquitous computing and networks[17]. Watsi, an impressive Y Combinator-backed non-profit, is working to deploy the infrastructure to operate universal health insurance in less developed countries[18].

From a regulatory point of view, it's becoming clearer how the current approach to social insurance should be upgraded. A mandate still seems necessary in every field where individuals are confronted with critical risks. Like in the case of car insurance, this is clearly the key to making insurance more affordable. As for exclusion, more data-driven regulations should be designed to make sure that insurers don't practice exclusion or eviction through pricing, effectively nudging them into welcoming new customers as part of the multitude and harnessing the related increasing returns to scale rather than selecting their customers based on personal data.

Beyond that, the key advantages of a single-payer system are effectively replicated by the winner-takes-most dynamics driven by increasing returns to scale. Indeed a major overhaul of the system should be made with regards to bargaining with providers or even having the insurers deliver certain products themselves instead of relying on third parties. Instead of restricting insurers from bargaining with providers, governments should support the superior market power of those lifted up by increasing returns, using this new breed of insurers to force the overhaul of entire industries through full-stack integration (rather than enacting prohibition on Medicare negotiating drug prices).

Clayton Christensen has worked a great deal on how to make healthcare more welcoming for disruptive innovation[19], which will go through retrofitting the old care providing industry by diversifying the way prevention and treatment are provided. As he wrote, *"Hospitals have become extraordinarily capable of dealing with very complicated problems. But in the process of adding all of that capability and its attendant costs, the hospital has overshot what patients with straightforward disorders can utilize when they are admitted"*[20]. Like in consumer finance, we can count on entrepreneurs to tackle the challenge of imagining new ways to serve individuals in the field of social insurance.

This vision for social insurance is indeed optimistic. It can only be realized if the right institutions are not only imagined but are actually established for this purpose. Two dangers must be identified and prevented: the first is the temptation to focus on an obsolete approach to social insurance, one that doesn't account for the radical changes brought about by ubiquitous computing and networks. The other would be neglecting to implement a policy designed to encourage the birth and development of a new breed of insurers and providers. Not taking advantage of the transition in the insurance industry would be a serious industrial policy mistake and a terrible missed opportunity. If we are committed to the principle of hedging people against most risks, then dealing a new hand in insurance must be a key part of building the Great Safety Net 2.0.

We should all be taxed like Donald Trump

During the 2016 presidential campaign, the press was abuzz with information on Donald Trump's income history—and the conclusions we could derive from his taxes (or lack thereof). According to a widely read *New York Times* article[21], Trump recorded a net loss of almost $1 billion in 1995, which could have enabled him to offset his income taxes for a very long time afterwards.

The reason why Trump was able to do so is that he records his income not like any other ordinary citizen or household, but instead as a kind of individual entrepreneurial venture. The net loss was probably generated by various business partnerships that he was part of, notably in real estate and casinos[22], whose expenses that year were (much) higher than income.

As opposed to a corporation, which is governed by the fundamental rule of limited liability[23], a partnership's shareholders are usually accountable for both the profits and the losses. When the partnership generates a profit, it can be transferred to the partners and will be taxed at a personal level. But when the partnership generates a loss, it will also be transferred to the partners who, due to the business nature of that negative income, are able to spread the loss across multiple years to cancel out future taxes on earnings. This is called a *"loss carryforward"*, *"an accounting technique that applies the current year's net operating losses to future years' profits"*[24].

Assessing a loss on one's personal tax returns doesn't necessarily mean that one is a bad entrepreneur (although it clearly appears as if Trump is precisely that[25]). Say that your partnership spends $2 million this year to build a business that begins generating revenues in the coming years, with the corresponding expenses generating a loss for the initial fiscal year. Carrying that loss forward means that the first $2 million generated will be tax-free, as they're making up for the previous 'loss' which is actually an investment and the only reason that the partnership was able to generate those future returns. It seems quite normal that the initial investment can be recovered before you start being taxed on the profits, doesn't it?

Yet many denounced the Trump tax situation, claiming that we should close those tax loopholes that only profit millionaires and billionaires. And it's true that no ordinary person, whose sources of income are mostly wages and any interest earned in their savings account, belongs to a business partnership for which they're accountable for both profits and losses. When ordinary households' expenses exceed their income, they borrow money and the interest they pay is certainly not deductible from their next tax bill (except if it's for buying a home, but that's another story[26]).

Should someone choose to replace their labor contract with a partnership that bills their employer in exchange for their services and thus claim the right to adjust for the difference between income and professional-related losses? After all, many expenses that are directly related to work (such as transportation, business lunches, devices such as a laptop and a mobile phone, and even some clothing and services like childcare) could be subtracted off their personal income so that, like a corporation, they're only taxed on their profit instead of their gross income. Why don't we all do that?

Two reasons, mostly. First, we still live in a world of settlers rather than hunters. For most of us operating like Donald Trump would mean losing a lot of benefits that are attached to being an employee[27], notably health insurance, the right to a pension, and the security that is generally provided to an employee under labor law. Unlike some salaried workers, a contractor can always be fired without cause and is solely responsible for anything related to covering risks such as illness and old age. For that reason, people usually prefer a labor contract as opposed to structuring their work as a partnership. (And moreover up until now most employers would probably refuse to hire someone as a contractor instead of an employee.)

The second reason why we don't all use tax loopholes like Donald Trump is that it is too complicated at the small scale of a middle-class household to account for all the needed information related to income and expenses. Anyone wanting to do that would have to perform double-entry accounting on all their personal finances so that they're only taxed on what more or less corresponds to their savings (the amount available for future personal investments).

Yes, that would allow individuals to subtract expenses as well as interest and depreciation from income so as to calculate their personal profit. But it is awfully hard to keep track of all those tiny expenses in their everyday life in the world of what Venkatesh Rao calls *"paperware"*[28]. The tax authorities could simply refuse their accounting since an ordinary household wouldn't likely have the robust information system, accountants and auditors to certify that they're providing a true and fair view of their finances and operating results. Right now, you need to be wealthy to deploy the necessary infrastructure and hire the accounting and law firms that keep track of your personal finances.

Donald Trump wasn't punished by voters for his tax situation—not during the campaign[29], nor, obviously, on election day. Meanwhile, many among his opponents and critics called to close that tax loophole[30]. But allow me to play the contrarian here. Instead of closing that particular loophole that is so well exploited by billionaires, why not expand it for everyone else? After all, in the Entrepreneurial Age more individuals are seeing a growing porosity between household spending and professional expenses, for the simple reason that there are more and more self-employed workers and entrepreneurs who have to buy equipment and draw on their savings to finance daily expenses when they start a business.

As we're converting to the hunting way of life, shouldn't we all be allowed to subtract more expenses from our personal income—expenses that in a broad sense are directly linked to our professional life? In the Entrepreneurial Age, aren't we all confronted with a more unstable professional life that, at various points, will see us dedicate a substantial part of our resources to personal training or founding a startup? As Peter Drucker once wrote, the *"entrepreneurial society"* is one *"in which innovation and entrepreneurship are normal, steady, and continuous"*[31].

It's true that there are already some mechanisms that favor that approach. There's the 401(k) account, which enables individuals to exempt income set aside for retirement from taxation with the potential for matching by employers. And there are tax credits to pay for tuition if you go back to school. But those mechanisms don't really account for the radical paradigm shift of the Entrepreneurial Age. For hunters, retirement doesn't happen only once in today's life: it happens many times, every time you switch jobs. As for learning, as we've seen in the previous chapter, it can't be reduced to going back to school—in fact, it could simply involve watching videos on YouTube, joining a learning community on Facebook, or giving gigs a try on a platform.

In the Entrepreneurial Age, we should have a hunter-friendly tax system that allows for a broader interpretation of earnings and losses over time. We need a system more like the one that's used by Donald Trump, not one designed for people who generally have a stable income from one year to the next throughout an entire career.

This would have been a crazy idea in the world of *"paperware"*[32], in which fraud and mismanagement would surely be widespread. But in the world of software, every transaction can be tracked and documented in the cloud, as illustrated by Intuit's solutions for the self-employed[33] or, in a more un-Western way, by the intriguing Chinese system of government-sponsored social credit[34]. In most cases it will become ever easier to separate business-related expenses from personal ones, thus opening the possibility that we all use that famous loophole: we wouldn't pay taxes, and would even be able to spread potential losses out over multiple years, if our business-related expenses exceed our income in a given year. On the other hand, taxes would be due when our personal *"startup of you"*[35] becomes profitable over the long term.

Overall, my sense is that the vast majority of people are under the illusion that the tax system is a given. But like is the case for many institutions, this is far from being true. Most components of our modern tax system were imagined as recently as in the twentieth century, in line with the specificities of value creation in the age of the automobile and mass production. Personal income tax was invented to account for the rise of salaried work, which made it easy to assess what people earned in a given period and then apply a tax rate to it. Its proponents were progressive politicians like Woodrow Wilson in the US, who helped pass the 16th Amendment to the US Constitution in 1913, and finance minister Joseph Caillaux in France (one of my *inspecteur des finances* predecessors in the French government).

Corporate tax levied on corporate profits was then tailored by economists working for the League of Nations following World War I. The idea was to support the development of multinational enterprises while making sure that their profits wouldn't be taxed more than once by the various countries where they had a permanent establishment. As for value added tax (VAT), now a major source of fiscal revenue, it was invented in 1951 by French senior civil servant Maurice Lauré (another *inspecteur des finances!*) to make it easier to tax value added in the presence of the lengthening value chains of the post-war boom (and of widespread cheating on income taxes). VAT was soon adopted by all developed countries in the world except for the US, which continues to rely upon a distortion-prone sales tax system.

In essence, our modern tax system was invented in reaction to the development of a now-exhausted techno-economic paradigm. Now that we're entering a new paradigm, that of the Entrepreneurial Age, there's no reason not to imagine a new tax system that accounts for the dominant way of life and earning income—that of hunters rather than settlers. It is true for businesses, with the rise of tech companies calling for radical change in the fields of both corporate tax and value added tax. It is no less true for individuals, whose taxes need to be also upgraded to account for the current shift of household income. As we pass from a world of stable salaries to a world marked by instability at every level, income taxation should contribute to stabilizing personal income over time and hedging hunting individuals against the ups and downs of careers in the Entrepreneurial Age.

Key takeaways

• *The shift to the Entrepreneurial Age calls for a new breed of consumer finance, one that is focused on facilitating career shifts rather than buying physical assets like houses and cars on credit.*

• *We need to harness technology to provide better insurance against critical risks. With adequate regulations, the market has the potential to deliver outcomes similar to those of social insurance.*

• *The tax system, too, must be upgraded to account for the ups and downs of the Entrepreneurial Age. We need to align personal income taxation with principles that govern corporate taxation.*

Chapter 12
A Hedge for
the Networked Individual

"Providing protection against... risks is a way of ensuring that the dynamism of our economy is politically sustainable and morally defensible. It is also a way of ensuring that Americans feel secure enough to take the risks necessary for them and their families to get ahead. Corporations enjoy limited liability, after all, precisely to encourage risk-taking. But while today we still have limited liability for American corporations, increasingly we have full liability for American families."
—Jacob Hacker[1]

The corporate world in retreat

One of the major changes of our time is how the corporate world has moved from the center to the periphery of the economy. We're leaving a world in which the large corporation was the epicenter of our lives. We're entering one in which more and more shots will be called by an even stronger party: the multitude.

Why were corporations so central until recently? Venkatesh Rao, of *Ribbon Farm*, has an interesting take:

"In the 1780s, only a small fraction of humanity was employed by corporations, but corporations were shaping the destinies of empires. In the centuries that followed the crash of 1772, the power of the corporation was curtailed significantly, but in terms of sheer reach, they continued to grow, until by around 1980, a significant fraction of humanity was effectively being governed by corporations"[2].

Indeed the reach of the corporate world increased greatly during most of the age of the automobile and mass production. In the tech-no-economic paradigm of the day, the corporation proved a superior mechanism when it came to delivering certain outcomes. In many cases, it was simply more efficient and more effective than either the state and the market. It was so effective, in fact, that the state used the corporation as a proxy for implementing the Great Safety Net 1.0: social insurance was mostly provided through employers; most of labor law was effectively bargained for at the company level; consumer finance relied on corporations providing steady, salaried jobs.

An entire discipline, *corporate strategy*, was developed to help corporations consolidate their position in the economy. Most people assume that the corporation's edge is derived from simply being bigger, as the bigger the size, the more value it can create and capture. But we tend to overlook the fact that scaling up demands difficult trade-offs. In practice, a corporation can grow in size only if it offloads some weight by outsourcing certain assets, functions, and risks to other businesses. This is what corporate strategy is all about: helping corporations expand their reach and scale up without becoming overweight.

Today we're way past the time when large corporations were verti-cally integrated. The Standard Oil Co. was one large corporation that was present all along its industry's value chain, from upstream (extracting crude oil from the Lima-Indiana fields in Ohio) all the way to downstream (selling gas to consumers)[3]. Rockefeller's empire was a precedent suggesting that a corporation could successfully address large consumer markets while operating each line of busi-ness in the industry.

Following the Standard Oil example, Henry Ford designed the Ford Motor Company to be just as integrated, with the assembly lines at the core and the company selling directly to consumers through department stores, mail order, and sales representatives. But then General Motors, Ford's nemesis, broke with that model. As discovered by its CEO Alfred P. Sloan, it only needed to control a few strong links in the value chain to impose conditions on third parties operating the other links. Owning certain strategic assets, the 'one ring to rule them all', was more than enough for GM to domi-nate the car industry.

Corporate strategy grew more sophisticated during the following decades, helping corporations such as GM make the many trade-offs that would allow them to scale even more. Following Bruce Henderson's *"Experience Curve"*[4] and *"Growth/Share Matrix"*[5], corporations started to divest non-core businesses. Then came the time of Michael Porter's *"strategic positioning"*[6], with which large firms realized that focusing on one line of business made it very difficult to achieve a competitive advantage.

As a compromise, it became common practice for large firms to pick two or three links in their value chain while leaving the rest to others. Car manufacturers had the assembly lines and the brands that they marketed to the public; the rest (manufacturing parts, selling cars) could be abandoned to weaker links submitted to their willpower. Large publishing houses had the editing and the distribution, but they obviously let authors write manuscripts and preferred that books be sold to the general public through independent bookstores. Insurance companies had the balance sheet to underwrite most risks, but they let insurance agents and brokers do the hard work of selling policies to businesses and consumers. Likewise, McDonald's had the trademark and, famously, the real estate[7], while most other assets, functions, and risks were carried out by its franchisees.

The idea that corporations are now in retreat may sound odd in a world so obviously dominated by large tech companies. And it's true that the story of the corporate world is still all about scaling up—at least in terms of market capitalization and number of customers served. But something has changed since we left the age of the automobile and mass production and entered the Entrepreneurial Age. With ubiquitous computing and networks, the strategic trade-off of the day is that corporations offload more assets, functions, and risks not to other businesses, but to us—the *users*.

This is a radical shift from the corporation's point of view. First of all, consumers are simply more powerful thanks to technology. They are not scattered, non-coordinating agents anymore. They're equipped with increasing computing power and connected with one another, forming the multitude—a networked organization whose exponential power eventually exceeds that of most corporations, however large and tech-savvy.

A recent example of that unprecedented pressure from the bottom up is how the #DeleteUber hashtag initiated the takedown of Uber's Travis Kalanick in 2017[8]. Another is how a revolt of Netflix's customers in 2011 led the company to renounce splitting its DVD-by-mail and streaming businesses into two separate entities[9]. Even traditional, brick-and-mortar companies are feeling the heat of consumers being empowered by technology, such as when Gap chose to cancel its ill-fated brand redesign in 2010[10], or when Delta had to rescind its partnership with the National Rifle Association following the Marjory Stoneman Douglas High School shooting in Parkland, Florida in 2018[11].

But the shift is about more than mere consumer empowerment. Again, in an economy in which production and consumption are increasingly blurred, we users are more than consumers. As we provide data, capital, and labor that is reintroduced into the supply chain, we're also an essential resource that large firms rely on. As a result, we now have a *grip* over corporations because we control two points of their value chain: as customers at the bottom, and as suppliers somewhere at the top. With those two points of support, individuals within the multitude can begin to apply Michael Porter's strategic positioning and secure a sustainable competitive advantage. And this further changes the balance of power between corporations and individuals, with the former retreating to the periphery while the latter take center stage in value creation.

We can draw many conclusions regarding prosperity and economic security from this. In the age of the automobile and mass production, the corporate world was so central to the economy that the main risks of the day could be mitigated by simply providing stability to corporations. Firms had to change and rebound at the pace of market competition. But the Great Safety Net 1.0 was there to help them absorb the shock and thus preserve households from the adverse effects of market instability. By making corporations more stable and resilient, the Great Safety Net 1.0 provided most individuals with opportunities to resist the ups and downs of the economic cycle.

Today's Entrepreneurial Age creates a new range of problems. There's the overall pressure on workers' income—the 'Greater Wal-Mart Effect'. With the rise of multitude-driven increasing returns, instability is of such magnitude that it has become impossible to count on corporations to absorb shocks for individuals. We need to imagine new ways of empowering individuals in a world that exposes them to more risks but also where technology provides them with unprecedented capacities.

The center of gravity of our entire economy has irreversibly moved. It is no longer the corporation and the rigid, stable relationships it entertained with individuals as shareholders, workers, and consumers. It is instead the individual as an entity, connecting with others (mostly individuals) on borderless networked markets. It is worth re-reading the prescient and lasting words of the *Cluetrain Manifesto*: "*Networked markets are beginning to self-organize faster than the companies that have traditionally served them. Thanks to the web, markets are becoming better informed, smarter, and more demanding of qualities missing from most business organizations*"[12].

Many twentieth-century institutions were set up with the underlying thinking that individuals were a faceless mass, incapable of self-organizing. But in the Entrepreneurial Age individuals are active, not passive. They're organized, not blended away into the mass. They're constantly on the move, not stuck in one place. In the Entrepreneurial Age, it becomes more and more difficult to fit individuals into rigid categories. The Great Safety Net 2.0 has to comply with this unprecedented difficulty in fitting any one individual into a particular box.

This explains the idea of promoting a Greater Safety Net for networked individuals rather than for corporations—a *hedge* designed to cover us against all critical risks and empower us in our many interactions with other economic agents, all without the intermediation of the proxies (large corporations, the state) on which the Great Safety Net 1.0 had to rely in the age of the automobile and mass production. In a world where corporations are now prospering at the margin rather than the center of the economy, the corporate world alone has neither the power nor the influence to initiate designing and implementing the Great Safety Net 2.0.

If the connected individual is now at the center, with everything constantly moving around them due to the features of the Entrepreneurial Age, then this calls for grounding economic security in the new paradigm: not institutions designed to manage the balance of power between individuals and corporations, but institutions designed to hedge individuals in the many connections they constantly make and break with organizations and other individuals in their various capacities.

This calls for radical imagination when it comes to harnessing the power of the multitude in the interests of the many instead of the few. Technology-driven capacities are now available for individuals in various guises: as voters, as users of public services, as self-employed workers, and even as employees. The multitude explains the adverse consequences of the Entrepreneurial Age, the widespread instability, the 'Greater Wal-Mart Effect'. Can it also be a dynamic positive force, like trade unions in the past, using the power of technology in the interest of economic security and prosperity?

The new frontier in collective bargaining

One issue with technology is what I have previously called 'downward augmentation': the fact that technology compensates for a lack of skills when executing many tasks. The more technology there is, the less educated you need to be to provide high quality services in a more productive way. For less educated workers, this is good news indeed. It means that the barriers will be lower when they try to access the job market. And once they have a job, they'll be able to deliver a greater output and will (in theory) be rewarded with an accordingly higher wage.

But there's a catch. With more people being able to occupy many jobs, technology also contributes to Karl Marx's *"reserve army of labor"* becoming wider than ever. Thanks to technology, employers tend to have an infinite pool of job-seekers into which they can tap to replace those who have the nerve to organize and demand better working conditions. How can workers restore their bargaining power in the presence of both increased consumer power and this infinite reserve army of labor?

As is often the case, there are many lessons to be drawn from the past. The rise of assembly lines at the end of the nineteenth century was similarly seen as a major threat for the well-being of workers.

Since working on these assembly lines required less skills than traditional craftsmanship, factory bosses could maintain pressure on wages and force their employees into accepting degraded conditions. Union leaders answered by breaking with the corporatist approach of the old craft unions and organizing industrial workers no matter their skills or the sector in which they worked[13].

To create a sense of shared destiny between their heterogenous members, innovative union leaders had to inspire their troops with radical messages and, in some cases, revolutionary views. But above all, they designed a new value proposal: joining a union was no longer about entering a closed corporation of skilled craftsmen; rather it was about taking a path towards inclusion in society. Thus much like the infamous political machines[14], industrial unions in the US were a preferred destination for minorities and immigrants since they provided their members with services covering critical risks and taught them the soft skills necessary to find their place in an otherwise antagonistic society.

My view is that such a cooperative model (call it a union, a guild, or a federation) is bound to rise in the future as the most effective way to empower workers in the Entrepreneurial Age. But a paradigm shift is needed in terms of what the goals are and what kind of methods and tools should be used by those trade unions of the Entrepreneurial Age.

Indeed the great Albert Hirschman told us about what it takes to move the needle: voice *and* exit[15]. Voice is obviously about making your voice heard: participating in a town hall meeting, demonstrating on the streets, or demanding to see the shop's manager. Exit is about taking refuge in the other option: you vote for the other candidate, or go to that other shop across the street where prices are cheaper, inventory is larger, and employees are nicer.

Historically, trade unions have been concerned mostly with supporting workers so that their voice is heard by employers. This was consistent with what jobs were all about in the settling model of a continuous career spanning decades. Because workers had the same employer for years, voice was their preferred option, with quitting their job the solution of last resort.

But now jobs have radically changed to the hunting model. We switch jobs more often. Some, notably many high-skilled workers and millennials, are even enjoying it. And as pointed out in 2014 by Adam Davidson, in our current *"Failure Age"*[16], businesses close down at a higher frequency anyway, so you can't plan on spending your entire career with one single employer anymore.

As a result, exit has become less frightening than it used to be. Quitting your current job is about precipitating the inevitable and switching jobs is the new normal[17]. This changes the relative opportunity of the two Hirschman levers: exit is not the last resort anymore. And with more of us becoming hunters in the Entrepreneurial Age, it has even become the more desirable.

So how come unions keep on supporting workers on the voice front only—bargaining with employers, going on strike, demonstrating, doing everything they can to save their members' jobs? I think it's time we imagine unions that support workers as they switch jobs, unions that would provide their members with all the resources necessary to find inspiration (*"What should I do?"*), train (*"How can I acquire new skills?"*), find a new employer (*"When do I start?"*), relocate (*"I need an affordable house close to my new workplace"*).

I can hear your doubts: that's not what unions do, they should stick to what they know. And yet it won't be the first time that unions reinvent themselves. Again, in the US, they once went from defending skilled (mostly white) craftsmen to defending the interests of all industrial workers whatever their skills, sectors, and origins. The industrial union paradigm was so different that a new entity had to be founded (the Congress of Industrial Organizations, which only later merged with the old craftsmen's American Federation of Labor).

So why not convert to supporting the growing population of workers for whom exit has become a viable and desirable option? The job of those new 'exit unions' would be to make employers feel the pain of their employees leaving instead of bargaining. They would support workers in their transition from one job to another, ideally at the pan-industrial level. They would organize the draining of entire industries that treat workers badly: good luck with retaining workers in low-quality jobs (e.g. coal[18]) when powerful unions orchestrate their switching to a more attractive, faster-growing industry (e.g. solar [19]).

More generally these new unions will invest heavily in professional training to attract and convert individuals willing to enter the profession. As explained in Chapter 10, they will become instrumental in attracting amateurs and growing the pool of future members willing to defend their collective interests. They will also complement these activities with insurance mechanisms designed for their members: mutual insurance against critical risks such as illness, platforms to make it easier for hunting workers to afford housing in the dense urban areas where most jobs and opportunities are now concentrated, services facilitating childcare and elder care.

Indeed 'exit unions' would carry a great deal of weight in the endless debate on affordable housing[20]. With strong, innovative unions joining the fight, my guess is that many obstacles to building more housing lots, loosening zoning rules, and maintaining rents at a sustainable level will disappear.

This new form of union will also be able to bargain directly with consumers—the most powerful party—to better establish the terms of the Great Safety Net 2.0. Recent victories on the minimum wage front[21] in the US, however limited, were obtained through an unprecedented alliance between workers and consumers, all connected individuals pursuing a common agenda rather than a corporatist group seeking to advance its own interests. Indeed for the first time in over three decades—admittedly before the advent of the Trump administration—, workers seemed to be regaining some of their long-lost influence thanks to the new alliances enabled by ubiquitous computing and networks[22].

This new approach to organizing workers need not serve only the interests of one kind of worker. As proven in the retail and food industries, you need motivated and caring employees at every level of the income ladder[23]. This is especially true in an economy dominated by proximity services (food, retail, hospitality, healthcare, personal care, last-mile logistics), where the majority of jobs will be about caring for people rather than making things[24].

Relying on networked organizations to implement the Great Safety Net 2.0 would not be unprecedented. Individuals trying to solve their own problems on the ground happened many times before, even in the recent past. One well-documented episode came when those who were dying of AIDS in the 1980s and '90s hacked a system that ignored and rejected them[25]. They eventually forced healthcare professionals to make the patient an active player in their own treatment, imposing a paradigm shift that had an impact far beyond that particular disease. A less well-known story is that of the Black Panthers and how they took charge of providing affordable healthcare to African-American families in Oakland, California, and many other places instead of waiting for the government to overcome its racial and social prejudices[26].

It is true that it is generally difficult to grow larger communities without weakening the bonds that tie everyone together. Public choice theorists have long demonstrated why special interests, when conflicting with the interests of a larger group (such as the entire middle class), tend to win in the end—namely, because it's easier to organize a small group of determined people with an acute realization of their common self-interest. Conversely, it is much more difficult to organize a larger group, as coordination and management becomes a practical challenge and the number of people involved increases the chance of marginal divergences that eventually affect morale.

There are various reasons why things could change in the Entrepreneurial Age. The first is lower barriers to entry. Harnessing the power of ubiquitous computing and networks makes it easier to cover many kinds of risks. This was an argument made in 2003 by Robert J. Shiller, a winner of the Nobel Prize in Economics, in *The New Financial Order*, a book dedicated to explaining how a *"an electronically integrated risk management culture"* could be *"designed to work in tandem with the already existing economic institutions of capitalism to promote wealth"*[27]. Shiller's proposal was somewhat obscured by the financial crisis that followed. But now various factors—increased processing power, regular and systematic monitoring of user activity, the strength of peer-to-peer networks—suggest that pooling resources at the scale of the multitude has become easier and less costly than in the past.

What's more, communities that were impossible to organize due to geographic distance have become viable as the basis of a new system thanks to today's technology. In the old days, people needed to live close to one another to form the bonds of a solid socio-institutional framework. Today they can connect with one another via the Internet and form a network that is as tight and resilient as a community of fellow villagers. This has practical consequences on the process of building the Great Safety Net 2.0. Suddenly, collectively organized networks can rapidly form around issues and interests for which it was previously impossible to advocate due to the distance between potential members. Distance and geographic frictions are no longer standing in the way of organizing.

A third factor is, once again, increasing returns to scale. As the multitude organizes to pool risks or offer shared services, individuals can be far away from each other while being very similar in terms of profiles and interests. As compared to self-organized communities in the past, *"cloud communities"*[28] have a major advantage due to their networked structure: the power of networks tends to increase instead of diminishing as the underlying community grows. In the past state intervention was needed to deploy institutions beyond a certain scale; in the future increasing returns to scale could be enough for technology-based initiatives to reach a universal scope. When it comes to discovering and imposing new institutions as part of the Great Safety Net 2.0, there could be cases in which technology-driven network effects replace and even surpass the authority of governments.

I'm convinced unions played the most critical part in building the middle class in the past age of the automobile and mass production. Now we have to reinvent unions so that workers gain leverage in the current age of ubiquitous computing and networks. Designing policy to do so will be one of the most critical political challenges of the coming decades—and just like collective bargaining was critical during the post-war boom, it is absolutely necessary to creating the Great Safety Net 2.0.

The equation for creating good jobs

Today's inertia can be explained by one simple fact: most people who genuinely care about promoting economic security and prosperity are looking backward instead of forward. Their dream is to 'make the safety net great again', as it was during the post-war boom, rather than imagining a new kind of safety net. Alas their pining for the Great Safety Net of the past cannot be converted into beneficial action. We're in a new paradigm now.

Today's challenge is not about securing the old working class of the age of the automobile and mass production. Rather it is to create more, better jobs for the new working class in urban proximity services. It consists in making those jobs more attractive while making those services more affordable for a larger number of customers. The solution will not come from the government simply subsidizing supply or demand. Rather it will be in designing a macro mechanism that helps the market find a new balance, with institutions that better fit the needs of today's workers and a new breed of unions as the dynamic force to make it all grow. It's about constructing a virtuous circle like once existed with the post-war boom.

What Zeynep Ton and Roger L. Martin call the *"good jobs solution"*[29] concerns the entire economy. But if it is to have a significant impact on the job market, including for less educated workers, it should start with creating more value in proximity services and reinvesting that value to create those good jobs. Conversely, if there is no additional value created in proximity services, then no surplus can ever be shared with proximity workers so as to turn them into the new middle class.

Creating additional value rarely happens by letting the private sector off the hook. Rather, businesses need to be pushed into using technology. In many cases, pressure comes from an increased level of competition. This is why a sound antitrust policy, one that aims to counter rent-seeking, is so important. Pressure can also be imposed by making inputs more expensive. This is one reason why the Great Safety Net 1.0 contributed so much to increasing productivity. Because it made labor more expensive, it eventually became an incentive for business leaders to try and produce more with fewer workers, thus creating additional value that helped pay for the whole mechanism!

This worked especially well in one particular part of the economy: large corporations ruled by scientific management. Meanwhile, the proximity service industry has resisted efforts to embrace such practices. In sectors taken over by the government, such as education, proximity workers secured middle class status because wages were decoupled from productivity, with the difference paid for using taxpayer dollars. But in other sectors such as hospitality and personal care, the preferred option has always been to exert pressure on workers so that they work longer hours and consent to lower wages.

And so in a typical feature of William Baumol's *"cost disease"*, most proximity services have been made into a zero-sum game that hasn't translated into either higher wages for workers or better services for customers. On the contrary, the absence of additional value in proximity services has been a self-reinforcing phenomenon. Business owners don't pursue higher quality at scale. In turn, consumers don't expect improvement in terms of the quality or the positioning of the service rendered. As they themselves are subject to the 'Greater Wal-Mart Effect', they only seek one thing: ever lower prices.

Absent high quality at scale, workers in proximity services are not expected to get better at what they do. Instead, they are *dispensable*, replaced in the blink of an eye while management keeps the business afloat. This explains the high employee turnover in most proximity services (think about restaurants, for instance). These sectors have always functioned without counting on more qualified and productive workers. And if anyone can be inserted to do the job at what is considered to be an adequate level, it becomes difficult for those already working to bargain for a higher share of the value added.

Fortunately, a radical change is happening. As we go further into the Entrepreneurial Age, technology is finally providing us with levers to create more value in *all* proximity services. The corollary is that it makes it possible to improve the quality of jobs in proximity services, even if they're not operated (and paid for) by the government. Clearly this is where entrepreneurs can make a difference by harnessing the power of technology and forging a bond with the multitude.

It takes time. Tech companies with an entrepreneurial approach don't serve large markets yet. As explained by economist James Bessen[30], productivity always slows down at the beginning of a technological revolution: entrepreneurs must experiment with the technology of the day and discover the new markets that it contributes to opening. Then those markets grow larger, triggering a virtuous circle as higher demand leads to a higher level of investment, which increases labor productivity, brings down prices, and sustains an even higher demand.

One early step to enter that virtuous circle is using technology to *augment* workers[31]. It makes it possible to generate higher productivity and quality while requiring less training for the job. If you increase output while relying on less qualified workers, you can employ more of them and pay them more as compared to what they earned in previous jobs, all while serving more consumers at a cheaper price[32].

This 'downward augmentation' doesn't mean that everybody, however unskilled, will be good at their job. Rather, it means that more workers will be able to execute the routine tasks required for many jobs in proximity services (for instance when real-time geolocation spares a driver from having to know the map of the city by heart). As for qualitative differences, they will be found in non-routine, human capabilities such as punctuality, attention, memory, kindness, empathy, literacy, energy, and warmth[33].

Beyond this 'downward augmentation', entrepreneurs can radically improve resource allocation by harnessing the power of the multitude. In a way, it's what Ikea has long done by putting customers in charge of assembling furniture[34], thus generating a surplus that could then be redistributed. Only now harnessing such power can be done at a much larger scale, powered by network effects and vast amounts of user-generated data. That's because in the Entrepreneurial Age the multitude contributes to creating value through three complementary channels: auxiliary amateur workers (as discussed in Chapter 10), free peer-to-peer contributions (as when people submit reviews on TripAdvisor), and casual user-generated data collection (performed by all tech companies, as explained in Chapter 5). All contribute to increasing and diversifying the output in proximity services. This creates an economic surplus to be redistributed according to the socio-institutional framework of the day.

This is why institutions must be designed to bring together the Great Safety Net 2.0. The stake is to shape the corporate contract in proximity services in a more favorable manner for workers. This can't be done by going against the mighty multitude. Rather it consists in harnessing its power to change the equation and align the interests of workers with those of the multitude. If the socio-institutional framework is favorable to the development of proximity services, then the multitude-driven surplus will be allocated to expanding the business by lowering prices and/or improving the quality. It will make it possible to address a

MOVING TOWARDS A VIRTUOUS CIRCLE

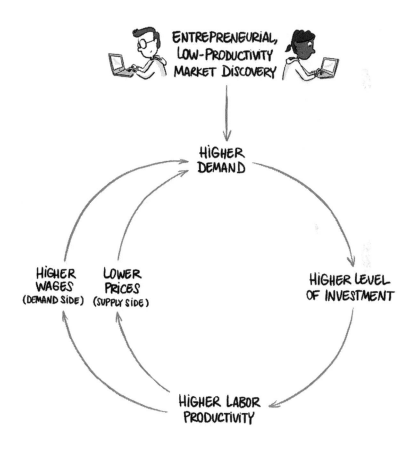

(INSPIRED BY JAMES BESSEN)

larger market thanks to a classical supply-side multiplier effect. In turn, greater, more diverse demand will require hiring more workers. And because of the augmentation facilitated by technology, those workers' higher productivity will make it possible to pay them more.

Creating more, better-paid jobs will also trigger a typical Keynesian demand-side multiplier effect as those numerous, better-paid workers consume more proximity services themselves. The city of Seattle is a case in point. Its fifteen-dollars-an-hour minimum wage has made proximity service jobs more appealing and revitalized the city's economy[35]. With higher pay, proximity service workers become consumers of other proximity services, triggering a positive feedback loop and leading the economy towards prosperity and increased economic security.

The goal of using technology in proximity services is not to standardize tasks, repress workers' initiative, or ignore their individuality. On the contrary, in proximity services, technology should make it easier for workers to take charge, make their own data-driven choices, and add value in their preferred approach, creating a partnership with customers that much resembles the spirit of craftsmanship. We must remember that such services are all about frequent and direct interactions with customers[36]. Connecting workers with customers makes a difference because it is then possible for businesses to be even more sensitive and responsive to the demand-side. With empowered proximity service workers, customer relationship management can be converted into a constant, data-driven dialogue. Demand can be managed and oriented based on the collected data and available resources, and high quality services can be supplied at scale by harnessing the additional power of the multitude.

For example, how do you provide affordable 24/7 service in personal care? By doing two things: having well-equipped workers come to the customer's home every working day while also complementing those workers with a call center, instant messaging, amateur workers as backup, and a social network of other customers. The stake is to have all those involved rely on an information system that shares knowledge, improves resource allocation, and provides customers with a seamless, customized experience. In this more favorable context, proximity workers can get better at what they do, manage their activity in a sound manner, and enjoy higher wages and better working conditions.

How the Multitude Generates Value in Proximity Services

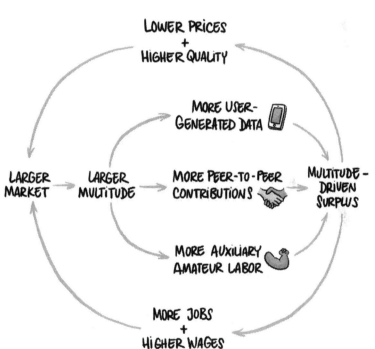

(SUPPLY-SIDE MULTIPLIER)

LOWER PRICES
+
HIGHER QUALITY

MORE USER-
GENERATED DATA

LARGER
MARKET

LARGER
MULTITUDE

MORE PEER-TO-PEER
CONTRIBUTIONS

MULTITUDE-
DRIVEN
SURPLUS

MORE AUXILIARY
AMATEUR LABOR

MORE JOBS
+
HIGHER WAGES

(DEMAND-SIDE MULTIPLIER)

All in all, technology doesn't make jobs irrelevant—far from it, as suggested by the uninterrupted growth of proximity services in expanding urban areas. But with the Entrepreneurial Age comes the new working class that we discussed earlier, and this new working class calls for a Great Safety Net 2.0. Two things are at stake: hedging networked individuals against the critical risks of the day and providing businesses with the steady, growing demand they need to invest. Will we be up to that challenge?

Key takeaways

• *The Great Safety Net 1.0 used to be built for and around the corporate world. But now our economy revolves around the networked individual: this is a Copernican revolution.*

• *With individuals harnessing the power of networks, it's time to reinvent trade unions. As workers convert to the hunting way of life, bargaining becomes less about voice and more about exit.*

• *The institutional stakes are clear: we need to create more jobs in proximity services and make them more attractive and rewarding. This is what the Greater Safety Net is all about.*

Conclusion

THE GREAT SAFETY NET 2.0
(ENTREPRENEURIAL AGE)

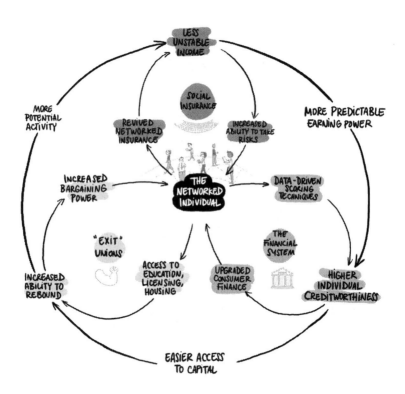

Basic Income Isn't Enough

"I came to believe that Monsieur Teste had managed to discover laws of the mind we know nothing of. Certainly he must have devoted years to this research; even more certainly, other years and many more years had been set aside for maturing his inventions, making them his instincts. Finding is nothing. The difficulty is in acquiring what has been found."

—Paul Valéry[1]

In September of 2016, I published an issue of our in-house series *The Family Papers*, for which I chose a splashy title: "Enough With This Basic Income Bullshit"[2]. Thanks to the piece being touted by Tim O'Reilly[3] and then discussed on *Hacker News*[4], I was pulled into heated arguments around the future of the safety net. And while my paper was initially written rather hastily in reaction to something I had read[5], the subsequent discussions helped me clarify why exactly I have so many misgivings about universal basic income.

One of my criticisms concerns the idea that universal basic income would be simpler. It's true that simplicity exerts a welcome fascination on tech entrepreneurs. After all, entrepreneurship is the art of making things simple. But we shouldn't forget that the safety net is complex for a reason, namely because it must provide economic security at the scale of entire nations to both households and businesses. And I still don't get how distributing a fixed amount of money to everyone can cover the entire economy against the many adverse consequences of the Entrepreneurial Age. The main problem, after all, is the difficulty most households have in coping with the rising and oftentimes unpredictable cost of healthcare, housing, higher education, and other critical expenses.

Another criticism derives from political history. The strength of an institution such as a social insurance program can be measured in its capacity to withstand the inevitable conservative backlash[6]. A retrospective of redistributive government programs suggests that universal basic income wouldn't pass that test. If a liberal government put it in place, soon enough the conservative opposition would succeed in discrediting it (along the lines of *"It makes the poor lazy and the rich don't need that money anyway"*), dismantling it as soon as they were back in power.

A third argument in my piece was echoed last year by *Vox*'s Matthew Yglesias: *"Silicon Valley's basic income fans should spare a minute to defend the actual safety net"*[7]. Like Yglesias, I think that the heated (and abstract) discussions around universal basic income distract powerful voices in the tech industry from considering the more pressing social challenges of the moment. And as those in power in the US seem to be busy dismantling what's left of the safety net of the past, the most pressing challenge in the US seems to be defending the very principle of the existence of a Great Safety Net.

Because really, where are tech entrepreneurs and venture capitalists when it comes to weighing in on safety net issues? Apart from discussing universal basic income, I find that they're nowhere to be found, heard, or read. I suspect there are several reasons for this. For one, they don't feel personally concerned. Well-educated white men from privileged backgrounds working in a rapidly expanding part of the economy have no reason to express an interest in the complicated and rough world of the welfare state or trade unions. Also, many entrepreneurs and venture capitalists, especially in Silicon Valley, mistrust the state as a matter of principle and have long preferred to stay away from industries as highly regulated as healthcare, consumer finance, or housing. Finally, there's the reluctance to join a public conversation that is so polarized on both sides of the political spectrum.

But let me lay out at least three reasons why US entrepreneurs and venture capitalists—in fact, the entire US tech industry—should very much care about building a *Greater Safety Net for the Entrepreneurial Age*.

First, consumers need purchasing power. As US Senator Elizabeth Warren explained in discussing Obamacare at the 2017 *Wall Street Journal* CFO Network conference[8], once individuals lose healthcare coverage, it drives costs up and creates problems for the entire economy. If people spend all they have on healthcare (or don't spend because they're worried about the potential for a future catastrophe), how can they subscribe to the tech industry's latest product, however cheap and convenient? Less healthcare coverage eventually means less revenue flowing to all businesses, including tech companies, that aren't in the insurance and healthcare industries. And the same is true for many other parts of the Great Safety Net.

Second, there are benefits in people's switching jobs and founding startups more easily. As former Obama economic advisor Jason Furman explained in a 2014 blog post, again discussing Obamacare,

"Access to health insurance outside the workplace allows people... to take risks that further their careers and benefit the economy as a whole, like going part-time in order to go back to school, leaving a job in order to start a business, or moving to a better job, perhaps at an employer that does not offer coverage"[9].

Third, it's actually caring about what matters for people and society. As of today, as revealed by the *"tech backlash"*, Silicon Valley has a major image problem with ordinary people who fear that they'll lose their jobs or won't be able to make ends meet. I'm not sure that a bunch of billionaires discussing the singularity and immortality provides the best impression when millions of ordinary people are feeling the inequality gap widen, their sense of economic security plummeting as most of their safety net disappears.

Above all, it's about truly shaping the future. Whatever the outcome of the current administration, many people expect the Democratic Party to strike a determined counter-attack, polarizing the debate on the safety net even more. Instead of looking back at the past with nostalgia, the opportunity that we must all seize together is to imagine a Great Safety Net 2.0 that is more in line with the Entrepreneurial Age. Doing that well requires serious, determined input from many parties, including tech entrepreneurs and venture capitalists. The world will remain open and business will flourish only if pro-business policies go hand-in-hand with building the Great Safety Net 2.0. Once again, it's about making what Will Wilkinson calls *"the freedom lover's case for the welfare state"*[10].

Now, the Great Safety Net is a complex solution to a complex set of problems. And as stated by John Gall in his landmark (and fun) book *Systemantics*, we can't try to design a complex system from the start:

"A complex system that works is invariably found to have evolved from a simple system that worked. A complex system designed from scratch never works and cannot be patched up to make it work. You have to start over with a working simple system."[11]

It's easy enough to draw the Great Safety Net 2.0 on the back of a napkin. But once the overall concept becomes clear, the challenge isn't to build the entire macro mechanism in just one round. Rather it is to invent solutions to an infinity of simple problems in fields as diverse as lifelong training, occupational licensing, housing, transportation, consumer finance, insurance, the tax system, collective bargaining, and many others.

Entrepreneurs have a lot to contribute in that regard. Their obsession is not with expressing ideas but with implementing them. Many good entrepreneurs are unable to easily explain what they do because their primary focus is on building things. Why not harness that unrivaled capacity to build things and have entrepreneurs build the Great Safety Net 2.0 one piece at a time?

It doesn't mean that governments have no role to play—quite the contrary. But my overall impression is that we've witnessed a sharp reversal in who has the capacity to explore, discover, and deliver. In the past, only governments could break the constraints and pull it off at a large scale. Now it looks like governments (at least in the West) are stuck in bureaucratic inertia and partisan gridlock at the very moment when entrepreneurs allied with the multitude are best positioned to harness the power of ubiquitous computing and networks.

The US is probably the most saddening case. It's both unable and unwilling to explore the path to building a Great Safety Net 2.0. At best, a significant part of the US electorate is deluded into thinking that they can restore the Great Safety Net of the past. At worst, as in the case of Donald Trump and the Republican Party, it's actively working on dismantling it. Only in certain limited if large parts of the country such as California can we see the signs of radical imagination[12]. It's a reason for hope, but hardly a sign that the US as a whole is ready for a collective radical effort.

Europe is another story. I think my continent is marked by a genuine attachment to the idea of promoting economic security and prosperity simultaneously. However the absence of a thriving local tech industry makes it difficult to promote the narrative of Europe leading the way into the socio-institutional phase of the Entrepreneurial Age. Not only is it not forward-looking enough, it's also encumbered by the remains of the Great Safety Net of the past. We Europeans were once the most advanced in sustained prosperity and economic security. But now it's as if we're condemned to lag behind as the new great surge of development forces us to revisit our entire socio-institutional framework.

Meanwhile, China is making progress in building its own version of the *Greater Safety Net for the Entrepreneurial Age*. The Chinese government may not be interested in embracing Western liberal democratic values. Yet the flourishing of the People's Republic depends on the majority of citizens sharing the fruits of prosperity with a reasonable level of economic security. So just as the American Republic saved itself with the New Deal from 1933 onward, China has a vital interest in deploying a Great Safety Net 2.0, as it is a necessary condition for the perpetuation of the Communist Party and the flourishing of the People's Republic. And the Chinese government knows it[13].

Why does it matter for us Westerners? Because as discussed in Chapter 3, China is racing ahead in making the most of the techno-economic paradigm of the day. The Chinese version of the Great Safety Net 2.0 could very well serve as a precedent and inspiration for all countries interested in combining economic security and prosperity in the Entrepreneurial Age. The problem is that it would lead to a very different global socio-institutional framework in terms of liberal democratic values than most in the West would find desirable.

Having ideas is not enough to create the durable and lasting institutions that would form a new Great Safety Net. Building such institutions is usually a long and painful fight, rooted in a clear and intimate understanding of what the new techno-economic paradigm is about and led in a strategic manner over the long term. We owe the Great Safety Net of the past mostly to the labor movement, which fought for more than a century to force both employers and governments to provide workers with economic security and a fair share of value added. The key players in that fight were not the intellectuals who wrote books and spoke at conferences. They were union leaders and activists who lived and worked at the forefront of the new age, organized against powerful adverse forces, established a balance of power with other parties, and sacrificed a great deal over the course of this long quest—including, in some cases, their own lives.

What's more, the violence and destruction didn't stop with clashes between unions and various forces of the established order. The consensus around the Great Safety Net of the age of the automobile and mass production was also a result of the widespread geo-political violence that swept away the decrepit institutions of the nineteenth-century age of steel and heavy engineering. The war effort in the US as well as the post-war *tabula rasa* in Europe and Japan freed the leaders of those countries from the dilemma of dealing with legacy policies and institutions. In the wake of two world wars, it was simply impossible to hold to the illusions of the past.

I certainly don't wish for people to die as a price to pay in designing and implementing the Great Safety Net 2.0. But the importance of starting at the bottom when addressing elementary problems and completely redefining the status quo is the reason why I think imagining this Great Safety Net 2.0 is a challenge that entrepreneurs should tackle. They know what it's like to start from zero and move up, fast. They need to find ways to reverse the *"tech backlash"* that puts their businesses at risk. They can maximize the fast spread of knowledge, which makes it easier to design and implement large-scale solutions to today's many problems. They intuitively understand the mighty multitude, always the entrepreneurs' best ally when it comes to radical innovation and delivering quality at scale.

The needed Western version of the *Greater Safety Net for the Entrepreneurial Age* won't rise from a magic-bullet mechanism such as universal basic income. It won't emerge from the murky depths of exhausted neoliberal or libertarian thinking. It won't be born from the top-down technocratic approach of most progressive government officials. In this new age, entrepreneurs look like the ones best positioned to do the hard, dirty work with levers such as technology and the multitude rather than weapons and propaganda.

If we only look at how history has progressed to this point, one would be forgiven for coming to the conclusion that a new World War is needed before we can radically upgrade the Great Safety Net from 1.0 to 2.0. But if we also look at the new tools furnished by today's technology, one could decide that another path is possible. I, for one, believe we should all bet on the latter, and hope this book serves as a contribution that tilts the odds in our favor.

TAKING ACTION: GETTING TO A GREATER SAFETY NET

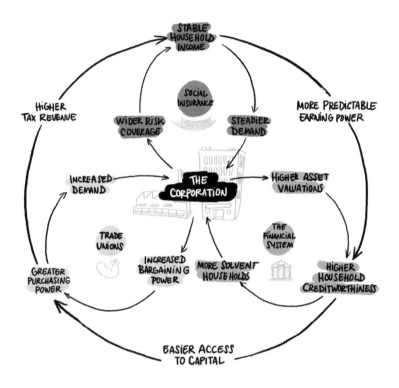

THE GREAT SAFETY NET 1.0
(AGE OF THE AUTOMOBILE & MASS PRODUCTION)

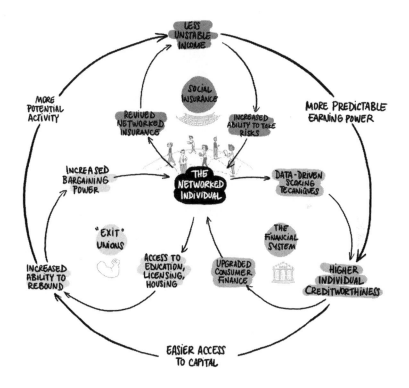

THE GREAT SAFETY NET 2.0
(ENTREPRENEURIAL AGE)

Acknowledgments

I would like to first express my love and gratitude to my wife Laetitia Vitaud. Over the past 12 years, she has been so much to me: a friend, a lover, a teacher, a supporter, a fellow traveller, a comrade-in-arms, a co-author, an advisor. This book, to which she contributed a great deal, is dedicated to her and our two inspiring children Béatrice and Ferdinand, as well as to my late uncle Eckhard Strohschänk.

Hedge also wouldn't exist without the contributions and support of my cofounders at The Family. Oussama Ammar had the idea of my writing a book addressing the tech industry on issues related to the safety net. Alice Zagury, CEO of The Family, has been an astute contributor in topics ranging from branding and positioning to making sure that the book would be readable beyond the small circle of policy wonks. I'm deeply indebted to Alice and Oussama's friendship and support. We still have a lot to do together to turn The Family into something even greater and I very much look forward to it.

Instrumental were those who encouraged the project from the start and were here all along to contribute with remarks and advice. I'm especially grateful to William H. Janeway for being an informal advisor, even approaching something close to a research director. Five years ago, Bill's own book, *Doing Capitalism in the Innovation Economy*, opened my eyes to the importance of bringing institutional discussions into the tech world. Later on, as we got to know each other, he contributed with advice on positioning my book and was among the few who read through the entire manuscript.

I'm also immensely grateful to Carlota Perez, who since 2016 has offered continuous guidance during rich conversations over meals at her favorite Thai restaurant in Lewes (Sussex). In many aspects, this book is a tribute to and a furtherance of her foundational work *Technological Revolutions and Financial Capital*. Carlota has helped a great deal in my writing *Hedge*, despite having quite a lot on her own plate. The tribute I wanted to pay to her has been returned tenfold by her kind and inspiring support.

No book is the work of one person only. During the past 18 months, I've enjoyed the help and support of key people in my team. Kyle Hall has been a masterful reviewer and editor, contributing with much more than correcting my language. Laurène Tran has been another pillar of this enterprise, assisting me with research, marketing, the tedious process of publishing, and her unique talent at spotting interesting people, works and ideas. Before her, Virgile Goyet helped bring a first, rough manuscript into existence, which was then reviewed by Sandrine Lacout. Finally, Camille Dubreuil and Camille Rigou-Chemin have contributed by creating the book's beautiful cover and helping with design choices.

Beyond The Family, Florent Masson has dedicated himself as an informal outside editor, contributing with thorough remarks. Martin Schmidbaur has also been involved in reviewing the manuscript, providing enthusiasm and support on top of crucial editing and marketing insights. Julie Colin did a wonderful job laying out the book. The brilliant Marguerite Deneuville drew all the illustrations to help me make many ideas clearer for a wide audience—a task for which I owe her a great deal! I'm also thankful to Miranda Bertram for her help in burnishing the book's storytelling and presentation.

Many others have been part of the writing process through in-depth discussions or by reviewing some of the book's draft chapters. I'm especially thankful to Kim-Mai Cutler, D-J Collins, Sarah O'Connor, Vivek Wadhwa, and Philippe Suchet, as well as Younès Rharbaoui, Jasper Sala, and Emilie Maret. I have also benefited from the supportive efforts of Chris Lehane, Guy Levin, Daniel Korski, John Thornhill, Alex Margot-Duclos, Philippe Platon, Marc-David Choukroun, Jonathan Hall, Balaji S. Srinivasan, Tim O'Reilly, Azeem Azhar, Eric Schmidt, Nick Clegg, J. Bradford Delong, and Marc Andreessen.

Writing a book on the safety net with a mostly American perspective wouldn't have been possible without all those who have had an influence on me in social policy, American studies, and politics and policy in general. I'm especially thankful to Hayet Zeggar, Gwénaële Calvès, the late Richard Descoings, Thierry Bert, Cyril Piquemal, Jérôme Marchand-Arvier, Elise Colette, Maxime Marzin, Gérôme Truc, Laurent Bigorgne, Patrick Weil, Pascal Saint-Amans, Thierry Pech, Laurent Cytermann, and my parents Thérèse Bécue and Jean-Marie Colin.

Learning more about China has been made easier by the incredible support of Jean-Jacques Augier, Wang Dadong, Zhang Wei, Mylène Hardy-Zhang, Fanglu Sun, Justin Vaïsse, Sébastien Badault,

François Godement, Nicolas de Mascarel, Alisée Pornet, Geoffrey Harris, Benjamin Joffe, Romain Aubert, and Yann Pouëzat.

Also influential were those who've guided me into the world of tech policy through advice and shared works: Charlotte Baratin, Pauline Mispoulet, Sébastien Soriano, Yann Algan, Andrew Wyckoff, Dirk Pilat, Teddy Pellerin, Lionel Ferreira, Grégory Edberg, Vicki Nash, Nathalie Collin, Augustin Landier, Anne Perrot, Pierre Mohnen, Bénédicte Tilloy, Duc Ha Duong, Yanai Zaicik, Raffaele Russo, Jérôme Giusti, Pierre Collin, Pierre Pezziardi, Alexandre Pikiakos, Patrick Zelnik, Jacques Toubon, Guillaume Cerutti, Constance Rivière, Jean-Marc Benoit, Godefroy Dang Nguyen, and Ioannis Kanellos.

Many thanks also go to Béatrice Lecerf, Richard Straub, Sophie Fay, Dominique Nora, Jonathan Derbyshire, Anne-Sylvaine Chassany, Philippe Escande, Antoine Reverchon, Renaud Thillaye, Sophie Pedder, and Matthieu Croissandeau for providing me with various opportunities to share my thoughts.

A special mention goes to Henri Verdier, as our book *L'Âge de la multitude* became the natural precursor to this one, and to my old accomplice Bruno Palier, with whom I published an article in *Foreign Affairs* in 2015 called "The Next Safety Net". In a way, those were the works that started it all!

Hedge is the result of all these wonderful relationships and interactions; any errors remain, of course, my own.

Notes

Introduction—From Europe With Love

1. Carlota Perez, *Technological Revolutions and Financial Capital: The Dynamics of Bubbles and Golden Ages* (Cheltenham: Edward Elgar Publishing, 2003), 165.

2. Nicolas Colin, "Les fossoyeurs de l'innovation," republished with a foreword February 18, 2016 (in French), https://salon.thefamily.co/les-fossoyeurs-de-l-innovation-6a754d1e8e35.

3. Bryan Burrough and John Helyar, Barbarians at the Gate: *The Fall of RJR Nabisco* (New York: Harper & Row, 1989).

Chapter 1—The Tech Backlash

1. Matt Bai, "What Steve Jobs Understood That Our Politicians Don't," *The New York Times,* October 6, 2011, https://thecaucus.blogs.nytimes.com/2011/10/06/what-steve-jobs-understood-that-our-politicians-dont/.

2. In 1998, at the peak of the optimism inspired by the *"new economy"*, the Bureau of Labor Statistics (BLS) predicted that 1.87 million jobs would be created in IT services by 2008, but just over 500,000 were actually created, even before the 2008 financial crisis. In communications, 150,000 jobs were destroyed by productivity gains, while the BLS had forecast the creation of nearly 300,000 additional jobs. Marc Giget, "Réflexions autour de l'innovation industrielle", *Le numérique dans la réindustrialisation*, Rencontres de Cap Digital, March 27, 2012, http://www.dailymotion.com/video/xsnbn5.

3. Pierre Collin and Nicolas Colin, "Taxation and the Digital Economy" (Task force report commissioned by the French Government, January 2013), https://www.dropbox.com/s/6w2divhpv3dcegj/Taxation_Digital_Economy.pdf?dl=0.

4. Jesse Drucker, "Google 2.4% Rate Shows How $60 Billion Is Lost to Tax Loopholes," *Bloomberg*, 2010, July 21, https://www.bloomberg.com/news/articles/2010-10-21/google-2-4-rate-shows-how-60-billion-u-s-revenue-lost-to-tax-loopholes.

5. Tim O'Reilly, "This New York Times piece on the Amazon-Cali-

fornia sales tax dispute," Google Plus, September 5, 2011, https://plus.
google.com/+TimOReilly/posts/QypNDmvJJq7.

6. Erik Brynjolfsson & Andrew McAfee, *The Second Machine Age:
Work, Progress, and Prosperity in a Time of Brilliant Technologies* (New
York: W. W. Norton & Company, 2014).

7. Matt Novak, "Did Al Gore Invent the Internet?," *Gizmodo*,
October 18, 2013, http://paleofuture.gizmodo.com/did-al-gore-invent-
the-internet-1447761524.

8. Jeff Madrick, *Age of Greed: The Triumph of Finance and the
Decline of America, 1970 to the Present*, Reprint edition (New York:
Vintage Books, 2012).

9. Thomas Ferguson and Joel Rogers, *Right Turn: The Decline of
the Democrats and the Future of American Politics* (New York: Hill &
Wang, 1987), 46-48.

10. Ira Katznelson, *Fear Itself: The New Deal and the Origins of Our
Time* (New York: Liveright, 2014).

11. Molly Reden, "Wall Street Failed To Crush The Democrats.
Now What?," *The New Republic*, November 6, 2012, https://www.
evernote.com/l/AOzuzVbsa7BBo4bjT3NT5Wu2FJ2YK1C_9oI.

12. Jonathan D. Salant, "Goldman Sachs Leads Split With Obama,
as GE Jilts Him Too," *Bloomberg*, August 9, 2012, https://www.
bloomberg.com/news/articles/2012-08-09/goldman-sachs-leads-split-
with-obama-as-ge-jilts-him-too.

13. Rahaf Arfoush, *Yes We Did! An inside look at how social media
built the Obama brand* (San Francisco: New Riders, 2009).

14. Carla Marinucci, "Bay Area money fills Obama campaign
coffers," *The San Francisco Chronicle*, November 3, 2012, https://
www.sfgate.com/politics/article/Bay-Area-money-fills-Obama-cam-
paign-coffers-4005151.php.

15. Nate Silver, "In Silicon Valley, Technology Talent Gap Threatens
G.O.P. Campaigns," *FiveThirtyEight*, November 28, 2012, https://
fivethirtyeight.blogs.nytimes.com/2012/11/28/in-silicon-valley-tech-
nology-talent-gap-threatens-g-o-p-campaigns/.

16.   Steven Brill, "Obama's Trauma Team," *Time*, February 27, 2014, http://time.com/10228/obamas-trauma-team/.

17.   Alas only Travis Kalanick, then CEO of Uber, once voiced the express support that others tech executives ultimately chose to keep for themselves. See Erin Mershon, "Uber and the gig economy used to love Obamacare. What happened?," *Stat*, July 20, 2017, https://www.statnews.com/2017/07/20/uber-lyft-gig-economy-obamacare/.

18.   The Economist, "Fighting fit: Obamacare is inspiring a horde of hopeful entrepreneurs," *The Economist,* December 1, 2012, https://www.economist.com/news/business/21567402-obamacare-inspiring-horde-hopeful-entrepreneurs-fighting-fit.

19.   Jonathan Chait, "Looking to Harry Truman to Understand Hillary Clinton," *New York Magazine*, May 17, 2016, http://nymag.com/daily/intelligencer/2016/05/harry-truman-hillary-clinton.html.

20.   Nicolas Colin, "Hillary's Problem, Explained by Technology," *The Family Papers*, July 18, 2016, https://salon.thefamily.co/software-eating-politics-the-case-for-picking-elizabeth-warren-3c22477c5d9a.

21.   Henry Kissinger, *On China* (New York: Penguin Books, 2012).

22.   Martin Jacques, *When China Rules the World* (New York: Penguin Books, 2012).

23.   Evan Osnos, "Making China Great Again," *The New Yorker*, January 8, 2018, https://www.newyorker.com/magazine/2018/01/08/making-china-great-again.

24.   National Committee on U.S.-China Relations, "Town Hall Meeting With Dr. Henry Kissinger," October 18, 2016, https://www.youtube.com/watch?v=dHoHN2Zgme (at 22:00).

25.   Martin Jacques, "One Belt One Road," *People's Daily*, May 12, 2017, http://www.martinjacques.com/articles/one-belt-one-road/.

26.   Roger Crowley, *Conquerors: How Portugal Forged The First Global Empire* (New York: Simon & Schuster, 2016).

27.   Carlota Perez, *Technological Revolutions and Financial Capital* (see Introduction, note 1).

28.   Martin Jacques, "The beginning of a new world order," *The New*

Statesman, April 18, 2012, http://www.martinjacques.com/essays/the-beginning-of-a-new-world-order/.

Chapter 2—Technology and Institutional Change

1.   Adam Davidson, "Welcome to the Failure Age!," *The New York Times,* November 12, 2014, https://www.nytimes.com/2014/11/16/magazine/welcome-to-the-failure-age.html.

2.   William H. Janeway, *Doing Capitalism in the Innovation Economy: Reconfiguring the Three-Player Game between Markets, Speculators and the State,* 2nd edition (Cambridge: Cambridge University Press, 2018), 229.

3.   Erik S. Reinert and Benjamin Sagalovsky, "Carlota Perez—Her Biography and the Origins of Her Ideas," *Techno-Economic Paradigms, Essays in Honour of Carlota Perez* (London: Anthem Press, The Other Canon, 2009).

4.   Carlota Perez, *Technological Revolutions and Financial Capital* (see Introduction, note 1).

5.   Fred Wilson, "The Carlota Perez Framework," *AVC,* February 8, 2015, http://avc.com/2015/02/the-carlota-perez-framework/.

6.   Alexia Tsotsis, "Marc Andreessen: Tech Is Still Recovering From A Depression," *TechCrunch,* February 12, 2014, https://techcrunch.com/2014/02/12/marc-andreessen-tech-is-still-recovering-from-a-depression/.

7.   Chris Dixon, "The computing deployment phase," *cdixon blog,* February 10, 2013, http://cdixon.org/2013/02/10/the-computing-deployment-phase/.

8.   Carlota Perez, "The Double Bubble at the Turn of the Century: Technological Roots and Structural Implications," *Cambridge Journal of Economics* 33, no. 4 (July 2009), https://www.researchgate.net/publication/227464491_The_Double_Bubble_at_the_Turn_of_the_Century_Technological_Roots_and_Structural_Implications.

9.   Carlota Perez, *Technological Revolutions and Financial Capital,* 8 (see Introduction, note 1).

10.   Robert Wilde, "Canals Were at Their Height during the Indus-

trial Revolution. This Is Why," *ThoughtCo*, November 24, 2016, https://www.thoughtco.com/development-of-canals-the-industrial-revolution-1221646.

11. Edmund S. Phelps, *Mass Flourishing: How Grassroots Innovation Created Jobs, Challenge, and Change,* 1st edition (Princeton: Princeton University Press, 2013).

12. Frank Dobbin, *Forging Industrial Policy: The United States, Britain, and France in the Railway Age* (Cambridge: Cambridge University Press, 1997).

13. Daniel Yergin, *The Prize: The Epic Quest for Oil, Money & Power,* Reissue edition (New York: Free Press, 2008).

14. Olivier Zunz, *Why the American Century?,* 1st edition (Chicago: University Of Chicago Press, 1998).

15. Leslie Berlin, *The Man Behind the Microchip: Robert Noyce and the Invention of Silicon Valley,* 1st edition (New York; Oxford: Oxford University Press, 2006).

16. Matt Novak, "Did Al Gore Invent the Internet?" (see Chapter 1, note 7).

17. See "Ten Theses on the Multitude and Post-Fordist Capitalism" in Paolo Virno, *A Grammar of the Multitude: For an Analysis of Contemporary Forms of Life,* trans. (Cambridge, MA ; London: Semiotext, 2004).

18. Friedrich A. Hayek, "The Use of Knowledge in Society," *The American Economic Review* 35, no. 4 (September 1945), http://home.uchicago.edu/~vlima/courses/econ200/spring01/hayek.pdf.

19. André Gorz, *The Immaterial,* trans. Chris Turner (London: Seagull Books, 2010).

20. Carl Shapiro and Hal R. Varian, *Information Rules: A Strategic Guide to the Network Economy* (Cambridge, MA: Harvard Business School Press, 1998).

21. Don Tapscott, *The Digital Economy, Anniversary Edition: Rethinking Promise and Peril in the Age of Networked Intelligence,* 2d edition (New York: McGraw-Hill Education, 2014).

22. Tim O'Reilly, "Next:Economy Summit: Future of Work Confer-

ence" (San Francisco: *O'Reilly Media*, 2016), https://conferences. oreilly.com/nextcon/economy-us.

23.   Ben Casselman, "Americans Don't Miss Manufacturing — They Miss Unions," *FiveThirtyEight*, May 13, 2016, https:// fivethirtyeight.com/features/americans-dont-miss-manufacturing-they-miss-unions/.

24.   Amy Bernstein and Anand Raman, "The Great Decoupling: An Interview with Erik Brynjolfsson and Andrew McAfee," *Harvard Business Review*, June 1, 2015, https://hbr.org/2015/06/the-great-decoupling.

25.   Bryan Appleyard, "The New Luddites: Why Former Digital Prophets Are Turning Against Tech," *The New Republic*, September 6, 2014, https://newrepublic.com/article/119347/neo-luddisms-tech-skepticism.

26.   Nelson Lichtenstein, *State of the Union: A Century of American Labor,* Revised and Expanded edition with a new preface and two new chapters by the author (Princeton, New Jersey: Princeton University Press, 2013), 23.

27.   Karl Polanyi, *The Great Transformation: The Political and Economic Origins of Our Time,* 2nd edition (Boston, MA: Beacon Press, 2001).

28.   Patrick Iber and Mike Konczal, "Karl Polanyi for President," *Dissent Magazine,* May 23, 2016, https://www.dissentmagazine.org/online_articles/karl-polanyi-explainer-great-transformation-bernie-sanders.

29.   Patrick Iber and Mike Konczal, *Ibid.*

30.   Karl Polanyi, *The Great Transformation,* 21 (see note 27).

31.   "Upton Sinclair's The Jungle: Muckraking the Meat-Packing Industry," *Constitutional Rights Foundation,* Fall 2008 (Volume 24, No. 1), accessed April 20, 2017, http://www.crf-usa.org/bill-of-rights-in-action/bria-24-1-b-upton-sinclairs-the-jungle-muckraking-the-meat-packing-industry.html.

32.   Karl Polanyi, *The Great Transformation,* foreword (see note 27).

33.   Karl Polanyi, *Ibid.*, foreword.

34.   Will Wilkinson, "The Freedom Lover's Case for the Welfare State,"

Vox, September 1, 2016, https://www.vox.com/2016/9/1/12732168/economic-freedom-score-america-welfare-state.

35.   Nelson Lichtenstein, *State of the Union*, 25 (see note 26).

36.   Nelson Lichtenstein, *Ibid.*, 6, 32.

37.   David Leonhardt, "The Economics of Henry Ford May Be Passé," *The New York Times*, April 5, 2006, https://www.nytimes.com/2006/04/05/business/the-economics-of-henry-ford-may-be-passe.html.

38.   Daniel Gross, "Henry Ford Understood That Raising Wages Would Bring Him More Profit," *The Daily Beast,* January 6, 2014, https://www.thedailybeast.com/henry-ford-understood-that-raising-wages-would-bring-him-more-profit.

39.   Albert O. Hirschman, *Exit, Voice, and Loyalty: Responses to Decline in Firms, Organizations, and States* (Cambridge, MA: Harvard University Press, 1970).

40.   Jonathan Cohn, "How They Did It," *The New Republic*, May 21, 2010, https://newrepublic.com/article/75077/how-they-did-it.

41.   Carlota Perez, *Technological Revolutions and Financial Capital*, 153 (see Introduction, note 1).

42.   Patrick Iber and Mike Konczal, "Karl Polanyi for President" (28 note 59).

Chapter 3—Stuck in the Dark Ages

1.   Karl Polanyi, *The Great Transformation*, 246 (see Chapter 2, note 27).

2.   Simon Kuper, "The Great Middle-Class Identity Crisis," *The Financial Times*, November 8, 2013, https://www.ft.com/content/04179370-4741-11e3-b4d3-00144feabdc0.

3.   Robert M. Solow, "Hayek, Friedman, and the Illusions of Conservative Economics," *The New Republic*, November 16, 2012, https://newrepublic.com/article/110196/hayek-friedman-and-the-illusions-conservative-economics.

4.   To be more precise: Keynesianism under the form of Paul Samuelson's neoclassical synthesis. See William H. Janeway, *Doing Capitalism*

in the Innovation Economy, 15 (see Chapter 2, note 2).

5.   William H. Janeway, *Ibid.,* 227-229, 361-363.

6.   Matthew Yglesias, "The tax reform debate is stuck in the 1970s," *Vox,* November 14, 2017, https://www.vox.com/policy-and-politics/2017/11/14/16634930/tax-reform-debate-stuck-1970s.

7.   Markus K. Brunnermeier, Harold James and Jean-Pierre Landau, *The Euro and the Battle of Ideas* (Princeton, NJ: Princeton University Press, 2016).

8.   William H. Janeway, *Doing Capitalism in the Innovation Economy,* 175 (see Chapter 2, note 2).

9.   Mark Blyth, *Great Transformations: Economic Ideas and Institutional Change in the Twentieth Century* (New York: Cambridge University Press, 2002).

10.   Noah Smith, "Free-Market Failure Has Been Greatly Exaggerated," *Bloomberg View,* November 15, 2017, https://www.bloomberg.com/view/articles/2017-11-15/free-markets-improved-more-lives-than-anything-ever.

11.   Kevin Drum, "Want a More Dynamic Economy? Rein in the Size of Big Market Incumbents," *Mother Jones,* June 21, 2016, http://www.motherjones.com/kevin-drum/2016/06/want-more-dynamic-economy-rein-size-big-market-incumbents.

12.   Pankaj Ghemawat, "Competition and Business Strategy in Historical Perspective," *Business History Review* 76, no. 1 (Spring 2002).

13.   David Weil, *The Fissured Workplace: Why Work Became So Bad for So Many and What Can Be Done to Improve It* (Cambridge, MA: Harvard University Press, 2014).

14.   Nelson Lichtenstein, *State of the Union,* 48 (see Chapter 2, note 26).

15.   Sarah Krouse and Austen Hufford, "BlackRock Assets Pass $5 Trillion as Earnings Climb," *The Wall Street Journal,* October 18, 2016, http://www.wsj.com/articles/blackrock-earnings-rise-as-assets-under-management-peak-1476788361.

16.   Clayton M. Christensen, Stephen P. Kaufman, and Willy C. Shih, "Innovation Killers: How Financial Tools Destroy Your Capacity to Do

New Things," *Harvard Business Review*, January 1, 2008, https://hbr. org/2008/01/innovation-killers-how-financial-tools-destroy-your-ca- pacity-to-do-new-things.

17. Edmund S. Phelps, "Mass Flourishing: How It Was Won, and Then Lost," *Reuters Blogs*, August 16, 2013, http://blogs.reuters.com/ great-debate/2013/08/16/mass-flourishing-how-it-was-won-and-then- lost/.

18. Thomas Piketty, *Capital in the Twenty First Century*, trans. Arthur Goldhammer (Cambridge, MA: Belknap Press, 2014).

19. Jacob S. Hacker, *The Great Risk Shift: The New Economic Inse- curity and the Decline of the American Dream*, Revised edition (Oxford: Oxford University Press, 2008).

20. John B. Judis, *The Populist Explosion: How the Great Recession Transformed American and European Politics* (New York: Columbia Global Reports, 2016).

21. Rana Foroohar, *Makers and Takers: The Rise of Finance and the Fall of American Business*, First edition (New York: Crown Business, 2016).

22. Clayton M. Christensen, "A Capitalist's Dilemma, Whoever Wins the Election," *The New York Times*, November 3, 2012, http:// www.nytimes.com/2012/11/04/business/a-capitalists-dilemma-who- ever-becomes-president.html.

23. Jonathan Chait, "Barack Obama's Legacy Is More Secure Than You, or the GOP, Think," *The New York Magazine*, January 10, 2017, http://nymag.com/daily/intelligencer/2017/01/obama-legacy-more-se- cure-than-you-think.html.

24. Jacob Hacker, "The New Economic Insecurity—And What Can Be Done About It," *Harvard Law & Policy Review*, vol. 1, 2007, http:// www.hlpronline.com/Vol1No1/hacker.pdf.

25. Jacob Hacker, *Ibid.*

26. Alana Semuels, "This Is What Life Without Retirement Savings Looks Like," *The Atlantic*, February 22, 2018, https://www. theatlantic.com/business/archive/2018/02/pensions-safety-net-cali- fornia/553970/.

27. Steve Blank, "What's a Startup? First Principles," *Steve Blank's Blog*, January 25, 2010, https://steveblank.com/2010/01/25/whats-a-startup-first-principles/.

28. Rebecca Traister, "Single Women Are Now the Most Potent Political Force in America," *New York Magazine*, February 22, 2016, http://nymag.com/thecut/2016/02/political-power-single-women-c-v-r.html.

29. Enrico Moretti, *The New Geography of Jobs* (Boston: Mariner Books, 2012).

30. Vanessa Brown Calder, "Why Do People Move and Why Don't They?," *Cato at Liberty*, Cato Institute, November 3, 2017, https://www.cato.org/blog/why-do-people-move-why-dont-they.

31. Nelson Lichtenstein, *State of the Union*, 32 (see Chapter 2, note 26).

32. Nelson Lichtenstein, *Ibid.*, 25.

33. Kevin Drum, "Why Screwing Unions Screws the Entire Middle Class," *Mother Jones*, April 2011, http://www.motherjones.com/politics/2011/02/income-inequality-labor-union-decline.

34. Kevin Drum, *Ibid.*

35. Adam Davidson, "Welcome to the Failure Age!" (see Chapter 2, note 32).

36. Pankaj Ghemawat, "Competition and Business Strategy in Historical Perspective" (see note 12).

37. "Global Value Chains," https://www.oecd.org, accessed March 29, 2017, https://www.oecd.org/sti/ind/global-value-chains.htm.

38. David Weil, *The Fissured Workplace* (see note 13).

39. Sara Horowitz, "America, Say Goodbye to the Era of Big Work," *The Los Angeles Times*, August 25, 2014, http://www.latimes.com/opinion/op-ed/la-oe-horowitz-work-freelancers-20140826-story.html.

40. David Leonhardt, "The Economics of Henry Ford May Be Passé" (see Chapter 2, note 37).

41. Colin Crouch, "Privatised Keynesianism: An Unacknowledged Policy Regime," *The British Journal of Politics & International Relations* 11, no. 3 (August 1, 2009): 382–99.

42. Louis Hartz, *The Liberal Tradition in America* (San Diego: Harvest Books, 1991).

43. David Roberts, "The US coal industry is going out, not with a whimper, but with a burst of rent-seeking," *Vox*, August 26, 2017, https://www.vox.com/energy-and-environment/2017/8/25/16201218/us-coal-industry-handouts.

44. Alan Wolfe, "Nobody Here but Us Liberals," *The New York Times*, July 3, 2005, http://www.nytimes.com/2005/07/03/books/review/nobody-here-but-us-liberals.html.

45. Nicolas Colin, "A Valley Divided: Do Startups Widen the Inequality Gap?," *The Family Papers*, February 4, 2016, https://salon.thefamily.co/a-valley-divided-do-startups-widen-the-inequality-gap-7bb783237eb8.

46. Julia Belluz, "Why the white middle class is dying faster, explained in 6 charts," *Vox*, March 23, 2017, https://www.vox.com/science-and-health/2017/3/23/14988084/white-middle-class-dying-faster-explained-case-deaton.

47. German Lopez, "The opioid epidemic, explained," *Vox*, August 3, 2017, https://www.vox.com/science-and-health/2017/8/3/16079772/opioid-epidemic-drug-overdoses.

48. Lynn Parramore, "America is Regressing into a Developing Nation for Most People," Institute for New Economic Thinking, April 20, 2017, https://www.ineteconomics.org/perspectives/blog/america-is-regressing-into-a-developing-nation-for-most-people.

49. Thomas Hale, "Saving for old age: the global story (part II)," *The Financial Times*, February 14, 2018, https://ftalphaville.ft.com/2018/02/14/2198793/saving-for-old-age-the-global-story-part-ii/.

50. Chun Han Wong & Eva Dou, "Foreign Companies in China Get a New Partner: The Communist Party," *The Wall Street Journal*, October 29, 2017, https://www.wsj.com/articles/foreign-companies-in-china-get-a-new-partner-the-communist-party-1509297523.

51. Don Weinland, "Deregulation creates China consumer loans boom," *The Financial Times*, July 23, 2017, https://www.ft.com/content/9d7d9460-5cb4-11e7-9bc8-8055f264aa8b.

52.   Lulu Yilun Chen, "Why Tencent and Sequoia Are Pouring Millions Into China's Rental Space," *Bloomberg*, January 28, 2018, https://www.bloomberg.com/news/articles/2018-01-29/china-s-start-ups-use-technology-to-target-young-renters-vc-cash.

53.   Linda Lew, "How Tencent's medical ecosystem is shaping the future of China's healthcare," *Technode*, February 11, 2018, https://technode.com/2018/02/11/tencent-medical-ecosystem/.

54.   Simina Mistreanu, "Life Inside China's Social Credit Laboratory," *Foreign Policy*, April 3, 2018, http://foreignpolicy.com/2018/04/03/life-inside-chinas-social-credit-laboratory/.

55.   Kevin Rudd, "On China's Rise and a New World Order," conference at La Trobe University, October 26, 2017, https://www.youtube.com/watch?v=psErow4xaIo.

56.   Kevin Rudd, *Ibid.*

57.   Laetitia Vitaud, "Back To Craftsmanship: Lessons from the Arts and Crafts Movement," *Medium*, June 6, 2017, https://medium.com/want-more-work/back-to-craftsmanship-lessons-from-the-arts-and-crafts-movement-e1aa5f09ec16.

58.   Oussama Ammar, "No Passport Needed: Launching in Internet Nation," The Family, October 17, 2016, https://salon.thefamily.co/no-passport-needed-launching-in-internet-nation-27440ff5a9e4.

59.   Balaji Srinivasan, "Software Is Reorganizing the World," *Wired*, November 2013, https://www.wired.com/2013/11/software-is-reorganizing-the-world-and-cloud-formations-could-lead-to-physical-nations/.

60.   Benedict Anderson, *Imagined Communities: Reflections on the Origin and Spread of Nationalism* (London: Verso Book, 2016).

Chapter 4—Entrepreneurs and the New Corporate World

1.   Babak Nivi, "No Tradeoff between Quality and Scale," *Venture Hacks*, February 18, 2013, http://venturehacks.com/articles/there-is-no-finish-line-for-entrepreneurs.

2.   The Family, *La Transition numérique au coeur des territoires*, 2014, https://www.dropbox.com/s/n2wxkkxdrkw9xz4/TheFamily_

Territoires.pdf?dl=0 (in French).

3. A critical source was Steve Blank, "The Secret History of Silicon Valley," *Steve Blank's Blog*, March 23, 2009, https://www. evernote.com/shard/s236/sh/2152575f-0376-470b-87c6-e2c78f-c0f584/8ae24372478485aa.

4. Olivier Zunz, *Why the American Century?*, 8 (see Chapter 2, note 14).

5. Olivier Zunz, *Ibid.*, 9.

6. Naomi R. Lamoreaux and Kenneth L. Sokoloff, eds., *Financing Innovation in the United States, 1870 to Present*, Reprint edition (Cambridge, MA: The MIT Press, 2009).

7. Naomi R. Lamoreaux and Kenneth L. Sokoloff, "Inventors, Firms, and the Market for Technology in the Late Nineteenth and Early Twentieth Centuries," Working Paper (National Bureau of Economic Research, April 1997), http://www.nber.org/papers/h0098.

8. Carlota Perez, *Technological Revolutions and Financial Capital*, 11 (see Introduction, note 1).

9. Tim Wu and Will Oremus, "The Great American Information Emperors," *Slate*, November 7, 2010, http://www.slate.com/articles/technology/technology/features/2010/the_great_american_information_emperors/how_theodore_vail_built_the_att_monopoly.html.

10. Steve Blank, "The Secret History of Silicon Valley" (see note 3).

11. Vannevar Bush, "Science: The Endless Frontier. A Report to the President" (Washington, DC, July 1945), https://www.nsf.gov/od/lpa/nsf50/vbush1945.htm.

12. Amar Bhidé, "Don't Expect Much From the R&D Tax Credit," *The Wall Street Journal*, September 11, 2010, http://www.wsj.com/articles/SB1000142405274870464404575481534193344088.

13. Paul A. Gompers, "The Rise and Fall of Venture Capital," *Business and Economic History*, Volume 23, no. 2, Winter 1994, http://www.thebhc.org/sites/default/files/beh/BEHprint/v023n2/p0001-p0026.pdf. See also Brad Feld, "Why The SBIC Doesn't Work For Venture Capital Anymore," *FeldThoughts*, July 28, 2014, https://www.feld.com/archives/2014/07/sbic-doesnt-work-venture-capital-anymore.html.

14. C. Stewart Gillmor, *Fred Terman at Stanford: Building a Discipline, a University, and Silicon Valley,* First edition (Palo Alto, CA: Stanford University Press, 2004).

15. Tom Wolfe, "The Tinkerings of Robert Noyce: How the Sun Rose on the Silicon Valley," *Esquire Magazine,* December 1983, https://web.stanford.edu/class/e145/2007_fall/materials/noyce.html.

16. Dan Gillmor and Daniel Gross, "Intel's Andy Grove Was Brilliant, Paranoid, and Prophetic. No Wonder Silicon Valley Reveres Him," *Slate,* March 22, 2016, http://www.slate.com/blogs/moneybox/2016/03/22/andy_grove_who_led_intel_has_died_he_was_brilliant_paranoid_and_prophetic.html.

17. Jaron Lanier, "Early Computing's Long, Strange Trip: A Book Review," *American Scientist,* August 2005, http://www.americanscientist.org/bookshelf/pub/early-computings-long-strange-trip.

18. Andrew S. Grove, *Only the Paranoid Survive* (London: Profile Books, 1998).

19. Clayton M. Christensen, *The Innovator's Dilemma: When New Technologies Cause Great Firms to Fail,* Reprint edition (Cambridge, MA: *Harvard Business Review* Press, 2016).

20. William H. Janeway, *Doing Capitalism in the Innovation Economy,* 45 (see Chapter 2, note 2).

21. William H. Janeway, *Ibid.,* 260-261.

22. Andrew McAfee and Erik Brynjolfsson, "Investing in the IT That Makes a Competitive Difference," *Harvard Business Review,* July 1, 2008, https://hbr.org/2008/07/investing-in-the-it-that-makes-a-competitive-difference.

23. The Economist, "Another Game of Thrones," *The Economist,* December 1, 2012, http://www.economist.com/news/21567361-google-apple-facebook-and-amazon-are-each-others-throats-all-sorts-ways-another-game.

24. Erik Brynjolfsson and Andrew McAfee, "The Big Data Boom Is the Innovation Story of Our Time," *The Atlantic,* November 21, 2011, https://www.theatlantic.com/business/archive/2011/11/the-big-data-boom-is-the-innovation-story-of-our-time/248215/.

25. Michael Mandel, "Scale and Innovation in Today's Economy," Progressive Policy Institute, December 2011, http://www.progressive-policy.org/wp-content/uploads/2011/12/12.2011-Mandel_Scale-and-Innovation-in-Todays-Economy.pdf.

26. William H. Janeway, *Doing Capitalism in the Innovation Economy*, 190 (see Chapter 2, note 2).

27. Babak Nivi, "No Tradeoff between Quality and Scale" (see note 1).

28. Carlota Perez, "Technological Revolutions and Techno-Economic Paradigms," *Working Papers in Technology Governance and Economic Dynamics* 20 (January 2009), http://technologygovernance.eu/files/main/2009070708552121.pdf.

29. Tim O'Reilly, "Gov 2.0: It's All About The Platform", *TechCrunch*, September 4, 2009, https://techcrunch.com/2009/09/04/gov-2-0-its-all-about-the-platform/.

30. Philip Evans, Patrick Forth, "Borges' Map: Navigating a World of Digital Disruption", *BCG Perspectives*, 2015, http://digitaldisrupt.bcgperspectives.com/.

31. Clayton M. Christensen, "A Capitalist's Dilemma, Whoever Wins the Election" (see Chapter 3, note 22).

32. Carlota Perez, "The Direction of Innovation after the Financial Collapse" (Technology, 9th Triple Helix Conference, Stanford, July 2011), https://www.slideshare.net/fredwilson/carlota-perez-talk-at.

33. Edmund S. Phelps, "Mass Flourishing: How It Was Won, and Then Lost" (see Chapter 3, note 17).

34. Steve Blank, "Fear of Failure and Lack of Speed In a Large Corporation," *Steve Blank's Blog*, March 11, 2015, https://steveblank.com/2015/03/11/fear-of-failure-and-lack-of-speed-in-a-large-corporation/.

35. Scott D. Anthony, "The New Corporate Garage," *Harvard Business Review*, September 1, 2012, https://hbr.org/2012/09/the-new-corporate-garage.

36. Brad Templeton, "On the Invention of the Internet," *Brad Ideas*, May 4, 2005, http://ideas.4brad.com/archives/000204.html.

37. Babak Nivi, "The Entrepreneurial Age," *Venture Hacks*,

February 25, 2013, http://venturehacks.com/articles/the-entrepreneurial-age.

38.   Susan Reid, "The Numbers Are In: Most People Want To Be Their Own Boss," *Forbes*, October 12, 2015, https://www.forbes.com/sites/susanreid/2015/10/12/the-numbers-are-in-most-people-want-to-be-their-own-boss/#62cf43071451.

39.   Simon Kuper, "The Great Middle-Class Identity Crisis" (see Chapter 3, note 2).

40.   Dominic Rossi, "The Global Savings Glut," Fidelity, May 2015, http://www.fidelity.com.au/insights-centre/investment-articles/the-global-savings-glut/.

41.   William H. Janeway, *Doing Capitalism in the Innovation Economy*, 52 (see Chapter 2, note 2).

42.   Tim O'Reilly, *WTF: What's the Future and Why It's Up to Us,* 1st edition (New York: Harper Business, 2017).

Chapter 5—Behind Entrepreneurs: The Multitude

1.   Carl Shapiro and Hal R. Varian, *Information Rules*, 179 (see Chapter 2, note 20).

2.   Nicolas Colin and Henri Verdier, *L'Âge de la multitude, Entreprendre et gouverner après la révolution numérique,* Second edition (Armand Colin, 2015). For an overview in English, read Nicolas Colin and Henri Verdier, "The Economics of the Multitude," *Paris Innovation Review*, June 7, 2012, http://parisinnovationreview.com/2012/06/07/economics-multitude/.

3.   Antonio Negri and Michael Hardt, *Multitude: War and Democracy in the Age of Empire* (New York: Penguin Books, 2009).

4.   Tim O'Reilly, "Why The Game of Business Needs to Change Its Rules," *WTF?*, August 9, 2016, https://wtfeconomy.com/why-the-game-of-business-needs-to-change-its-rules-4332ee4917de.

5.   Charles Fishman, *The Wal-Mart Effect: How the World's Most Powerful Company Really Works and How It's Transforming the American Economy,* Reprint edition (New York: Penguin Books, 2006).

6. Pankaj Ghemawat and Ken A. Mark, "The Real Wal-Mart Effect", *Working Knowledge*, Harvard Business School, August 23, 2006, http://hbswk.hbs.edu/item/the-real-wal-mart-effect.

7. Roger Cheng, "Why Technology Companies Loathe Dividends," *CNET*, March 19, 2012, https://www.cnet.com/uk/news/why-technology-companies-loathe-dividends/.

8. Tim O'Reilly, "Networks and the Nature of the Firm," *WTF?*, August 14, 2015, https://medium.com/the-wtf-economy/networks-and-the-nature-of-the-firm-28790b6afdcc.

9. Clayton M. Christensen, Stephen P. Kaufman, and Willy C. Shih, "Innovation Killers: How Financial Tools Destroy Your Capacity to Do New Things" (see Chapter 3, note 16).

10. The Economist, "A New Idolatry," *The Economist*, April 22, 2010, http://www.economist.com/node/15954434. See also Michael C. Jensen and William H. Meckling, "Theory of the Firm: Managerial Behavior, Agency Costs and Ownership Structure," *SSRN Scholarly Paper* (Rochester, NY: Social Science Research Network, July 1, 1976), https://papers.ssrn.com/abstract=94043.

11. Sam Walton and John Huey, *Made In America: My Story* (New York: Bantam America, 1993).

12. Sebastian Mallaby, *More Money Than God: Hedge Funds and the Making of a New Elite,* Reprint edition (New York: Penguin Books, 2011), 123.

13. James Hawes, *The Shortest History of Germany* (London: Old Street Publishing, 2017), 194.

14. Matt Phillips, "Germany's Bizarre Version of Capitalism—where Bosses and Workers Actually Cooperate—is Winning," *Quartz*, accessed May 6, 2017, https://qz.com/452076/this-just-in-german-capitalism-has-won/.

15. Wired Staff, "Mark Zuckerberg's Letter to Investors: 'The Hacker Way,'" *Wired*, February 2012, https://www.wired.com/2012/02/zuck-letter/.

16. Marcus Wohlsen, "What Uber Will Do With All That Money From Google," *Wired*, January 2014, https://www.wired.com/2014/01/uber-travis-kalanick/.

17. William Mellor, Lulu Yilun Chen, and Zijing Wu, "Ma Says Alibaba Shareholders Should Feel Love, Not No. 3," *Bloomberg*, November 9, 2014, https://www.bloomberg.com/news/articles/2014-11-09/ma-says-alibaba-shareholders-should-feel-love-not-no-3.

18. Henry Blodget, "14 Years Ago Jeff Bezos Told You How To Take Over The World," *Business Insider*, November 16, 2011, http://www.businessinsider.com/jeff-bezos-told-you-how-to-take-over-the-world-2011-11.

19. Roger L. Martin, "The Age of Customer Capitalism," *Harvard Business Review*, January 1, 2010, https://hbr.org/2010/01/the-age-of-customer-capitalism.

20. Gus Lubin and Vivian Giang, "The 19 Most Hated Companies In America," *Business Insider*, June 2011, http://www.businessinsider.com/most-hated-companies-america-2011-6.

21. Andrew McAfee and Erik Brynjolfsson, "Investing in the IT That Makes a Competitive Difference" (see Chapter 4, note 22).

22. Nicolas Colin and Henri Verdier, "The Economics of the Multitude" (see note 2).

23. Venkatesh Rao, "A New Soft Technology," *Breaking Smart*, February 7, 2015, https://breakingsmart.com/en/season-1/a-new-soft-technology/.

24. Kevin Kelly, "1,000 True Fans," *Kevin Kelly Blog*, 2008, http://kk.org/thetechnium/1000-true-fans/.

25. Nicolas Colin and Bruno Palier, "The Next Safety Net," *Foreign Affairs*, June 16, 2015, https://www.foreignaffairs.com/articles/2015-06-16/next-safety-net.

26. Tim O'Reilly, "Workers in a World of Continuous Partial Employment," *WTF?*, August 31, 2015, https://medium.com/the-wtf-economy/workers-in-a-world-of-continuous-partial-employment-4d7b53f18f96.

27. Tim O'Reilly, "Networks and the Nature of the Firm" (see note 8).

28. Nilofer Merchant, "We need a new language for the collaborative age," *Wired UK*, March 8, 2013, http://www.wired.co.uk/article/we-need-a-new-language-for-the-collaborative-age.

29.   Nicolas Colin, "A New Corporate Contract for the Digital Age," *The 8th Global Drucker Forum Blog*, October 19, 2016, https://www.druckerforum.org/blog/?p=1364.

30.   Rick Levine et al., *The Cluetrain Manifesto: The End of Business as Usual* (New York: Basic Books, 2000), http://www.cluetrain.com/book/95-theses.html.

31.   Named after Gordon Moore, a co-founder of Intel, *"whose 1965 paper described a doubling every year in the number of components per integrated circuit, and projected this rate of growth would continue for at least another decade"*. In fact Moore's law has remained true until at least 1998. "Moore's law – Wikipedia." Accessed October 28, 2016, https://en.wikipedia.org/wiki/Moore%27s_law/.

32.   Pierre Collin and Nicolas Colin, "Taxation and the Digital Economy" (see Chapter 1, note 3).

33.   Nicolas Colin, "In Search of Scalability," *The Family Papers*, August 26, 2016, https://salon.thefamily.co/in-search-of-scalability-5c495f8f4f0.

34.   Jeff Howe, *Crowdsourcing: Why the Power of the Crowd Is Driving the Future of Business* (New York: Crown Business, 2009).

35.   Don Tapscott and Anthony D. Williams, *Wikinomics: How Mass Collaboration Changes Everything*, Expanded edition (New York: Portfolio, 2010).

36.   Yochai Benkler, *The Wealth of Networks: How Social Production Transforms Markets and Freedom* (New Haven: Yale University Press, 2007).

37.   Shoshana Zuboff, "Creating Value in the Age of Distributed Capitalism," *McKinsey Quarterly*, September 2010, http://www.mckinsey.com/business-functions/strategy-and-corporate-finance/our-insights/creating-value-in-the-age-of-distributed-capitalism.

38.   Clay Shirky, *Cognitive Surplus: How Technology Makes Consumers into Collaborators,* Reprint edition (New York: Penguin Books, 2011).

39.   Yann Moulier Boutang, *Cognitive Capitalism*, First edition (Cambridge, UK: Polity, 2012).

40. Trebor Scholz, ed., *Digital Labor: The Internet as Playground and Factory,* First edition (New York: Routledge, 2012).

41. Nicolas Colin and Henri Verdier, *L'Âge de la multitude* (see note 2).

42. .Tim O'Reilly, "What Is Web 2.0: Design Patterns and Business Models for the Next Generation of Software," *O'Reilly Media,* September 30, 2005, http://www.oreilly.com/pub/a/web2/archive/what-is-web-20.html.

43. Babak Nivi, "The Entrepreneurial Age" (see Chapter 4, note 37).

44. Philip Evans and Patrick Forth, "Borges' Map: Navigating a World of Digital Disruption" (see Chapter 4, note 30).

45. Benedict Evans, "Ways to Think about Cars," *Benedict Evans' Blog,* July 27, 2015, http://ben-evans.com/benedictevans/2015/7/27/ways-to-think-about-cars.

46. Carl Shapiro and Hal R. Varian, *Information Rules,* 179 (see Chapter 2, note 20).

47. Bruce Henderson, "The Rule of Three and Four," *BCG Perspectives,* accessed May 6, 2017, https://www.bcgperspectives.com/content/Classics/strategy_the_rule_of_three_and_four/.

48. Andrew Odlyzko and Benjamin Tilly, "A refutation of Metcalfe's Law and a better estimate for the value of networks and network interconnections," Digital Technology Center, University of Minnesota, March 2, 2005, http://www.dtc.umn.edu/~odlyzko/doc/metcalfe.pdf.

49. Sangeet Paul Choudary, "Reverse Network Effects: Why Today's Social Networks Can Fail As They Grow Larger," *Wired,* March 2014, https://www.wired.com/insights/2014/03/reverse-network-effects-todays-social-networks-can-fail-grow-larger/.

50. W. Brian Arthur, "Increasing Returns and the New World of Business," *Harvard Business Review,* July-August 1996, https://hbr.org/1996/07/increasing-returns-and-the-new-world-of-business.

51. W. Brian Arthur, *Ibid.*

52. Fred Wilson, "Winner Takes Most," *AVC,* October 2015, http://avc.com/2015/10/winner-takes-most/.

53.   Erik Brynjolfsson and Andrew McAfee, "The Big Data Boom Is the Innovation Story of Our Time" (see Chapter 4, note 24).

Chapter 6—Consumer Power: The Modern-Day Janus

1.   W. Brian Arthur, "Increasing Returns and the New World of Business" (see Chapter 5, note 50).

2.   Sam Walton and John Huey, *Made In America* (see Chapter 5, note 11).

3.   Mark Whitehouse, "How Wal-Mart's Price Cutting Influences Both Rivals and Inflation," *The Wall Street Journal*, November 25, 2006, http://www.wsj.com/articles/SB116441560746932358.

4.   Charles Fishman, *The Wal-Mart Effect* (see Chapter 5, note 5).

5.   Thomas Wailgum, "45 Years of Wal-Mart History: A Technology Time Line," *CIO*, October 17, 2007, http://www.cio.com/article/2437873/infrastructure/45-years-of-wal-mart-history--a-technology-time-line.html.

6.   Jodi Kantor and David Streitfeld, "Inside Amazon: Wrestling Big Ideas in a Bruising Workplace," *The New York Times*, August 15, 2015, https://www.nytimes.com/2015/08/16/technology/inside-amazon-wrestling-big-ideas-in-a-bruising-workplace.html.

7.   Jeffrey Pfeffer, "Here's Why Amazon Is More Ruthless Than Walmart," *Time*, June 11, 2014, http://time.com/2850505/amazon-walmart-suppliers/.

8.   David Greenberg, "How Teddy Roosevelt Invented Spin," *The Atlantic*, January 24, 2016, https://www.theatlantic.com/politics/archive/2016/01/how-teddy-roosevelt-invented-spin/426699/.

9.   Louis Hartz, *The Liberal Tradition in America* (see Chapter 3, note 42).

10.   Franklin Foer, "Amazon Must Be Stopped," *The New Republic*, October 10, 2014, https://newrepublic.com/article/119769/amazons-monopoly-must-be-broken-radical-plan-tech-giant.

11.   Michael Pollan, "Why Did the Obamas Fail to Take On Corporate Agriculture?," *The New York Times*, October 5, 2016, https://

www.nytimes.com/interactive/2016/10/09/magazine/obama-administration-big-food-policy.html.

12. Keith Naughton, Alex Webb, and Mark Bergen, "Silicon Valley Just Realized How Hard It Is to Make a Car," *Bloomberg*, October 25, 2016, https://www.bloomberg.com/news/articles/2016-10-25/bill-ford-to-silicon-valley-the-future-of-cars-is-in-detroit.

13. Issie Lapowsky, "Tech's Next Big Legal Clash Will Be Over Selling Insurance," *Wired*, July 15, 2015, https://www.wired.com/2015/05/zenefits-funding/.

14. Tim O'Reilly, "Networks and the Nature of the Firm" (see Chapter 5, note 8).

15. Kim-Mai Cutler, "How Burrowing Owls Lead To Vomiting Anarchists (Or SF's Housing Crisis Explained)," *TechCrunch*, April 14, 2014, http://social.techcrunch.com/2014/04/14/sf-housing/.

16. Nicolas Colin and Antoine Zins, "Why Entrepreneurship Is Harder in Healthcare, and How We Can Make It Easier," *The Family Papers*, November 18, 2015, https://salon.thefamily.co/why-entrepreneurship-is-harder-in-healthcare-and-how-we-can-make-it-easier-d53dd94d94c1.

17. Cameron Albert-Deitch, "The Single Biggest Barrier to Entrepreneurship Among Millennials," *Inc*, June 7, 2016, https://www.inc.com/cameron-albert-deitch/2016-30-under-30-student-loans.html.

18. Philippe Aghion et al., "Competition and Innovation: An Inverted-U Relationship," *The Quarterly Journal of Economics* 120, no. 2 (May 2005), http://www.jstor.org/stable/25098750.

19. George Packer, "Cheap Words," *The New Yorker*, February 17, 2014, http://www.newyorker.com/magazine/2014/02/17/cheap-words.

20. Franklin Foer, "Amazon Must Be Stopped" (see note 10).

21. Ylan Q. Mui and Michael S. Rosenwald, "Wal-Mart's New Tack: Show 'Em the Payoff," *The Washington Post*, September 13, 2007, http://www.washingtonpost.com/wp-dyn/content/article/2007/09/12/AR2007091202513.html.

22. Megan McArdle, "Beware: Wal-Mart's Raises Are Not a Victory," *Bloomberg*, January 26, 2016, https://www.bloombergview.com/arti-

cles/2016-01-26/beware-wal-mart-s-raises-are-not-a-victory.

23. Tim O'Reilly, "The Architecture of Participation," *O'Reilly Media*, June 2004, http://archive.oreilly.com/pub/a/oreilly/tim/articles/architecture_of_participation.html.

24. Nelson Lichtenstein, *State of the Union*, 22 (see Chapter 2, note 26).

25. W. Brian Arthur, "Increasing Returns and the New World of Business" (see Chapter 5, note 50).

26. Fred Wilson, "Winner Takes Most" (see Chapter 5, note 52).

27. Marcus Wohlsen, "What Uber Will Do With All That Money From Google" (see Chapter 5, note 16).

28. Babak Nivi, "No Tradeoff between Quality and Scale" (see Chapter 4, note 1).

29. Steve Blank, "Why Uber Is the Revenge of the Founders," *Steve Blank's Blog*, October 24, 2017, https://steveblank.com/2017/10/24/uber-the-revenge-of-the-founders/.

30. J. Bradford Delong, "Profits of Doom," *Wired*, April 1, 2003, https://www.wired.com/2003/04/profits-of-doom-2/.

31. Rachel Sherman, "What the Rich Won't Tell You," *The New York Times*, September 8, 2017, https://www.nytimes.com/2017/09/08/opinion/sunday/what-the-rich-wont-tell-you.html.

32. Edmund S. Phelps, "Corporatism Not Capitalism Is to Blame for Inequality," *The Financial Times*, July 24, 2014, https://www.ft.com/content/54411224-132c-11e4-8244-00144feabdc0.

33. Clayton M. Christensen, "A Capitalist's Dilemma, Whoever Wins the Election" (see Chapter 3, note 22).

34. Clayton M. Christensen, Stephen P. Kaufman, and Willy C. Shih, "Innovation Killers: How Financial Tools Destroy Your Capacity to Do New Things" (see Chapter 3, note 16).

35. William Lazonick, "Profits Without Prosperity," *Harvard Business Review*, September 1, 2014, https://hbr.org/2014/09/profits-without-prosperity.

36. Edmund S. Phelps, "Less Innovation, More Inequality," *The New York Times*, Opinionator, https://opinionator.blogs.nytimes.

com/2013/02/24/less-innovation-more-inequality/.

37.   Dan Wang, "Why Is Peter Thiel Pessimistic About Technological Innovation?," September 10, 2014, https://danwang.co/why-is-peter-thiel-pessimistic-about-technological-innovation/.

38.   David Graeber, *The Utopia of Rules: On Technology, Stupidity, and the Secret Joys of Bureaucracy,* Reprint edition (New York: Melville House, 2016).

39.   Marc Andreessen, "Why Software Is Eating The World," *The Wall Street Journal,* August 20, 2011, https://www.wsj.com/articles/SB10001424053111903480904576512250915629460.

40.   Lauren Friedman, "IBM's Watson Supercomputer May Soon Be The Best Doctor In The World," *Business Insider*, April 22, 2014, http://www.businessinsider.com/ibms-watson-may-soon-be-the-best-doctor-in-the-world-2014-4.

41.   Kim-Mai Cutler, "YC's ROSS Intelligence Leverages IBM's Watson To Make Sense Of Legal Knowledge," *TechCrunch,* July 2017, http://social.techcrunch.com/2015/07/27/ross-intelligence/.

42.   Seth Godin, "I Spread Your Idea Because...," *Seth's Blog,* October 27, 2010, http://sethgodin.typepad.com/seths_blog/2010/10/ideas-spread-when.html.

43.   James Bessen, "How Technology Creates Jobs for Less Educated Workers," *Harvard Business Review,* March 21, 2014, https://hbr.org/2014/03/how-technology-creates-jobs-for-less-educated-workers.

44.   Tim O'Reilly, "Don't Replace People. Augment them," *WTF?,* July 17, 2016, https://wtfeconomy.com/dont-replace-people-augment-them-8bea60cb80ac.

45.   Chris Taylor, "Sorry, Taxis: You're History," *Mashable UK,* June 12, 2014, http://mashable.com/2014/06/11/sorry-taxis/#e.63w_lKGEqI.

46.   James Bessen, "How Technology Creates Jobs for Less Educated Workers" (see note 43).

Chapter 7—The Safety Net in an Open World

1. Dani Rodrik, "The inescapable trilemma of the world economy," *Dani Rodrik's weblog*, June 27, 2007, http://rodrik.typepad.com/dani_rodriks_weblog/2007/06/the-inescapable.html.

2. Rex Storgatz, "The Internet Really Has Changed Everything. Here's the Proof," *Backchannel*, April 19, 2016, https://www.wired.com/2016/04/the-internet-really-has-changed-everything-heres-the-proof/.

3. Kevin Baker, "Democrats Should Bring Back the Political Machines," *The New Republic*, August 17, 2016, https://newrepublic.com/article/135686/soul-new-machine.

4. Thomas Ferguson and Joel Rogers, *Right Turn*, 46-51 (see Chapter 1, note 9).

5. Clark Clifford, "The Politics of 1948, Memorandum from Clark Clifford to Harry S. Truman," 1947, https://www.trumanlibrary.org/dbq/res/1948/1948Campaign_CliffordMemo.pdf.

6. Clark Clifford, *Ibid.*

7. Janan Ganesh, "Who Is Paying for the Global City?," *The Financial Times*, August 4, 2017, https://www.ft.com/content/e7067ffc-7834-11e7-90c0-90a9d1bc9691.

8. W. Brian Arthur, "Where is technology taking the economy?," *McKinsey Quarterly*, October 2017, https://www.mckinsey.com/business-functions/mckinsey-analytics/our-insights/where-is-technology-taking-the-economy.

9. Corin Faife, "The Rebirth of the City-State," *How We Get To Next*, April 12, 2016, https://howwegettonext.com/the-rebirth-of-the-city-state-1d005f7c4eb7.

10. Balaji Srinivasan, "Silicon Valley's Ultimate Exit", Y Combinator's Startup School, October 2013, https://genius.com/Balaji-srinivasan-silicon-valleys-ultimate-exit-annotated. See also Albert O. Hirschman, *Exit, Voice, and Loyalty* (see Chapter 2, note 39).

11. Dan Zak, "This Is California in the Era of Trump," *The Washington Post*, March 22, 2017, https://www.washingtonpost.com/lifestyle/style/this-is-california-in-the-era-of-

trump/2017/03/22/04e349e2-02b0-11e7-b1e9-a05d3c21f7cf_story.html?utm_term=.693ce04e0621.

12. Richard Florida, "The Most Disruptive Transformation in History," *Medium*, December 1, 2016, https://medium.com/@Richard_Florida/the-most-disruptive-transformation-in-history-80a50ef89b4d.

13. Claire Cain Miller, "Liberals Turn to Cities to Pass Laws and Spread Ideas," *The New York Times*, January 26, 2016, https://www.nytimes.com/2016/01/26/upshot/liberals-turn-to-cities-to-pass-laws-and-spread-ideas.html.

14. David Osborne, *Laboratories of Democracy: New Breed of Governor Creates Models for National Growth* (Boston: Harvard Business School Press, 1990).

15. Debora MacKenzie, "End of Nations: Is There an Alternative to Countries?," *New Scientist*, September 3, 2014, https://www.newscientist.com/article/mg22329850-600-end-of-nations-is-there-an-alternative-to-countries/.

16. Hugo Pratt, *Corto Maltese: Fable of Venice* (San Diego, CA: IDW Publishing, 2017).

17. Roger Crowley, *City of Fortune: How Venice Ruled the Seas*, Reprint edition (New York: Random House Trade Paperbacks, 2013).

18. Piero Formica, "Why Innovators Should Study the Rise and Fall of the Venetian Empire," *Harvard Business Review*, January 2017, https://hbr.org/2017/01/why-innovators-should-study-the-rise-and-fall-of-the-venetian-empire.

19. "Venetian Statute on Industrial Brevets, Venice (1474)" (Manuscript from the Venetian State Archives, 1474), accessed April 29, 2018, http://www.copyrighthistory.org/cam/tools/request/showRepresentation?id=representation_i_1474.

20. Friedrich List, *The National System of Political Economy*, contemporary edition (Memphis, TN: General Books LLC, 2012).

21. Fernand Braudel, *The Wheels of Commerce* (Civilization and Capitalism: 15th-18th Century—Volume 2) (Oakland, CA: University of California Press, 1992).

22. Hervé Coutau-Bégarie, « Le problème de la thalassocratie », in

Jean Pagès, *Recherches sur les thalassocraties antiques : L'exemple grec* (Paris: Economica, coll. « Hautes Études Militaires », octobre 2001).

23.   Michael E. Porter, "What Is Strategy?," *Harvard Business Review*, November 1, 1996, https://hbr.org/1996/11/what-is-strategy.

24.   Roger Crowley, *City of Fortune: How Venice Ruled the Seas* (see note 17).

25.   Hervé Coutau-Bégarie, « Le problème de la thalassocratie » (see note 22).

26.   Dan Senor and Saul Singer, *Start-up Nation: The Story of Israel's Economic Miracle*, Reprint edition (New York: Twelve, 2011).

27.   Ben Hammersley, "Concerned about Brexit? Why Not Become an E-Resident of Estonia," *Wired UK*, March 27, 2017, http://www.wired.co.uk/article/estonia-e-resident.

28.   Daron Acemoglu and James Robinson, *Why Nations Fail: The Origins of Power, Prosperity, and Poverty*, Reprint edition (New York, NY: Crown Business, 2013).

29.   Steve Blank, "The Secret History of Silicon Valley" (see Chapter 4, note 3).

30.   Tim O'Reilly, "Gov 2.0: It's All About The Platform" (see Chapter 4, note 29).

31.   Carl Schmitt, *Land and Sea: A World-Historical Meditation*, ed. Samuel Garrett Zeitlin and Russell A. Berman (Candor, NY: Telos Press Publishing, 2015).

32.   Brad Templeton, "On the Invention of the Internet" (see chapter 4, note 36).

33.   The Economist, "The First Venture Capitalists: Before there were tech startups, there was whaling," *The Economist*, December 30, 2015, http://www.economist.com/news/finance-and-economics/21684805-there-were-tech-startups-there-was-whaling-fin-tech.

34.   Ben Schiller, "Why The Future Will Be Dictated By Cities, Not Nations," *Fast Company*, September 1, 2016, https://www.fastcodesign.com/3062884/why-the-future-will-be-dictated-by-cities-not-nations.

35. Thomas Ferguson and Joel Rogers, *Right Turn* (see Chapter 1, note 9).

36. "Nixon and the End of the Bretton Woods System, 1971–1973," Office of the Historian (US Department of State), accessed March 30, 2017, https://history.state.gov/milestones/1969-1976/nixon-shock.

37. John B. Judis, *The Populist Explosion* (see Chapter 3, note 20).

38. The Economist, "The New Political Divide," *The Economist*, July 30, 2016, http://www.economist.com/news/leaders/21702750-farewell-left-versus-right-contest-matters-now-open-against-closed-new.

39. Staffan Kumlin, "Blaming Europe: Why Welfare State Dissatisfaction Breeds Euroscepticism", Paper presented at the annual meeting of the American Political Science Association, Hilton Chicago and the Palmer House Hilton, Chicago, IL, Sep 02, 2004, http://citation.allacademic.com/meta/p_mla_apa_research_citation/0/6/1/4/6/p61468_index.html.

40. The Economist, "George Bush, protectionist," *The Economist*, May 7, 2002, http://www.economist.com/node/1021395.

41. Alec Russell, "Bush risks Rust Belt backlash as steel tariffs are ended," *The Telegraph*, December 5, 2003, http://www.telegraph.co.uk/education/3323794/Bush-risks-Rust-Belt-backlash-as-steel-tariffs-are-ended.html.

42. Jonathan Cohn, "How They Did It" (see Chapter 2, note 40).

43. Mark Blyth, "The Austerity Delusion," *Foreign Affairs*, May 1, 2013, https://www.foreignaffairs.com/articles/2013-04-03/austerity-delusion.

44. Sarah Kendzior, "Why America's impressive 5% unemployment rate feels like a lie for so many," *Quartz*, April 20, 2016, https://qz.com/666311/why-americas-impressive-5-unemployment-rate-still-feels-like-a-lie/.

45. Joel D. Hirst, "The Suicide of Venezuela," Joel D. Hirst's Blog, April 23, 2016, https://joelhirst.wordpress.com/2016/04/23/the-suicide-of-venezuela/.

46. Dani Rodrik, "Why Do More Open Economies Have Bigger Governments?," *Journal of Political Economy*, February 1996, http://

drodrik.scholar.harvard.edu/files/dani-rodrik/files/why-do-more-open-economies-have-bigger-governments.pdf.

47.   Dani Rodrik, *The Globalization Paradox: Democracy and the Future of the World Economy*, Reprint edition (New York: W. W. Norton & Company, 2012).

48.   Edmund S. Phelps, "Less Innovation, More Inequality" (see Chapter 6, note 36).

Chapter 8—From the Old to the New Working Class

1.   Tamara Draut, *Sleeping Giant: How the New Working Class Will Transform America* (Doubleday, 2016).

2.   Nicolas Colin, "Hillary's Problem, Explained by Technology," *The Family Papers*, July 18, 2016, https://salon.thefamily.co/software-eating-politics-the-case-for-picking-elizabeth-warren-3c22477c5d9a.

3.   Betsy Woodruff, "Goodbye West Virginia," *Slate*, October 29, 2014, http://www.slate.com/articles/news_and_politics/politics/2014/10/republicans_are_turning_west_virginia_red_how_the_democrats_lost_control.html.

4.   Jim Edwards, "Alan Greenspan Just Explained How 'Productivity' Caused Brexit and Trump, in 10 Elegant Sentences," *Business Insider Australia*, February 20, 2017, https://www.businessinsider.com.au/alan-greenspan-productivity-brexit-trump-2017-2.

5.   Marc Levinson, *The Box: How the Shipping Container Made the World Smaller and the World Economy Bigger* (Princeton, NJ: Princeton University Press, 2008).

6.   Alessandra Potenza, "In 1952 London, 12,000 people died from smog — here's why that matters now," *The Verge*, December 16, 2017, https://www.theverge.com/2017/12/16/16778604/london-great-smog-1952-death-in-the-air-pollution-book-review-john-reginald-christie.

7.   Paul Krugman, "The Gambler's Ruin of Small Cities (Wonkish)," *The New York Times*, December 30, 2017, https://www.nytimes.com/2017/12/30/opinion/the-gamblers-ruin-of-small-cities-wonkish.html.

8.   Kim Phillips-Fein, *Invisible Hands: The Businessmen's Crusade Against the New Deal* (New York: W. W. Norton & Company, 2010).

9.   Emily Badger, "What Happens When the Richest U.S. Cities Turn to the World?," *The New York Times*, December 22, 2017, https://www.nytimes.com/2017/12/22/upshot/the-great-disconnect-megacities-go-global-but-lose-local-links.html.

10.   Federica Cocco, "Most US manufacturing jobs lost to technology, not trade," *The Financial Times*, December 2, 2016, https://www.ft.com/content/dec677c0-b7e6-11e6-ba85-95d1533d9a62.

11.   Ben Casselman, "2016 Election Results Coverage," *FiveThirtyEight*, November 8, 2016, https://fivethirtyeight.com/live-blog/2016-election-results-coverage/.

12.   Richard Florida, "The New Urban Crisis," a conference hosted by LSE Cities and the Centre for London, attended by the author in London (UK), October 9, 2017, http://www.lse.ac.uk/Events/2017/10/20171009t1830vSZT/the-new-urban-crisis.

13.   Patrick Sharkey, "Two Lessons of the Urban Crime Decline," *The New York Times*, January 13, 2018, https://www.nytimes.com/2018/01/13/opinion/sunday/two-lessons-of-the-urban-crime-decline.html.

14.   Mark Gimein, "Why the High Cost of Big City Living Is Bad for Everyone," *The New Yorker*, August 25, 2016, https://www.newyorker.com/business/currency/why-the-high-cost-of-big-city-living-is-bad-for-everyone.

15.   Mason B. Williams, *City of Ambition: FDR, LaGuardia, and the Making of Modern New York* (New York: W. W. Norton, 2013).

16.   Michael Alan Wolff, *The Zoning of America: Euclid v. Ambler* (Lawrence, KS: University Press of Kansas, 2008).

17.   Richard Rothstein, *The Color of Law: A Forgotten History of How Our Government Segregated America* (New York: Liveright, 2017).

18.   Ross Anderson, "The Threat," *Edge*, May 8, 2017, https://www.edge.org/conversation/ross_anderson-the-threat.

19.   Jonathan Malher, "The Case for the Subway," *The New York Times*, January 3, 2018, https://www.nytimes.com/2018/01/03/maga-

zine/subway-new-york-city-public-transportation-wealth-inequality.
html.

20.   Patrick Sisson, "How cities can work with Uber and Lyft to create
bigger, better transportation networks," *Curbed,* September 8, 2016,
https://www.curbed.com/2016/9/8/12846470/uber-transporta-
tion-public-transit-lyft-report.

21.   Kim-Mai Cutler, "How Burrowing Owls Lead To Vomiting Anarchists" (see Chapter 6, note 15).

22.   Rick Wartzman, "Want engaged employees? It's easy—pay them,"
Fortune, July 10, 2015, http://fortune.com/2015/07/10/wages-pay-
middle-class/.

23.   Richard Florida, "It's Not (Just) the Working Class. It's the
Service Class," *Evonomics,* http://evonomics.com/richard-florida-not-
just-working-class-service-class/.

24.   Kathryn Stockett, *The Help* (New York: Penguin, 2010).

25.   Bill Bryson, *At Home: A Short History of Private Life* (New York:
Anchor, 2011).

26.   Laetitia Vitaud, "Why Taylorism Cannot Apply To the Cleaning
Craft," *Medium,* October 8, 2017, https://medium.com/@Vitolae/
why-taylorism-cannot-apply-to-the-cleaning-craft-864293bafabf.

27.   Tamara Draut, *Sleeping Giant* (see note 1).

28.   Richard Dobbs, Jaana Remes, Sven Smit, James Manyika, Jonathan Woetzel, and Yaw Agyenim-Boateng, *Urban World, The Shifting
Global Business Landscape,* McKinsey Global Institute, October 2013,
https://www.mckinsey.com/global-themes/urbanization/urban-world-
the-shifting-global-business-landscape.

29.   Kim-Mai Cutler, "How Burrowing Owls Lead To Vomiting Anarchists" (see Chapter 6, note 15).

30.   Ben Casselman, "Americans Don't Miss Manufacturing — They
Miss Unions" (see Chapter 2, note 23).

31.   Paul Graham, "The Refragmentation," *Paul Graham's Blog,*
January 2016, http://www.paulgraham.com/re.html.

32.   Thomas B. Edsall, "Why Is It So Hard for Democracy to Deal

With Inequality?," *The New York Times*, https://www.nytimes. com/2018/02/15/opinion/democracy-inequality-thomas-piketty.html.

33. Matthew Yglesias, "There's a New 'Silent Majority,' and It's Voting for Hillary Clinton," *Vox*, October 19, 2016, http://www.vox. com/policy-and-politics/2016/10/19/13288594/new-silent-majority.

34. Rebecca Traister, *All the Single Ladies: Unmarried Women and the Rise of an Independent Nation* (New York City, NY: Simon & Schuster, March 2016).

35. Louis Hartz, *The Liberal Tradition in America* (see Chapter 3, note 42).

36. Richard Florida, "The Most Disruptive Transformation in History" (see Chapter 7, note 12).

37. Nate Silver, "Will The Electoral College Doom The Democrats Again?," *FiveThirtyEight*, November 14, 2016, https://fivethirtyeight. com/features/will-the-electoral-college-doom-the-democrats-again/.

38. Mike Konczal, "The "new liberal economics" is the key to under-standing Hillary Clinton's policies," *Vox*, September 15, 2016, https:// www.vox.com/the-big-idea/2016/9/15/12923528/liberal-econom-ics-great-recession-policy-clinton.

39. As pointed out to me by Kim-Mai Cutler in a comment on my manuscript, *"minimum wage is still well behind a livable wage and isn't indexed to some type of peg. We repeatedly have to reset it through expensive and costly political fights."*

40. Sara Horowitz, "America, Say Goodbye to the Era of Big Work" (see Chapter 3, note 39).

41. Dov Seidman, "From the Knowledge Economy to the Human Economy," *Harvard Business Review*, November 12, 2014, https://hbr. org/2014/11/from-the-knowledge-economy-to-the-human-economy.

42. Noam Scheiber, "What It Feels Like to Be Washed Up at 35," *The New Republic*, March 23, 2014, https://newrepublic.com/ article/117088/silicons-valleys-brutal-ageism.

43. Katherine S. Newman and Hella Winston, *Reskilling America: Learning to Labor in the Twenty-First Century* (New York: Metropol-itan Books, 2016).

44.   Kim-Mai Cutler, "A Conversation on Future Urbanism, Tech Hubs," *TechCrunch*, October 9, 2014, http://social.techcrunch.com/2014/10/09/urbanism-tech-hubs/.

45.   Claire Cain Miller and Ruth Fremson, "'Forget About the Stigma': Male Nurses Explain Why Nursing Is a Job of the Future for Men," *The New York Times*, January 4, 2018, https://www.nytimes.com/interactive/2018/01/04/upshot/male-nurses.html.

46.   Mae M. Ngai, *Impossible Subjects: Illegal Aliens and the Making of Modern America* (Princeton, NJ: Princeton University Press, 2004).

47.   Cat Johnson, "The Power of Peers Inc: a Q&A with Robin Chase," *Shareable*, August 4, 2015, http://www.shareable.net/blog/the-power-of-peers-inc-a-qa-with-robin-chase.

48.   Edmund S. Phelps, "Corporatism Not Capitalism Is to Blame for Inequality" (see Chapter 6, note 32).

49.   Kathleen Pender, "California's unemployment rate falls to record low," *The San Francisco Chronicle*, January 19, 2018, https://www.sfchronicle.com/business/article/California-s-unemployment-rate-falls-to-record-12510752.php.

50.   Umair Haque, "Seven Lessons We Should Have Learned From History But Didn't," *Eudaimonia*, March 31, 2018, https://eand.co/seven-lessons-we-should-have-learned-from-history-but-didnt-14dde0929c29.

Chapter 9—The Lost Art of State Intervention

1.   Franklin Foer, "Obamacare's Threat to Liberalism," *The New Republic*, November 24, 2013, https://newrepublic.com/article/115695/obamacare-failure-threat-liberalism.

2.   Michael C. Janeway, *The Fall of the House of Roosevelt: Brokers of Ideas and Power from FDR to LBJ* (New York: Columbia University Press, 2004).

3.   Michael C. Janeway, *Ibid.*

4.   Nelson Lichtenstein, *State of the Union* (see Chapter 2, note 26).

5.   David Greenberg, "How Teddy Roosevelt Invented Spin," *The*

Atlantic, January 24, 2016, https://www.theatlantic.com/politics/archive/2016/01/how-teddy-roosevelt-invented-spin/426699/.

6.   Woodrow Wilson, "The Study of Administration," *Political Science Quarterly,* 1887, https://en.wikipedia.org/w/index.php?title=The_Study_of_Administration&oldid=747756994.

7.   Stephen Skowronek, *The Politics Presidents Make: Leadership from John Adams to Bill Clinton,* Revised Edition (Cambridge, MA: Belknap Press, 1997).

8.   Nelson Lichtenstein, *State of the Union* (see Chapter 2, note 26).

9.   Robert M. Solow, "Hayek, Friedman, and the Illusions of Conservative Economics" (see Chapter 3, note 3).

10.   Walter Kiechel III, "Seven Chapters of Strategic Wisdom," *Strategy+Business,* February 23, 2010, https://www.strategy-business.com/article/10109?gko=70983.

11.   Walter Kiechel III, *The Lords of Strategy: The Secret Intellectual History of the New Corporate World* (Boston, MA: *Harvard Business Review* Press, 2010).

12.   David Osborne, *Laboratories of Democracy* (see Chapter 7, note 14).

13.   Nick Pearce, "Missing Link," *Progress,* February 2014, http://www.progressonline.org.uk/2014/02/06/missing-link-2/.

14.   Tony Blair, "Full Text: Blair's Fabian Speech," *The Guardian,* June 17, 2003, https://www.theguardian.com/society/2003/jun/17/publicservices.speeches1.

15.   Mary D. Edsall and Thomas Byrne Edsall, *Chain Reaction: The Impact of Race, Rights, and Taxes on American Politics,* Revised edition (New York: W. W. Norton & Company, 1992).

16.   David Osborne, *Reinventing Government: How the Entrepreneurial Spirit Is Transforming the Public Sector,* New edition (New York, N.Y: Longman, 2000).

17.   Stanley B. Greenberg, *Middle Class Dreams: The Politics and Power of the New American Majority,* Revised and Updated Edition (New Haven: Yale University Press, 1996).

18.   David Graeber, "Capitalism's Secret Love Affair with Bureaucracy," *The Financial Times*, March 6, 2015, https://www.ft.com/content/73212b74-c1ba-11e4-8b74-00144feab7de.

19.   Tim O'Reilly, "Networks and the Nature of the Firm" (see Chapter 5, note 8).

20.   Clayton M. Christensen, *The Innovator's Dilemma* (see Chapter 4, note 19).

21.   Michael Grunwald, *The New New Deal: The Hidden Story of Change in the Obama Era*, Reprint edition (New York: Simon & Schuster, 2013).

22.   Jonathan Chait, *The Big Con: Crackpot Economics and the Fleecing of America* (Boston and New York: Houghton Mifflin, 2007).

23.   Brink Lindsey and Steven Teles, *The Captured Economy: How the Powerful Become Richer, Slow Down Growth, and Increase Inequality* (Oxford: Oxford University Press, 2017).

24.   Matt Bai, "What Steve Jobs Understood That Our Politicians Don't" (see Chapter 1, note 1).

25.   Babak Nivi, "The Entrepreneurial Age" (see Chapter 4, note 37).

26.   John Harris, "The Lesson of Trump and Brexit: A Society Too Complex for Its People Risks Everything," *The Guardian*, December 29, 2016, https://www.theguardian.com/commentisfree/2016/dec/29/trump-brexit-society-complex-people-populists.

27.   Franklin Foer, "Obamacare's Threat to Liberalism" (see note 1).

28.   Younès Rharbaoui, "Entrepreneurs, Let's Finance Businesses Better!," The Family, February 5, 2018, https://salon.thefamily.co/entrepreneurs-lets-finance-businesses-better-bf4a6e14df4b.

29.   Tim O'Reilly, "Government as a Platform," Innovations, *MIT Press Journals* 6, no. 1 (Winter 2011), http://www.mitpressjournals.org/toc/itgg/6/1.

30.   Jennifer Pahlka, "Beyond Tech: Policymaking in a Digital Age," *The Code for America Blog*, March 30, 2017, https://medium.com/code-for-america/beyond-tech-policymaking-in-a-digital-age-2776b9a17b69.

31. Ben Hammersley, "Concerned about Brexit? Why not become an e-resident of Estonia," *Wired UK,* March 27, 2017, http://www.wired.co.uk/article/estonia-e-resident.

32. Diego Piacentini, "Towards the new "operating system" of the country," *Team Per La Trasformazione Digitale,* December 21, 2016, https://medium.com/team-per-la-trasformazione-digitale/new-operating-system-country-technological-competence-plans-11b50a750ea7.

33. Romain Dillet, "France wants to rethink the state as a platform," *TechCrunch,* July 6, 2016, https://techcrunch.com/2016/07/06/france-wants-to-rethink-the-state-as-a-platform/.

34. Mariana Mazzucato, *The Entrepreneurial State: Debunking Public Vs. Private Sector Myths* (London: Anthem Press, 2015).

35. Rainer Kattel and Erkki Karo, "Start-Up Governments, or Can Bureaucracies Innovate?," Institute for New Economic Thinking, January 4, 2016, https://www.ineteconomics.org/perspectives/blog/start-up-governments-or-can-bureaucracies-innovate.

36. Patrick Sisson, "How cities can work with Uber and Lyft to create bigger, better transportation networks" (see Chapter 8, note 20).

Chapter 10—Always Be Rebounding

1. Critical Art Ensemble, *The Electronic Disturbance* (New York: Autonomedia, 1994).

2. Robert Reich, *The Work of Nations: Preparing Ourselves for 21st Century Capitalism* (New York: Vintage, 1992).

3. Anthony Giddens, *The Third Way: The Renewal of Social Democracy* (London: Polity Press, 1998).

4. Jeremy Rifkin, *The End of Work: The Decline of the Global Labor Force and the Dawn of the Post-Market Era* (New York: Tarcher, 1996).

5. John F. Harris, "Indispensable Or Irrelevant?," *The Washington Post,* January 18, 2001, https://www.washingtonpost.com/archive/politics/2001/01/18/indispensable-or-irrelevant/0c1028c4-1fc2-40fd-abea-a26da0e5bff5/?utm_term=.e8fdc3016ce0.

6. Paul Krugman, "Sympathy for the Luddites," *The New York Times,*

June 13, 2013, http://www.nytimes.com/2013/06/14/opinion/krug-man-sympathy-for-the-luddites.html.

7. Scott D. Anthony, S. Patrick Viguerie, Evan I. Schwartz, John Van Landeghem, 2018 *Corporate Longevity Forecast: Creative Destruction is Accelerating*, Innosight, 2018, https://www.innosight.com/insight/creative-destruction/.

8. Adam Davidson, "Welcome to the Failure Age!" (see Chapter 2, note 1).

9. Michael Mandel, "Can the Internet of Everything Bring Back the High-Growth Economy?," Policy Paper, Progressive Policy Institute, September 12, 2013, http://www.progressivepolicy.org/issues/economy/can-the-internet-of-everything-bring-back-the-high-growth-economy/.

10. The Economist, "Occupational licensing blunts competition and boosts inequality," *The Economist*, February 17, 2018, https://www.economist.com/news/united-states/21737053-how-high-earning-pro-fessions-lock-their-competitors-out-market-occupational.

11. Richard Susskind, Daniel Susskind, *The Future of the Professions: How Technology Will Transform the Work of Human Experts* (Oxford: Oxford University Press, 2016).

12. The Economist, "Occupational licensing blunts competition and boosts inequality" (see note 10).

13. Tim O'Reilly, "Networks and the Nature of the Firm" (see Chapter 5, note 8).

14. Gabrielle Gurley, "Underserved Communities Rely on Uber, but Challenges Remain," *Prospect*, October 5, 2016, http://prospect.org/article/underserved-communities-rely-uber-challenges-remain.

15. Sarah O'Connor, "Customers in the digital economy have the whip hand," *The Financial Times*, November 29, 2016, https://www.ft.com/content/c04ccc22-b584-11e6-961e-a1acd97f622d.

16. Barry Ritholtz, "Taxi Cab Owners and Regulators Created Uber," *Bloomberg*, May 4, 2018, https://www.bloomberg.com/view/articles/2018-05-04/taxi-cab-owners-and-regulators-created-uber.

17. Laetitia Vitaud, "The Age of Amateurs," Switch Collective,

August 22, 2016, https://medium.com/switch-collective/the-age-of-amateurs-d7eaa7d8f799.

18. Teddy Pellerin, "Heetch: 3 Years in Review and a Vision for the Future," *Medium*, November 22, 2016, https://medium.com/@teddypellerin/heetch-3-years-in-review-and-a-vision-for-the-future-b59ca1b6d2c6.

19. Chris Taylor, "Sorry, Taxis: You're History" (see Chapter 6, note 45).

20. Kim-Mai Cutler, "How Burrowing Owls Lead To Vomiting Anarchists" (see Chapter 6, note 15).

21. Kim-Mai Cutler, "Silicon Valley Lost, and Found," *TechCrunch*, January 4, 2014, https://techcrunch.com/2014/01/04/silicon-valley-lost-and-found/.

22. Olivier Zunz, *Why the American Century?* (see Chapter 2, note 14).

23. Kim-Mai Cutler, "Nothing Like This Has Ever Happened Before," *TechCrunch*, January 29, 2016, https://techcrunch.com/2016/01/29/nothing-like-this-has-ever-happened-before/.

24. David Levitus, "YIMBYism and the Cruel Irony of Metropolitan History," *StreetsBlog LA*, February 27, 2018, https://la.streetsblog.org/2018/02/27/yimbyism-and-the-cruel-irony-of-metropolitan-history/.

25. Statistisches Bundesamt, "Building, buying, renting: the situation on the German housing market", *STATMagazin*, January 21, 2014, https://www.destatis.de/EN/Publications/STATmagazin/Prices/2014_01/2014_01HousingMarket.html.

26. Jennifer Warburg, "Forecasting San Francisco's Economic Fortunes," *Spur*, February 27, 2014, http://www.spur.org/news/2014-02-27/forecasting-san-francisco-s-economic-fortunes.

27. Sarah Kendzior, "Expensive cities are killing creativity," *Al Jazeera*, December 17, 2013, https://www.aljazeera.com/indepth/opinion/2013/12/expensive-cities-are-killing-creativity-2013121065856922461.html.

28. Sarah Kendzior, "Geography is making America's uneven economic recovery worse," *Quartz*, April 29, 2016, https://qz.com/672589/geography-is-making-americas-uneven-economic-re-

covery-worse/.

29. Robert Caro, *The Power Broker: Robert Moses and the Fall of New York* (New York: Knopf, 1974).

30. Kim-Mai Cutler, "A Conversation on Future Urbanism, Tech Hubs" (see Chapter 8, note 44).

31. Sarah Buhr, "Ron Conway And Chamath Palihapitiya Debate SF Housing And Google At Next Big Thing Conference," *TechCrunch*, June 9, 2014, https://techcrunch.com/2014/06/09/eruption-over-sf-housing-and-google-breaks-out-at-next-big-thing-conference/.

32. Clayton M. Christensen, "How Healthcare Can Become Higher in Quality, Lower in Cost & Widely Accessible," *Faculty Perspectives on Healthcare*, Harvard Business School, February 8, 2012, https://youtu.be/yoW5x71vbJc?t=27m53s.

33. Sarah Goodyear, "A New Way of Understanding 'Eyes on the Street'," *City Lab*, July 22, 2013, https://www.citylab.com/equity/2013/07/new-way-understanding-eyes-street/6276/.

34. Frederic Laloux, "We are Wired to Raise Children in Community," *Medium*, December 11, 2017, https://medium.com/@fredlaloux/we-are-wired-to-raise-children-in-community-103cd4e9e9bf.

35. Kim-Mai Cutler, "Nothing Like This Has Ever Happened Before" (see note 23).

Chapter 11—Institutions for Hunters

1. Robert J. Shiller, *The New Financial Order: Risk in the 21st Century* (Princeton, NJ: Princeton University Press, 2003).

2. Adam Davidson, "Welcome to the Failure Age!" (see Chapter 2, note 1).

3. Natasha Lomas, "Lambda School aims to cash in by upskilling untapped talent," *TechCrunch*, August 7, 2017, https://techcrunch.com/2017/08/07/lambda-school-aims-to-cash-in-by-upskilling-untapped-talent/.

4. Alex Rampell, "Point," Andreessen Horowitz, September 13, 2016, https://a16z.com/2016/09/13/point/. For an overview of the

discussion around "shared equity", see Richard Morris, "Don't Reform Housing Finance – Reinvent It," *Knowledge@Wharton*, November 21, 2013, http://knowledge.wharton.upenn.edu/article/dont-reform-housing-finance-reinvent/.

5.   Richard Waters, "Data open doors to financial innovation," *The Financial Times*, December 13, 2012, https://www.ft.com/content/3c-59d58a-43fb-11e2-844c-00144feabdco.

6.   Nicolas Colin, "11 Notes on Goldman Sachs," *The Family Papers*, May 16, 2017, https://salon.thefamily.co/11-notes-on-goldman-sachs-d6103213759.

7.   Reena Jana, "Facebook's Design Strategy: A Status Update Behind the scenes with the team that's redefining human connection," *TBJ 100 Blog*, August 22, 2011, https://tbj100.wordpress.com/2011/08/22/facebook%E2%80%99s-design-strategy-a-status-update-behind-the-scenes-with-the-team-that%E2%80%99s-redefining-human-connection/.

8.   Colin Crouch, "Privatized Keynesianism: An Unacknowledged Policy Regime" (see Chapter 3, note 41).

9.   Charles D. Ellis, *The Partnership: The Making of Goldman Sachs* (New York: Penguin Books, 2009).

10.   Gillian Tett, *Fool's Gold: How Unrestrained Greed Corrupted a Dream, Shattered Global Markets and Unleashed a Catastrophe* (London: Abacus, 2010).

11.   Aaron Klein, "Why is Glass-Steagall so politically popular and what does it really mean?," The Brookings Institution, July 19, 2016, https://www.brookings.edu/opinions/why-is-glass-steagall-so-politically-popular-and-what-does-it-really-mean/.

12.   The Economist, "The great pruning," *The Economist*, May 9, 2015, http://www.economist.com/news/finance-and-economics/21650593-banks-are-thinning-their-branch-networks-more-drastic-cuts-may-come-great.

13.   Madison Marriage, "Tech giants pose threat to fund houses," *The Financial Times*, April 20, 2014, https://www.ft.com/content/oceee29c-c594-11e3-a7d4-00144feabdco.

14.   Matt Bai, "What Steve Jobs Understood That Our Politicians

Don't" (see Chapter 1, note 1).

15. Beth Seidenberg, "Obamacare Spurring A New Generation Of Startups," *TechCrunch*, February 22, 2014, http://techcrunch.com/2014/02/22/obamacare-spurring-a-new-generation-of-health-care-startups/.

16. Kim-Mai Cutler, "Oscar Raises $145M At A $1.5B Valuation To Build A New Healthcare, Insurance Giant," *TechCrunch*, April 20, 2015, https://techcrunch.com/2015/04/20/oscar-145m/.

17. Q Bio, "A Positive Feedback Loop for Humanity," *Medium*, November 2, 2016, https://medium.com/@qbio/a-positive-feedback-loop-for-humanity-437762f6725c.

18. Sam Altman, "YC Research: Universal Healthcare," Y Combinator, February 7, 2017, https://blog.ycombinator.com/yc-research-universal-healthcare/.

19. Clayton M. Christensen, Jerome H. Grossman, M.D., and Jason Hwang, M.D., *The Innovator's Prescription: A Disruptive Solution for Health Care* (New York: McGraw-Hill Education, 2009).

20. Clayton M. Christensen, Jerome H. Grossman, M.D., and Jason Hwang, "Disrupting The Hospital Business Model," *Forbes*, March 31, 2009, https://www.forbes.com/2009/03/30/hospitals-health-care-disruption-leadership-clayton-christensen-strategy-innovation.html#4a6e82b96512.

21. David Barstow, Susanne Craig, Russ Buettner, and Megan Twohey, "Donald Trump Tax Records Show He Could Have Avoided Taxes for Nearly Two Decades, The Times Found," *The New York Times*, October 1, 2016, http://www.nytimes.com/2016/10/02/us/politics/donald-trump-taxes.html.

22. Matthew Yglesias, "How Donald Trump made millions running failed casinos in Atlantic City," *Vox*, June 12, 2016, https://www.vox.com/2016/6/12/11909176/trump-atlantic-city-business.

23. The Economist, "The key to industrial capitalism: limited liability," *The Economist*, December 23, 1999, https://www.economist.com/node/347323.

24. As defined on https://www.investopedia.com/terms/l/losscarryforward.asp (accessed March 15, 2018). See also Low Incomes Tax

Reform Group, "What if I make a loss?", December 2, 2017, https://www.litrg.org.uk/tax-guides/self-employment/working-out-profits-losses-and-capital-allowance/what-if-i-make-loss.

25. Matthew Yglesias, "How Donald Trump made millions running failed casinos in Atlantic City" (see note 22).

26. Matthew Desmond, "How Homeownership Became the Engine of American Inequality," *The New York Times*, May 9, 2017, https://www.nytimes.com/2017/05/09/magazine/how-homeownership-became-the-engine-of-american-inequality.html.

27. Nick Grossman, Elizabeth Woyke, *Serving Workers in the Gig Economy, Emerging Resources for the On-Demand Workforce,* O'Reilly, October 2015, http://www.oreilly.com/iot/free/serving-workers-gig-economy.csp.

28. Venkatesh Rao, "Getting Reoriented," *Breaking Smart,* Season 1, 2015, https://breakingsmart.com/en/season-1/getting-reoriented/.

29. Ryu Spaeth, "The Trump tax story is a big, beautiful gift for Hillary Clinton," *The New Republic,* October 3, 2016, https://newrepublic.com/minutes/137374/trump-tax-story-big-beautiful-gift-hillary-clinton.

30. Matthew Yglesias, "Leaked tax documents reveal how Trump could have avoided paying income tax for a decade," *Vox,* October 1, 2016, https://www.vox.com/2016/10/1/13134976/trump-tax-documents.

31. Richard Straub, "The Promise of a Truly Entrepreneurial Society," *Harvard Business Review,* March 25, 2016, https://hbr.org/2016/03/the-promise-of-a-truly-entrepreneurial-society.

32. Venkatesh Rao, "Getting Reoriented" (see note 27).

33. Ryan Lawler, "Stripe Partners With Intuit To Help On-Demand Workers Keep Track Of Their Finances," *TechCrunch,* January 26, 2015, https://techcrunch.com/2015/01/26/stripe-intuit-on-demand-workers/.

34. Jacob Silverman, "China's Troubling New Social Credit System—And Ours," *The New Republic,* October 29, 2015, https://newrepublic.com/article/123285/chinas-troubling-new-social-credit-system-and-ours. For a more nuanced view, see Simina Mistreanu, "Life Inside

China's Social Credit Laboratory" (see Chapter 3, note 54).

35. Laetitia Vitaud, "In-Between Waves," Want More Work, September 13, 2016, https://medium.com/want-more-work/in-between-waves-79ecdbbdf8f9.

Chapter 12—A Hedge for the Networked Individual

1.   Jacob Hacker, "The New Economic Insecurity—And What Can Be Done About It" (see Chapter 3, note 24).

2.   Venkatesh Rao, "A Brief History of the Corporation: 1600 to 2100," *Ribbon Farm*, June 8, 2011, https://www.ribbonfarm.com/2011/06/08/a-brief-history-of-the-corporation-1600-to-2100/.

3.   Daniel Yergin, *The Prize: The Epic Quest for Oil, Money & Power*, Reissue edition (New York: Free Press, 2008).

4.   Bruce Henderson, "The Experience Curve," *BCG Perspectives*, January 1, 1968, https://www.bcg.com/en-gb/publications/1968/business-unit-strategy-growth-experience-curve.aspx.

5.   Bruce Henderson, "The Product Porfolio," *BCG Perspectives*, January 1, 1970, https://www.bcg.com/publications/1970/strategy-the-product-portfolio.aspx.

6.   Michael E. Porter, "What Is Strategy?" (see Chapter 7, note 23).

7.   Chase Purdy, "McDonald's isn't just a fast-food chain—it's a brilliant $30 billion real-estate company," *Quartz*, April 25, 2017, https://qz.com/965779/mcdonalds-isnt-really-a-fast-food-chain-its-a-brilliant-30-billion-real-estate-company/.

8.   Julie Bort, "The Takedown of Travis Kalanick: The untold story of Uber's infighting, backstabbing, and multi-million-dollar exit packages," *Business Insider*, March 11, 2018, https://www.businessinsider.in/THE-TAKEDOWN-OF-TRAVIS-KALANICK-The-untold-story-of-Ubers-infighting-backstabbing-and-multi-million-dollar-exit-packages/articleshow/63257918.cms.

9.   Nick Wingfield and Brian Stelter, "How Netflix Lost 800,000 Members, and Good Will," *The New York Times*, October 24, 2011, http://www.nytimes.com/2011/10/25/technology/netflix-lost-

800000-members-with-price-rise-and-split-plan.html?.

10.   Josh Halliday, "Gap scraps logo redesign after protests on Facebook and Twitter," *The Guardian*, October 12, 2010, https://www.theguardian.com/media/2010/oct/12/gap-logo-redesign.

11.   Josh Barro, "There's a simple reason companies are becoming more publicly left-wing on social issues," March 1, 2018, *Business Insider*, http://uk.businessinsider.com/why-companies-ditching-nra-delta-selling-guns-2018-2?r=US&IR=T.

12.   Rick Levine et al., *The Cluetrain Manifesto* (see Chapter 5, note 30).

13.   Olivier Zunz, *Why the American Century?*, 85 (see Chapter 2, note 14).

14.   Kevin Baker, "Democrats Should Bring Back the Political Machines" (see Chapter 7, note 3).

15.   Albert O. Hirschman, *Exit, Voice, and Loyalty* (see Chapter 2, note 39).

16.   Adam Davidson, "Welcome to the Failure Age!" (see Chapter 2, note 1).

17.   Ilana Gershon, "The quitting economy," *Aeon*, July 26, 2017, https://aeon.co/essays/how-work-changed-to-make-us-all-passionate-quitters.

18.   Gwynn Guilford, "The 100-year capitalist experiment that keeps Appalachia poor, sick, and stuck on coal," *Quartz*, December 30, 2017, https://qz.com/1167671/the-100-year-capitalist-experiment-that-keeps-appalachia-poor-sick-and-stuck-on-coal/.

19.   Brad Plumer, "There are now twice as many solar jobs as coal jobs in the US," *Vox*, February 7, 2017, https://www.vox.com/energy-and-environment/2017/2/7/14533618/solar-jobs-coal.

20.   Kim-Mai Cutler, "How Burrowing Owls Lead To Vomiting Anarchists" (see Chapter 6, note 15).

21.   Mike Konczal, "The 'new Liberal Economics' is the Key to Understanding Hillary Clinton's Policies," *Vox*, September 15, 2016, https://www.vox.com/the-big-idea/2016/9/15/12923528/liberal-economics-great-recession-policy-clinton.

22.   Mike Konczal, *Ibid.*

23.   Rick Wartzman, "Want engaged employees? It's easy—pay them" (see Chapter 8, note 22).

24.   Sarah O'Connor, "Never mind the robots; future jobs demand human skills," *The Financial Times*, May 16, 2017, https://www. ft.com/content/b893396c-3964-11e7-ac89-b01cc67cfeec.

25   .John Leland, "Twilight of a Difficult Man: Larry Kramer and the Birth of AIDS Activism," *The New York Times*, May 19, 2017, https://www.nytimes.com/2017/05/19/nyregion/larry-kramer-and-the-birth-of-aids-activism.html.

26.   Alondra Nelson, *Body and Soul: The Black Panther Party and the Fight against Medical Discrimination* (Minneapolis: University Of Minnesota Press, September 1, 2013).

27.   Robert J. Shiller, *The New Financial Order* (see Chapter 11, note 1).

28.   Balaji S. Srinivasan, "Software Is Reorganizing the World" (see Chapter 3, note 59).

29.   Zeynep Ton, Roger L. Martin et al., "The Good Jobs Solution," *Harvard Business Review*, December 4, 2017, https://hbr.org/2017/12/its-time-to-make-more-jobs-good-jobs.

30.   James Bessen, *Learning by Doing: The Real Connection Between Innovation, Wages, and Wealth* (New Haven, CT: Yale University Press, 2015).

31.   Tim O'Reilly, "Don't Replace People. Augment them" (see Chapter 6, note 44).

32.   Bill Gurley, "How to Miss By a Mile: An Alternative Look at Uber's Potential Market Size," *Above the Crowd*, July 11, 2014, http://abovethecrowd.com/2014/07/11/how-to-miss-by-a-mile-an-alternative-look-at-ubers-potential-market-size/.

33.   Dov Seidman, "From the Knowledge Economy to the Human Economy," *Harvard Business Review*, November 12, 2014, https://hbr.org/2014/11/from-the-knowledge-economy-to-the-human-economy.

34.   Thomas A. Stewart and Patricia O'Connell, "The Legacy of IKEA Founder Ingvar Kamprad," *Strategy+Business*, February 12, 2018, https://www.strategy-business.com/blog/The-Legacy-of-IKEA-Found-

er-Ingvar-Kamprad.

35.　Paul Constant, "Seattle's $15 Minimum Wage Experiment is Working," *International Policy Digest*, January 4, 2018, https://intpolicydigest.org/2018/01/14/seattle-s-15-minimum-wage-experiment-is-working/.

36.　Sarah O'Connor, "Never mind the robots; future jobs demand human skills" (see note 24).

Conclusion—Basic Income Isn't Enough

1.　Paul Valéry, "The Evening With Monsieur Teste," in *Monsieur Teste* (Princeton, NJ: Princeton University Press, 1973).

2.　Nicolas Colin, "Enough With This Basic Income Bullshit," *The Family Papers*, September 9, 2016, https://salon.thefamily.co/enough-with-this-basic-income-bullshit-a6bc92e8286b.

3.　Tim O'Reilly's comment (published on September 9, 2016) can be accessed here: https://medium.com/@timoreilly/this-is-utterly-brilliant-a90c52d0219b.

4.　The whole discussion on *Hacker News* can be accessed here: https://news.ycombinator.com/item?id=12473112.

5.　Tom Streithorst, "How Basic Income Solves Capitalism's Fundamental Problem," *Evonomics*, accessed May 5, 2018, http://evonomics.com/how-universal-basic-income-solves/.

6.　Olof Palme, "Employment and Welfare. The 1984 Jerry Wurf Memorial Lecture" (The Labor and Worklife Program, Harvard Law School, 1984), http://www.law.harvard.edu/programs/lwp/wurf_lectures/1984Palm.pdf.

7.　Matthew Yglesias, "Silicon Valley's basic income fans should spare a minute to defend the actual safety net," *Vox*, June 1, 2017, https://www.vox.com/policy-and-politics/2017/6/1/15694194/silicon-valley-ubi.

8.　The video can be accessed on https://www.facebook.com/senatorelizabethwarren/videos/798818593613969/.

9.　Jason Furman, "Six Economic Benefits of the Affordable Care Act,"

The White House Blog (President Barack Obama), February 6, 2014, https://obamawhitehouse.archives.gov/blog/2014/02/06/six-economic-benefits-affordable-care-act.

10.   Will Wilkinson, "The Freedom Lover's Case for the Welfare State" (see Chapter 2, note 34). See also Samuel Hammond, *The Free-Market Welfare State: Preserving Dynamism in a Volatile World*, Niskanen Center, May 2018, https://niskanencenter.org/blog/the-free-market-welfare-state-preserving-dynamism-in-a-volatile-world/.

11.   John Gall, *Systemantics: How Systems Work & Especially How They Fail* (New York: Times Books, 1977).

12.   Peter Leyden, "California Is The Future," *NewCo Shift*, accessed on May 15, 2018, https://medium.com/s/state-of-the-future.

13.   Peter Hartcher, "The surprising way the Chinese Communist Party keeps power," *The Sydney Morning Herald*, November 27, 2017, https://www.smh.com.au/opinion/the-surprising-way-the-chinese-communist-party-keeps-power-20171127-gztdqm.html.

Index

#DeleteUber, 236
9/11 attacks, 28, 68

A

Affordable Care and Patient Protection Act of 2010 (US), 33, 57, 175, 185, 222, 226, 254-255
Africa, 37-38, 75, 170
Âge de la multitude, L' (Colin & Verdier), 100, 109-110
Aghion, Philippe, 120
Airbnb, 17, 23, 106, 207-208, 210
Airbus, 151
Alibaba, 36-37, 39, 104
Alipay, 38, 220
Amazon, 24, 40, 95, 104, 110, 112, 117-118, 120, 121, 127, 187, 188, 189, 218
Amazon Web Services, 95
American Airlines, 118
American Recovery and Reinvestment Act of 2009 (US), 185
Ammar, Oussama, 35, 77
Amsterdam (Netherlands), 171
Andreessen-Horowitz, 226
Andreessen, Marc, 44
Anthemis, 44
antitrust, 53, 119-120, 126, 189, 244
Apple, 40, 47, 188
    App Store, 23
    iPhone, 23
Argentina, 144
Arkansas (US), 25, 118, 181-182
Arkwright, Richard, 45
Arthur, W. Brian, 117, 125, 142

Asian Infrastructure Investment Bank, 37
AT&T, 85
Au Bonheur des Dames (Zola), 203
austerity, 153, 179, 181, 185, 223
Australia, 76
automation, 25, 49, 139, 172
automobile, 18-19, 38, 44, 46-47, 50-51, 53, 55-57, 60, 64, 67, 69, 93-94, 99, 101-102, 104, 106, 109, 119, 127, 136, 157-158, 160, 163-164, 168, 176-177, 187, 203, 207-208, 212, 216-217, 221, 231, 234-237, 243-244, 258

B

Back to the Future (Zemeckis), 84
Badger, Emily, 160
Bai, Matt, 23
Baidu, 36
banks, 31, 103-104, 188, 216-217, 219
Bardeen, John, 86
Baumol, William, 245
Bay Area, 129, 202
Bear Stearns, 31
Beijing (China), 37
Beito, David T., 188
Bell Labs, 85-86
Bell Telephone Laboratories, Inc., 85
Bell, Alexander Graham, 85
Belt and Road Initiative (China), 37-39, 75, 143
Benkler, Yochai, 110
Bentonville (Arkansas, US), 118
Berlin Wall, 63
Bessemer, Henry, 85

Bessen, James, 245, 247

Beveridge, William, 59

Bezos, Jeff, 104

Bismarck, Otto von, 53, 59

BlaBlaCar, 106

Black Panthers, 89, 242

Blair, Tony, 181

Boeing, 151

Bork, Robert, 120

Boston Globe, The, 176

Boston (Massachusetts, US), 161

Brandeis, Louis, 120-121, 143, 177

Brattain, Walter, 86

Braudel, Fernand, 145

Brazil, 68

Bretton Woods system, 62, 150-152, 179

Brexit, 25, 125

Britain. *See* United Kingdom.

British maritime power, 147

Brynjolfsson, Erik, 25, 49

bubbles, 47, 125-127, 143
    dotcom bubble, 28, 80, 122, 129
    financial speculation, 44
    housing bubble leading to the 2008 crisis, 23, 28 major technology bubbles, 44, 47, 122, 126
    role of bubbles in financing startups, 44, 47, 122
    bubbles as a factor of instability, 68

Budapest (Hungary), 50

bureaucracy, 178-182, 226

Bush, George H.W., 25

Bush, George W., 152

Bush, Vannevar, 86

C

Caillaux, Joseph, 231

California (US), 87, 89, 242, 256

Cameron, David, 25, 77

Captured Economy, The (Lindsey & Teles), 186

Carnegie, Andrew, 84

Casanova, Giacomo, 144

Casselman, Ben, 161

Central Asia, 37, 39, 75, 144-145

Chaplin, Charlie, 51

Chesky, Brian, 88

Chicago (Illinois, US), 119, 159, 166

Chile, 153

China, 18, 35-41, 68, 75-77, 101, 143, 147, 148, 152, 159, 168-170, 220, 257
    and the Western world, 35,38,
    Chinese Communist Party (CCP), 75, 257
    history of, 36-41, 75
    international ambitions of, 37-39, 143,
    technology in, 37, 220

Christensen, Clayton M., 68, 89, 132, 183, 206, 227

cities, 65, 71, 143, 148, 158-162, 164-168, 170-173, 195, 206-208, 212
    city states, 143-144
    clustering, 65
    cohabitation of hunters and settlers in, 202, 207
    manufacturing and, 158-161
    tense real estate markets in, 206, 218

Civil War (US), 150

classical liberalism, 18, 50

Clay, Henry, 150

Clayton, William, 150
Clifford Memo, 140-141
Clinton, Bill, 25, 28, 74, 153, 180-182, 186, 196
Clinton, Hillary Rodham, 33-34, 157-158, 166
cloud communities, 243
Cluetrain Manifesto, The, 107, 237
Code for America, 189
Cold War, 92, 162
Collin & Colin Report on Taxation in the Digital Economy, 24, 109-110
Collin, Pierre, 109-110
communism, 75, 178, 257
Connally, John, 151
Conservative Revolution, 120, 180, 186
Constantinople, 145
consumer finance, 54, 75, 215-218, 220, 227, 232, 234, 254, 256
    credit cards, 68, 216
    innovation in, 75
    mortgages, 54, 217-218
    student loans, 68, 216, 218
consumption, 28, 38, 46-47, 51, 52, 54, 55-56, 59, 65, 68, 69, 73, 85, 106, 131, 216, 236
copyright law, 33
Corcoran, Tommy, 176
Corn Laws (UK), 147
corporate contract, 99, 101, 103, 107, 111, 121, 246
corporate world, 19, 31, 51, 64, 72-73, 77, 83, 96, 101-102, 111, 149, 166, 233, 235-237, 250
corporatism, 30, 59, 170, 185, 239, 241
counterculture, 28, 89, 178
Coutau-Bégarie, Hervé, 145

Craigslist, 107
crash of 1929, 123-124
creative class, 131, 142, 165, 195, 204
Critical Art Ensemble, 195
Cromford mill, 45
Crouch, Colin, 73, 218
crypto protocols, 215
Cultural Revolution (China), 75
customers, 59, 99, 101-107, 110, 111, 113-114, 118, 119, 121, 125-127, 134, 158, 163, 165-166, 198, 210, 215, 217, 219, 220-224, 226, 235-236, 245-248
Cutler, Kim-Mai, 202, 206, 211

D

Dark Ages (of financialization), 61, 65, 73, 78, 94, 102-104, 108-109, 134, 136, 141, 172, 180, 186, 208
data, 112-114, 118, 201, 211, 215, 218, 224, 226, 236, 246, 248
Davidson, Adam, 43, 72, 240
Deliveroo, 187
Delong, J. Bradford, 126
Delta, 236
democracy, 23, 25, 52, 56, 63, 74, 138, 143, 171, 180
Democratic Party, 31-34, 41, 140-141, 150, 158, 165-166, 180, 186, 226, 255
Denmark, 152
Detroit (Michigan, US), 67, 157, 159
Didi Chuxing, 36
Digital Equipment Corporation, 89
Dixon, Chris, 44
Djibouti, 37
Dodd-Frank Act of 2010 (US), 31, 68, 186

Doing Capitalism in the Innovation Economy (W.H. Janeway), 43

Douglas, William O., 176

downward augmentation, 134, 238, 246

Draut, Tamara, 157, 163

Drucker, Jesse, 24

Drucker, Peter, 230

Dukakis, Michael, 180

E

Eastern Europe, 38, 63, 76

eBay, 107

economic security, 18-19, 23, 30, 40, 51, 53-60, 61-62, 65, 73, 76, 78, 96, 106, 108, 120, 123, 129, 132, 136, 139, 144, 149-156, 164-166, 168, 171-172, 176-177, 185-186, 196, 198

economies of scale, 47, 93, 99, 111-112, 182

Economist, The, 199

Edgar Thomson Steel Works, 84

education, 18, 74, 120, 141, 163-164, 167-168, 175, 181-182, 195-198, 212, 217-219, 244, 253

    lifelong education, 196-197, 212

Eisenhower, Dwight, 177

Elections,

    1992 US presidential election, 25, 74, 153, 182

    2008 US presidential election, 24, 31, 33, 99, 165

    2012 US presidential election, 33, 165

    2016 US presidential election, 25, 34, 149, 157-158, 166, 186, 228

    Arkansas gubernatorial elections, 181-182

Ellis, Charles D., 219

energy, 34, 45-46, 62, 86, 106, 113, 151, 211

    coal, 45, 158, 167, 171, 240

    electricity, 46

    oil, 28, 46, 52, 62, 108, 127, 159, 179, 203, 234

    solar, 33, 106, 240

    steam, 44-46, 158

Entrepreneurial Age, 19, 87, 89, 94-96, 102, 104, 106-107, 109, 112, 117, 119-131, 133-136

    definition of, 94-96

    reasons for calling it, 94

entrepreneurial ecosystem, 17, 35, 37, 84, 126-129, 144, 147, 215

Entrepreneurial State, The (Mazzucato), 189

entrepreneurship, 17-18, 71, 83-84, 86, 88-89, 94-96, 189, 212, 215, 230, 253

    entrepreneurs, 16-19, 29-33, 35-37, 70, 83, 84, 87-89, 92-96, 99, 100, 102, 104, 110-111, 119, 122, 126, 131, 147-149, 165, 183, 186, 189, 191, 204, 215, 220, 227, 230, 245-246, 253, 254-256, 258

    as the pursuit of high quality at scale, 94, 102, 113, 245

Erhard, Ludwig, 103

Estonia, 144, 147, 189

Europe, 15, 17-18, 24, 30, 35-40, 50, 52, 55, 59, 63, 74-79, 94, 142-144, 150-153, 161-162, 164, 170-172, 185, 196, 215, 223, 257-258

European Union, 25, 63, 76, 152-153, 196

F

Facebook, 18, 24, 40, 100, 104, 110, 112, 141, 188, 198, 208, 218, 230

Fairchild Camera & Instrument, 87

Fairchild Semiconductor, 87-88

Fall of the House of Roosevelt, The (M.C. Janeway), 176

Fannie Mae, 54, 216-217

fascism, 40, 51-52, 61, 144

Federal Housing Administration (US), 162

Federal Reserve (US), 63

financial crisis of 2008, 23, 29, 31, 40-41, 47, 65, 68, 73, 123, 125, 136, 185-186, 218, 242

financial system, 40, 53-55, 57, 63, 65, 68, 73, 78, 134, 136, 199, 206, 217, 219-221
    as a pillar of the Great Safety Net, 53-55, 73, 78, 199
    role in financial crisis, 40, 65, 68

Financial Times, The, 62

financialization, 49, 68, 73, 78, 94, 102-103, 108, 141, 172, 180, 208

Fincher, David, 95

Fishman, Charles, 118

Florida, Richard, 131, 161, 163, 166, 195

Foer, Franklin, 121, 175, 187

Ford Model T, 46, 59

Ford Motor Company, 234

Ford, Henry, 30, 46, 56, 234

Fordism, 19, 25, 47, 51-52, 54, 55, 72-73, 93, 108, 123, 141, 163, 183, 188

Foroohar, Rana, 68

Fortas, Abe, 176

France, 17, 28, 35, 45, 53, 56, 59, 84, 101, 103, 123, 131, 147, 167, 171, 175, 185, 187-188, 189, 231
    Ancien Régime corporations in France, 188
    civil service in, 178
    criminal law in, 15-17
    French government, 16, 24, 100, 108, 109, 122, 179, 231
    Socialist Party of, 63

fraternal societies, 188

Freddie Mac, 54, 216-217

Freelancers Union, 166

Friedman, Milton, 63

Fugitive Slave Act of 1850 (US), 150

Furman, Jason, 255

G

G20, 24, 110

Gall, John, 256

Gap, 236

General Electric, 30

General Motors, 64, 99, 234

George, Henry, 203, 211

Germany, 40-41, 45, 53, 56, 59, 63-64, 101, 103, 142, 147, 167, 168, 177, 204

Giddens, Anthony, 195

Glass-Steagall Act (US), 28

globalization, 46, 49, 78, 139, 141, 143, 149-155, 161, 172, 196

Goldman, Henry, 219-220

Goldman, Marcus, 217, 219

Goldman Sachs, 217, 219

Google, 29, 40, 106, 111, 127, 141, 224

Google Translate, 141

Gore, Al, 28, 74

government, 16-17, 23-25, 29, 30, 33-35, 37, 44, 46-47, 52-56, 59-60, 68, 72, 74, 76-77, 86, 88-89, 100, 103, 109-110, 117, 119, 122, 131, 139, 141, 144, 148-149, 155, 162, 164, 166, 175-181, 187-189, 191,

199, 204, 206-297, 212, 126-222, 227, 231, 242-244, 254, 256-58
GPS, 93, 148
Graeber, David, 133
Great Britain. See United Kingdom.
Great Compression, 43
Great Decoupling, 49, 57
Great Depression, 40, 52, 54, 59, 124, 176, 190, 217
Great Moderation, 63, 123
Great Safety Net, 53-57, 60, 65, 68, 71-73, 75-78, 85, 95-96, 106, 108, 123, 129, 132, 136, 140-143, 149-155, 159, 166, 170-173, 177, 185, 190, 199, 203-204, 208, 212, 216, 218, 221, 227, 234, 236, 237, 241, 243-244, 246, 250
    Great Safety Net 1.0, 53, 59-60, 68, 72-73, 78, 123, 159, 170-172, 185, 199, 203, 208, 216, 234, 236-237, 244, 250
    Great Safety Net 2.0, 75-76, 129, 136, 155, 166, 171-172, 190, 208, 212, 218, 227, 237, 241, 243, 246, 250, 255-258,
    Greater Safety Net, 19, 36, 129, 136, 237, 250
Great surges of development, 18, 44-47, 60, 93, 158, 170, 257
    Industrial Revolution, 38, 45, 60, 93, 145
    age of steam and iron railways, 44, 158
    age of steel and heavy engineering, 38, 40, 50-52, 55, 84, 158, 168, 258
    age of the automobile and mass production, 19, 38, 46-47, 50-51, 53, 55-57, 64-65, 69, 93-94, 101, 102, 106, 109, 119, 127, 136, 158, 160, 163, 164, 168, 176, 177, 182, 187, 203, 207-208, 212, 216, 217, 221, 231, 234-237, 243, 244, 258

    age of ubiquitous computing and networks, 34, 40, 49, 60, 65, 76, 77, 92, 94, 100, 168, 183, 190, 226, 243. See also Entrepreneurial Age.
    Golden Ages as part of, 44, 129, 190
Great Transformation, The (Polanyi), 50
Greece, 76
Greenspan, Alan, 158
Groupe Rousselet (formerly Groupe G7), 15
Grove, Andrew, 88-89
Grunwald, Michael, 185

H

Hacker News, 253
Hacker, Jacob S., 69, 233
Hamilton, Alexander, 150
Hangzhou (China), 39, 168
Hartz reforms (Germany), 63
Hartz, Louis, 74
Harvard University, 68
Haussmann, Baron Georges-Eugène, 206
Hayek, Friedrich, 63
healthcare, 18, 25, 31, 33, 57, 69, 75, 77, 95, 120, 133, 153, 163, 164, 179, 185, 186, 199, 221-227, 241, 242, 253, 254, 255
Henderson, Bruce, 235
Herodotus, 195
Hirschman, Albert O., 57, 239-240
Hollywood, 31-33
Hong Kong (China), 24, 153, 203
Horowitz, Sara, 166
housing, 18, 23, 28, 71, 75, 95, 120,

162, 164, 165, 167, 190, 202-213, 216, 218, 219, 241, 253, 254, 256

Howe, Jeff, 110

HTTP, 94

hunters, 202, 207-213, 215-220, 229, 230, 232, 239-241, 250

I

IBM, 89, 133

Ikea, 107, 246

Illinois (US), 166

immigration, 34, 40, 168-170

Immigration Act of 1924 (US), 168

increasing returns to scale, 77, 93, 95, 104, 109, 112-115, 117, 123, 125-127, 131, 136, 147, 156, 226-227, 236, 243

industrial policy, 151-152, 189-190, 227

inequality, 23, 49, 51, 64-65, 72, 74, 132, 186, 204, 255

infrastructures, 37, 44-45, 47, 74, 93-94, 113, 148, 158, 160, 212

innovation, 16-17, 31, 33, 37, 43-45, 69, 71, 74-75, 83, 85-88, 92-94, 96, 120, 126, 132, 136, 143, 148, 182-185, 189, 190, 199, 203,220, 223, 227, 230, 258, 265

innovator's dilemma, 89, 183

Inspection générale des finances (France), 175

instability, 122-125, 127, 129, 131,134, 136, 153, 157, 176, 196-197, 213, 216-217, 232, 236, 238

Institute for Innovation and Public Purpose (University College London), 189

institutions, 15, 19, 30-31, 35, 40, 44,

46, 50-52, 59, 60, 70, 73, 75-78, 84, 94, 96, 101, 106, 127, 131, 136, 145, 149, 171-172, 185, 199, 212, 215, 221, 227, 231, 237, 242-244, 257-258

insurance, 53-60, 68-70, 72, 77, 120, 136, 142, 145, 152, 155, 179, 185, 186, 188, 199, 203, 219, 221-227, 229, 232, 234, 235, 241, 254-256

Intel, 46, 88-89

intermittency, 70-71

International Tax Review, 110

Internet, 23,28,36, 40, 47, 62-63, 77,89, 92-93,107, 121,127,148, 242

Intuit, 231

Ireland, 168

Israel, 143-144, 147

Italy, 63, 142, 168, 189

Ivy League, 175

J

Jacques, Martin, 36-37

Janeway, Eliot, 176

Janeway, Elizabeth, 176

Janeway, Michael C., 176

Janeway, William H., 43, 92, 95, 265

Japan, 101, 151, 258

jobs,
    bullshit jobs, 133
    good jobs, 29, 149, 166, 173, 243-250
    lousy jobs, 168, 169, 171, 199
    steady jobs, 25, 43, 64, 69, 87, 102, 207

Jobs, Steve, 88, 95

Johnson, Lyndon B., 31, 176

Juicero, 122

Jumpstart Our Business Startups (JOBS) Act of 2010 (US), 185

Jungle, The (Sinclair), 51, 119

K

Kalanick, Travis, 236
Kattel, Rainer, 190
Kennan, George, 150
Keynes, John Maynard, 177
Keynesianism, 63, 73, 218
Kissinger, Henry, 36
Kodak, 70
Krugman, Paul, 160, 196
Kuper, Simon, 62, 95

L

labor law, 152, 229
laboratories of democracy (states as), 143, 180
laissez-faire, 50, 52, 63, 150, 152-153, 176-177, 180
land, 147-148, 156, 159, 203, 211-212
Lauré, Maurice, 231
League of Nations, 231
legacy industries, 34, 147, 167
    difficulties of innovating in, 92, 131
    lobbying of, 34
    rent-seeking of, 132, 152, 201, 244
    workers in, 167
Lehman Brothers, 31
Lending Club, 107
LendUp, 217
Levine, Rick, 107
liberalism, 50, 175
Lichtenstein, Nelson, 50, 56, 72, 123
Lindsey, Brink, 186

Lisbon Strategy (European Union), 196
Liverpool (UK), 45
Locke, Christopher, 107
Lockheed Martin Corporation, 85
London (UK), 159, 170-171, 203
Luddism, 50
Lyft, 200

M

Ma, Jack, 104
machine learning, 113
Macintosh, 88
Macron, Emmanuel, 17, 175, 196
Magic Mike (Soderbergh), 61-62
Makers and Takers (Foroohar), 68
Maltese, Corto (comics character), 144
Manchester (UK), 45
Manchuria, 45
manufacturing, 46, 49-51, 64, 84, 99, 157, 161, 166, 235
Mao Zedong, 75
Marcus by Goldman Sachs, 217, 219
Marjory Stoneman Douglas High School shooting, 236
Marshall Plan, 75, 150-151
Martin, Roger L., 104, 244
Marx, Karl, 134, 199, 238
Marxism, 55, 100
mass consumption, 28, 46, 52, 55, 65, 68, 73, 85
mass production, 46, 51, 73, 93, 108
Mazzucato, Mariana, 189-190
McAfee, Andrew, 25, 49
McDonald's, 235
Medium, 133, 141, 198

Merchant, Nilofer, 107

Mexico, 152

Michigan (US), 157, 171

microprocessor, 40, 46-47, 88

Microsoft, 47

middle class, 23, 29, 49, 61-62, 64-65, 71, 72, 78, 119, 131, 132, 134, 159, 172, 180, 182, 203, 216, 242-244

Middle East, 63, 68

minimum wage, 53, 121, 123, 166, 171, 241, 248

mobility, 16, 69, 168, 179

Modern Times (Chaplin), 51

Monde diplomatique, Le, 28

Mongolia, 145

Moore, Gordon, 46, 88

Moore's Law, 109

Moretti, Enrico, 70, 165

Morris, William, 77

Moses, Robert, 206

Moulier Boutang, Yann, 110

multitude,
    as an ally of organizations, 36, 107, 246, 248-249
    as both an input and a consumption force, 36, 107, 113, 246, 248-249
    definition of, 100-102, 110, 114
    role in the current transition, 96, 104, 109-111, 245-246, 256

Munich (Germany), 171

N

Nader, Ralph, 120

Napoleon (North Dakota, US), 139, 141

Napster, 29

nation states, 77, 141-142, 152

National Aeronautics and Space Administration (NASA), 88

National Domestic Workers Alliance (US), 166

National Health Service (UK), 179, 223

National Insurance Act of 1911 (UK), 53

National Labor Relations Act of 1935 (US), 56

National Recovery Administration (US), 30

National Rifle Association (US), 236

Nationalsozialistische Deutsche Arbeiterpartei (NSDAP, or Nazi Party, Germany), 59

Navigation Acts (UK), 145

Negri, Antonio, 100

neoliberalism, 63, 136, 152, 178

net neutrality, 17, 33-34, 148

Netflix, 142, 236

Netherlands, The, 147, 152

network effects, 47, 104, 112-113, 226, 243, 246

New Covenant, 181

New Deal, 30-31, 56, 75, 77, 140, 150, 160, 176, 181, 185, 189, 257

New Financial Order, The (Shiller), 215, 242

New Republic, The, 121

New York Times, The, 228

New Yorker, The, 36

New York City (New York, US), 203

Niskanen Center, 54

Nivi, Babak, 83, 94

Nixon, Richard M., 62, 89, 151

North American Free Trade Agreement (NAFTA), 153

Noyce, Robert, 46, 87-88

O

Oakland (California, US), 242

Obama, Barack, 17, 23-25, 31-34, 57, 68, 75, 77, 99, 153, 165, 185-186, 255

Obamacare. *See* Affordable Care and Patient Protection Act of 2010 (US).

occupational licensing, 198-199, 201-202, 213, 222, 256

Ohio (US),157, 234

Old-Age Pensions Act of 1908 (UK), 53

O'Reilly, Tim, 96, 110, 121, 134, 188-189, 253, 255

Organisation for Economic Co-operation and Development (OECD), 24, 110, 204

Oscar, 226

Osnos, Evan, 36

Owen, Robert, 77

P

PageRank, 106

Palihapitiya, Chamath, 206

Palo Alto (California, US), 87

paradigm shift, 107, 131, 185, 198, 206, 215, 230, 239, 242

Paris (France), 15, 74, 171, 203, 206

Parkland (Florida, US), 236

Partnership, The (Ellis), 219

Pennsylvania (US), 157

pensions, 31, 95
    401(k) plans, 69

Perez, Carlota, 15, 43, 47, 58, 84, 93, 126, 190, 265

Perkins, Frances, 53

personal computing, 47, 88-89, 92, 178

Piacentini, Diego, 189

Pittsburgh (Pennsylvania, US), 84, 159, 167

platforms, 170, 189, 198, 201, 207, 241

Poland, 168

Polanyi, Karl, 50-52, 60-61
    double movement, 60
    life of, 50
    work of, 51

populism, 65, 76, 158, 187

Porter, Michael E., 235-236

Portugal, 156

Posner, Richard, 120

post-war boom, 123, 151, 190, 232, 243, 244

Pratt, Hugo, 144

privacy, 23-24

'Privatized Keynesianism' (Colin Crouch), 73, 218

productivity, 45, 49, 56-57, 108, 120, 134, 164, 177, 244-246, 248

Progressive Era, 119, 177

progressivism, 34

Prohibition, 30

prosperity, 18-19, 30, 35, 40, 45, 46, 51-53, 55, 57, 59-60, 62, 65, 73, 74, 76, 78, 96, 120, 129, 136, 139, 144, 149, 151, 153, 160, 165, 171-172, 185, 186, 207, 216, 236, 238, 243, 248, 257

proximity services, 162-173, 204, 206, 207, 211, 241, 244-250

Pure Food and Drug Act of 1906 (US), 119

Q

Q Bio, 226

Quora, 198

R

railways, 18, 45, 150

Ranchère, Yann, 44

Rao, Venkatesh, 229, 233

Reagan, Ronald, 25, 63

real estate, 71, 101, 159, 162, 203-204, 206, 208, 210-212, 218, 222, 228, 235

regulation, 16, 31, 56, 94, 101, 117, 119-120, 142, 170-171, 185, 198, 200, 204, 206, 226, 232

Reich, Robert, 195, 197

Renaissance, 65

Republican Party, 28, 31, 34, 150, 152, 157, 180, 186, 256

Rharbaoui, Younès, 187

Ribbon Farm, 233

Rifkin, Jeremy, 195

risks, 31, 43, 52-55, 60, 65, 68-70, 73, 78, 87, 129, 131, 136, 140, 145, 150, 155, 161, 176, 177, 181, 188, 210, 219, 221, 223, 226-227, 229, 232, 234, 235, 236-237, 239, 241-243, 250, 255

Robertson, Julian, 103

robotics, 25

Rockefeller, John D., 234

Rodrik, Dani, 139, 155

Rogers (Arkansas, US), 118

Roosevelt, Franklin D., 30, 33, 53, 57, 77, 150, 162, 176-177

Roosevelt, Theodore, 77, 119, 177

Ross (startup), 133

Rousselet, Nicolas, 15-16, 19

Rudd, Kevin, 76

Russia, 68

Rust Belt, 132, 157, 164, 166

S

San Francisco (California, US), 161, 171, 202, 206

Sanders, Bernie, 152

scale, 46, 47, 55, 56, 59, 64, 69, 77, 83, 93-95, 99, 102, 104, 109-114, 117, 118, 120, 123, 125-127, 131, 136, 140, 147, 156, 160, 168, 177, 179, 181-183, 186, 187, 188, 196, 199, 200, 201, 224, 226-227, 234-235, 243, 245, 246, 248, 256, 258

Scholz, Trebor, 110

Schröder, Gerhard, 63

Schumpeter, Joseph, 94, 134

science, 28, 74, 83-86, 122, 161, 177

Sciences Po (also known as Institut d'études politiques de Paris, France), 74

scientific management, 46, 51, 85, 132, 163, 244

Searls, Doc, 108

Seattle (Washington, US), 117, 248

segregation, 31, 140, 162

service class, 163-166, 172, 195

settlers, 202, 207-208, 210-213

Shanghai (China), 143, 168, 206

Shapiro, Carl, 99

shareholders, 64, 101-103, 107, 114, 121, 125, 126, 228, 237

Shenzhen (China), 37, 143

Sherman, Rachel, 129

Shiller, Robert J., 215, 242

Shirky, Clay, 110

Shockley Semiconductor Laboratory, 86-87

Shockley, William, 86-87

Silicon Valley, 17, 33, 34, 35, 50, 74, 83, 87, 104, 110, 117, 129, 143, 254, 255

Sinclair, Upton, 51, 119

Skunk Works (Lockheed Martin Corporation), 85

Sloan, Alfred P., 30, 64, 234

smartphones, 23, 92

Snowden, Edward, 24

Social Capital, 206

social contract, 49, 177, 201

social credit (China), 75, 231

Social Network, The (Fincher), 95

Social Security, 53, 56

socialism, 53, 59, 158

socio-institutional framework, 59, 143, 163, 189, 242, 246, 257

Soderbergh, Steven, 61

SolarCity, 106

Soviet Union, 89, 92, 190

Spain, 147

Srinivasan, Balaji S., 77, 143

Standard Oil Co., 119, 234

Stanford University, 87-88

state, 53, 57, 59, 63, 72, 75, 77, 96, 118, 141-144, 145-149, 151, 152, 155, 156, 175-191, 216, 218-219, 221, 223, 234, 237, 243, 254

state socialism (Germany), 53-59

steel, 28, 40, 46, 84-85, 152, 157

Stephenson, Robert, 45

Stiglitz, Joseph, 51-52

Storgatz, Rex, 139

Story of my Life, The (Casanova), 144

strategy, 37, 68, 92-93, 103, 112, 140, 143, 145, 188, 196, 234

Sweden, 152

Switzerland, 144

Systemantics (Gall), 256

T

Taft-Hartley Act of 1948 (US), 57, 160

Tapscott, Don, 110

taxation, 15, 24, 71-72, 109-110, 152, 230, 232, 271

taxi industry, 15-17, 170, 199-200

Taylor, Frederick, 85

Taylorism, 163-164

TCP/IP, 94

Tea Party, 186

tech backlash, 18, 23, 29, 34, 41, 255, 258

tech companies, 76-77, 89, 92-93, 102, 104, 109-115, 117, 119, 120, 121, 122, 123, 124, 125-127, 132, 134, 142, 145, 148-149, 156, 187-188, 206, 215, 232, 235, 245-246, 255

tech industry, 19, 24, 25, 29, 74, 119, 129, 132, 226, 254, 255
    European tech industry, 257
    US tech industry, 17-18, 34, 35, 38, 77, 254

TechCrunch, 202

techno-economic paradigm, 30, 45-47, 52, 59, 68, 75-76, 78

technological revolution, 40, 44, 59, 93, 122, 245

Technological Revolutions and Financial Capital (Perez), 44, 265

Tehran (Iran), 37

Teles, Steven, 186

Tencent, 36-37

Terman, Frederick T., 87-88

terrorism, 28

Tesla, 111

thalassocracy, 145, 147-149

Thatcher, Margaret, 63, 153

The Family, 15, 35, 83, 95, 215, 253

Theranos, 122

Thiel, Peter, 132

Tokyo (Japan), 203

Ton, Zeynep, 244

Toys "R" Us, 70

trade, 28, 30, 31, 32, 33, 34, 37-39, 64, 106, 108, 133, 142, 143-156, 158, 159

trade unions, 30-31, 53, 55-57, 59, 71-73, 75, 77, 102-104, 140, 150, 167, 177, 200, 203, 238-243, 244, 250, 252, 254, 258, 261
    American Federation of Labor (US), 240
    collective bargaining and, 51, 53, 55-56, 68, 71-72, 164, 199, 238-243, 256
    Congress of Industrial Organizations (US), 240
    'exit unions', 238-243, 252, 261
    labor movement, 52-53, 59, 77, 176, 257
    'right to work' laws (US), 72, 160

TransferWise, 208

transistor, 86-88

transportation, 16, 47, 158, 159, 162, 164, 167, 190, 206, 211, 229, 256

Tribune, La, 15

TripAdvisor, 106, 133, 246

Truman, Harry, 33, 140, 150

Trump, Donald,
    administration of, 17, 36, 74-75, 153, 161-162, 241
    attitude toward technology, 17, 34, 41, 143, 161
    election of, 17, 25, 34, 49, 157, 186, 228, 230-231
    impact on US standing, 74-75, 153, 161, 164, 229, 256

Tupperware, 107

Twitter, 17, 110, 141

U

Uber, 16-17, 24, 104, 110, 111, 121, 134, 142, 187, 199-200, 236

ubiquitous computing and networks, 34, 40, 49, 60, 65, 76-77, 92, 94, 96, 100, 108, 113, 121-122, 125, 141-143, 163, 168, 183, 190, 224, 226-227, 235, 241-243, 256

unemployment, 25, 53-54, 57, 62, 64, 68, 70, 108, 123, 134, 153, 166, 171, 177, 179, 197-198, 219, 221

UK. *See* United Kingdom.

Union of Automobile Workers (US), 157

United Kingdom, 44-45, 56, 59, 76, 123, 125, 142, 153, 147, 170-171, 175, 179, 181, 204

United States of America, 15, 17-18, 24, 25, 29, 30, 32-34 35, 36, 37, 38, 40, 41, 45, 47-49, 53-54, 56-57, 59, 62, 63, 68, 74-77, 86, 88, 101, 118-119, 123, 140, 142, 143-144, 147-152, 161-163, 166, 167, 168, 170-172, 175, 178-182, 185-186, 188-189, 196, 199, 204, 216, 223, 226, 231-232, 239, 240, 241, 254, 256, 258
    as the core of several great surges of development, 40-41, 47, 168
    federal government of, 30, 34, 54, 63, 88, 148, 186, 204
    in international affairs, 36, 38
    military in, 86, 88
    politics in, 25, 41, 74, 140, 152, 157-158, 180-182, 186, 196
    history of, 56-59, 74, 140, 150, 163, 175-176, 188, 231, 239-240

universal basic income, 50, 53, 253-254, 258

University College London (UK), 189

US. *See* United States of America.

US Bureau of Labor Statistics, 24

US Congress, 56, 153, 186

US Constitution, 30, 231
  Commerce Clause (Article I,
    Section 8, Clause 3), 30
  First Amendment, 15, 142

US Postal Service, 118, 179

US Supreme Court, 30, 120, 143,
176

user experience, 93, 226

V

Vail, Theodore, 85

Valéry, Paul, 253

value chains, 64, 72, 111, 119-120,
127, 161, 232

Varian, Hal R., 99

Venezuela, 44, 155

Venice (Italy), 144-145, 147-149, 156

venture capital, 35, 44, 92, 110, 131,
144, 148

Verdier, Henri, 189, 267

Victorian era, 38, 45, 77, 147

Vienna (Austria), 50

Vietnam War, 89

Vitaud, Laetitia, 207

Vladivostok (Russia), 37

voice and exit (Hirschman framework), 57, 239

Volcker, Paul, 63

Vox, 254

W

wages, 31, 49-50, 56-57, 64, 65, 87,
102, 108, 121, 123, 132, 143, 164,
167-168, 239, 244-245, 248, 250

Wagner Act of 1935 (US), 56

Wal-Mart Effect, 101, 117, 163
  'Greater Wal-Mart Effect', 120,
  129-131, 134, 136
  Wal-Mart Effect, The (Fishman),
  118

Wall Street, 31, 33, 123, 215, 254

Wall Street Journal, The, 254

Walmart (formerly Wal-Mart), 103,
118-121

Walton family, 118,

Walton, Sam, 118

War of Chioggia, 147

Warren, Elizabeth, 254

Washington Consensus, 63

Washington, DC, 17, 186

Washington Post, The, 196

Watergate scandal, 180

Watsi, 226

Watson (IBM), 133

Web 2.0, 110

WeChat, 37-38, 220

Weil, David, 64, 72

Weinberger, David, 108

welfare, 182

welfare state, 53-54, 64, 73, 150, 152,
254-255

West Virginia (US), 158, 167, 171

Western Electric Research Laboratories, 85

WeWork, 208

WhatsApp, 141

Wikipedia, 133, 198

Wilkinson, Will, 54, 255

Wilson, Fred, 44

Wilson, Woodrow, 177, 231

winner-takes-most, 112, 227
Wired, 139
Wisconsin (US), 157
women, 70, 157, 163, 164, 166, 168, 170
Work of Nations, The (Reich), 195
workers,
    amateur workers, 106, 135, 198-202, 213, 241, 246, 248
    gig economy, 24, 25
    reserve army of labor, 134, 199, 201, 238
working class, 52, 71-72, 140, 152, 157, 161, 162, 164-167, 171, 172, 173, 195, 199, 244, 250
World Trade Organization, 153
World War I (also known as the Great War), 50-52, 231
World War II, 37, 46, 52, 59, 60, 65, 76, 86, 120, 123, 151, 178
Wozniak, Steve, 88

X

Xerox, 85
Xerox PARC, 85
Xi Jinping, 37

Y

Y Combinator, 226
Yale University, 176
Yglesias, Matthew, 254
Young, Owen, 30
YouTube, 141, 198, 230
Yozma (Israeli government), 144
Yunnan (China), 178

Z

Zagury, Alice, 35, 265
Zola, Emile, 203
Zuboff, Shoshana, 110
Zuckerberg, Mark, 88, 95, 104
Zunz, Olivier, 84

32197355R00190

Printed in Poland
by Amazon Fulfillment
Poland Sp. z o.o., Wrocław